LEPAM

Crime: Local and Global

This book is one of two published by Willan Publishing in association with The Open University:

Crime: Local and Global (edited by John Muncie, Deborah Talbot and Reece Walters)

Criminal Justice: Local and Global (edited by Deborah Drake, John Muncie and Louise Westmarland)

These publications form part of The Open University course *Crime and justice* (DD301).
Details of this and other Open University courses can be obtained from the Student Registration and Enquiry Service, The Open University, PO Box 197, Milton Keynes, MK7 6BJ, United Kingdom (tel. +44 (0) 845 300 60 90; email general-enquiries@open.ac.uk).

Alternatively, you can visit the Open University website at www.open.ac.uk where you can learn more about the wide range of courses and packs offered at all levels by The Open University.

To purchase a selection of Open University materials visit www.ouw.co.uk or contact Open University Worldwide, Michael Young Building, Walton Hall, Milton Keynes, MK7 6AA, United Kingdom for a brochure (tel. +44 (0) 1908 858793; fax +44 (0) 1908 858787; email ouw-customer-service@open.ac.uk).

Crime: Local and Global

Edited by John Muncie, Deborah Talbot and Reece Walters

Published by

Willan Publishing
Culmcott House
Mill Street, Uffculme
Cullompton, Devon
EX15 3AT, UK
Tel: +44 (0) 1884 840337
Fax: +44 (0) 1884 840251
email: info@willanpublishing.co.uk
website: www.willanpublishing.co.uk

Published simultaneously in the USA and
Canada by

Willan Publishing
c/o ISBS, 920 NE 58th Ave, Suite 300
Portland, Oregon 97213-3786, USA
Tel: +001 (0) 503 287 3093
Fax: +001 (0) 503 280 8832
email: info@isbs.com
website: www.isbs.com

in association with

The Open University
Walton Hall, Milton Keynes
MK7 6AA
United Kingdom

First published 2010

Copyright © 2010 The Open University

The publisher has no responsibility for the persistence or accuracy of URLs for any external or
third-party internet websites referred to in this book, and does not guarantee that any content on
such websites is, or will remain, accurate or appropriate.

Edited and designed by The Open University.

Typeset in India by Alden Prepress Services, Chennai.

Printed and bound in the United Kingdom by Bell & Bain Ltd., Glasgow.

Library of Congress Cataloguing in Publication data: applied for

British Library Cataloguing in Publication data: applied for

ISBN 978-1-84392-516-3 (paperback)

ISBN 978-1-84392-515-6 (hardback)

1.1

Mixed Sources
Product group from well-managed
forests and other controlled sources
www.fsc.org   Cert no. TT-COC-002769
© 1996 Forest Stewardship Council

The paper used in this publication contains pulp sourced from forests
independently certified to the Forest Stewardship Council (FSC) principles and criteria. Chain of custody certification allows the pulp from
these forests to be tracked to the end use (see www.fsc-uk.org).

Contents

Notes on contributors

Deborah Drake is a Lecturer in Criminology at The Open University. She has conducted extensive prison research in the areas of resettlement, maximum-security and long-term imprisonment, and in secure settings for children. Her work has primarily focused on the experiences of prisoners, but has also included consideration of staff experiences and working practices.

Penny Green is Professor of Law and Criminology at King's College, London. She has published widely on a range of issues including state crime, state-corporate crime, and transnational crime. Her books include *The Enemy Without: Policing and Class Consciousness in the Miners' Strike* (Open University Press, 1990) and *Drug Couriers* (Quartet Books, 1991). She has also co-authored the books *Criminal Justice in Transition: Criminal Policy-Making Toward the New Millennium* (Hart Books, 2000), *State Crime: Governments, Violence and Corruption* (Pluto Press, 2004) and *Criminology and Archaeology: Studies in Looted Antiquities* (Hart Books, 2009).

Gerry Mooney is a Senior Lecturer in Social Policy at The Open University. He is co-author of *Rethinking Welfare* (Sage, 2002), and co-editor of *Exploring Social Policy in the 'New' Scotland* (Policy Press, 2005) and *New Labour/Hard Labour?* (Policy Press, 2007). He is also co-author of *Understanding Social Welfare Movements* (Policy Press, 2009) and co-editor of the forthcoming *Criminal Justice in Contemporary Scotland* (Willan, 2010).

John Muncie is a Professor of Criminology and Co-director of the International Centre for Comparative Criminological Research at The Open University. A third edition of his *Youth and Crime* (Sage, 2009) was published recently, and he has co-authored *The Sage Dictionary of Criminology* (Sage, 2006), *Youth Crime and Justice* (Sage, 2006), *Comparative Youth Justice* (Sage, 2006) and *The Student Handbook of Criminal Justice and Criminology* (Cavendish, 2004).

Sarah Neal is a Senior Lecturer in Social Policy at The Open University. She is the author of *The Making of Equal Opportunities Policies in Universities* (Open University Press, 1998), and *Rural Identities: Ethnicity and Community in the Contemporary English Countryside* (Ashgate, 2009). She has also co-authored the forthcoming *Race, Multiculture and Social Policy* (Palgrave, 2010) and co-edited *The New Countryside: Ethnicity, Nation and Exclusion in Contemporary Rural Britain* (Policy Press, 2006).

Deborah Talbot is a Lecturer in Criminology at The Open University, and author of *Regulating the Night: Race, Culture and Exclusion in the Making of the Night Time Economy* (Ashgate, 2007), co-editor of *Security: Crime, Welfare and Society* (Open University Press, 2008) and of the forthcoming book *Revisiting Criminology* (Pearson, 2009).

Steve Tombs is a Professor of Sociology at Liverpool John Moores University and Chair of the Centre for Corporate Accountability. Most recently, he co-authored *Safety Crimes* (Willan, 2007). He has co-edited various books including *Beyond Criminology? Taking Harm Seriously* (Pluto Press, 2004), *Criminal Obsessions* (Crime and Society Foundation, 2008), and *Unmasking the Crimes of the Powerful: Scrutinizing States and Corporations* (Peter Lang, 2003). He has also co-authored *Corporate Crime* (Longman, 1999) and *Toxic Capitalism* (Ashgate, 1998).

Reece Walters is a Professor of Criminology at The Open University. He has published widely in the areas of environmental crime, crimes of the powerful and the sociology of criminological knowledge. His books include *Eco-Crime and Genetically Modified Food* (Routledge, 2009), and *Deviant Knowledge, Criminology, Politics and Policy* (Willan, 2003). He is an editorial-board member of three international journals including *The British Journal of Criminology*.

Louise Westmarland is a Senior Lecturer in Criminology and Social Policy at The Open University. She has written widely on police and policing, specifically on various aspects of police culture – such as in her book *Gender and Policing: Sex, Power and Police Culture* (Willan, 2001) – and on violence and police culture, ethics and integrity. Most recently, she co-authored *Creating Citizen-Consumers: Changing Publics and Changing Public Services* (Sage, 2007).

David Whyte is a Reader in Sociology at the University of Liverpool. His research interests include state and corporate crime, the regulation of global markets, and the construction of the corporate veil. He has edited *Crimes of the Powerful: A Reader* (Open University Press, 2009), and co-authored *Safety Crimes* (Willan, 2007) and *Unmasking the Crimes of the Powerful: Scrutinizing States and Corporations* (Peter Lang, 2003). He is a board member of the Centre for Corporate Accountability and an advisory board member of Corporate Watch.

Preface

Crime: Local and Global is the companion textbook to the similarly titled *Criminal Justice: Local and Global*. Both are published by Willan Publishing in association with The Open University.

Across the world, crime, disorder and justice are increasingly pressing concerns. Fear of crime and proliferating global threats have contributed to a pervasive sense of insecurity. These books broaden the criminological imagination by *first* exploring the degree to which globalisation has created conditions for 'new' crimes to occur and how far different societies are collaborating to form a common criminal-justice response. *Second*, local concerns – for example, about street crime and violence – are now accompanied by twenty-first century global concerns about 'disorderly' cities, human trafficking, climate change, cyber-crime, terrorism, pollution, and human rights violations. *Third*, these 'threats' to safety and security have clear implications for justice, as the boundaries between crime control and civil liberties are being redrawn. *Finally*, it is increasingly assumed that not only does the threat of crime lie beyond the control of individual nation states, but that societies can freely learn from one another in the formulation of effective crime control policies. These appear as forms of zero tolerance, border controls, surveillance techniques, risk analyses, experiments in restoration and reconciliation, or through recourse to international conventions and declarations of universal human rights.

In these ways, the two books explore the meaning of 'crime' and 'criminal justice' in a globalising world. They do not assume, however, that a focus on 'the global' should replace any other mode of analysis. The idea that the 'global' simply creates homogeneity and convergence is seriously flawed. These books are just as concerned with the ways that (undeniable) international transformations can only fully be made sense of by recognising how they are imagined, reworked or resisted in local contexts. Developing a deeper understanding of how local and global initiatives intersect *and* collide – both in how crime is conceived and how it is responded to – is one of the major challenges facing contemporary criminological inquiry.

Crime: Local and Global
edited by John Muncie, Deborah Talbot and Reece Walters

This book broadens 'everyday' conceptions of crime by exploring the different ways in which 'crime' manifests itself in the diverse sites of the city, cyberspace, the body, the corporation, the environment, and the state. It is in these sites that this book begins to unravel how and why certain 'undesirable' behaviours, people, places and events are identified as deserving the criminal label (and thereby criminal sanction), while others are not. The book explores a number of examples – such as 'urban disorders', transgression in cyberspace, human trafficking, corporate violence, environmental pollution, genocide and state-sponsored torture – to consider how far 'the global' is challenging traditional criminological conceptions of the meaning and parameters of crime. Looking beyond the borders of 'crime' (as defined through the criminal law statutes of individual nation states) forces exploration of areas traditionally neglected by criminology. It requires a level of analysis that places 'crime' alongside alternative concepts such as 'harm', 'transgression', 'violence' and 'power'. It compels recognition of a wide range of troubling issues which remain hidden (and thereby unacknowledged) by traditional state-centred criminological perspectives. But what are the implications of this for criminological studies? Should we be seeking a 'global criminology'? And if so, how exactly might this be defined?

Criminal Justice: Local and Global
edited by Deborah Drake, John Muncie and Louise Westmarland

This book broadens 'everyday' conceptions of criminal justice by exploring the different ways in which 'criminal justice' manifests itself in cultures of control, experiments in restoration and conflict resolution, risk technologies, private security, techniques of surveillance, transnational policing and in conceptions of universal human rights. It is in these broad strategies of crime control and social ordering that the particular role of criminal justice systems is analysed and assessed. Looking beyond the borders of 'criminal justice' (as practised through the police, courts and prisons of individual nation states) forces reconsideration of the viability of viewing criminal justice systems as self-contained sovereign entities. Historically, law making and law enforcement have been the prerogative of the state. That sovereignty is now being challenged by international courts, human rights instruments, multinational private-security enterprises, and possibilities for global surveillance. It is no longer clear what the scope of criminal justice is and who exactly constitutes the subject of its gaze. This uncertainty creates a series of conundrums for the student of 'criminal justice'. 'Criminal justice' is being increasingly challenged not simply by the production of its own 'internal injustices', but also through disjuncture between domestic and international priorities and requirements. What role can individual states perform, on their own, in a world of global threats and insecurities? What meaning remains for state-specific concepts of criminal law and criminal justice?

Each book is a fully illustrated interactive teaching and learning resource. The chapters should be read sequentially, as each builds on preceding discussions and debates. A number of activities are built into each chapter in order to encourage active engagement and to develop a critical reflective analysis. Each activity is followed by a comments section where the authors offer their response to the questions posed and against which you can compare your own.

The production of these two books has been a long and complex process which has drawn on the expertise of many people. First and foremost, we are indebted to Kate Smith who, as course manager, has ensured that we never veered too far from our production schedules. The work of the central academic course team has been immeasurably enhanced by the advice of a panel of tutors made up of Elaine Ellis, Colin Rogers and Mari Woolfson. We are also grateful to the invaluable contributions made by our internal and external authors. All of this has been kept together (and more) by Louise Westmarland who chaired the production of the course from beginning to end, and all under the watchful eye of the external assessor, Suzanne Karstedt. Responsibility for the high quality of the books in this series also rests with a wide range of production staff, including Donna Collins (secretarial support), Fiona Harris and Adam Nightingale (editing), Paul Hillery (graphic design) and Margaret McManus (media assistance).

We thank them all.

Book Editors:

John Muncie, Deborah Talbot and Reece Walters

Chapter 1
Interrogating crime

John Muncie, Deborah Talbot and Reece Walters

Contents

1   Introduction

Crime appears as a constant source of anxiety, fascination and national and international despair. It is difficult to escape the seemingly endless political, media and popular debates about moral decline, growing anarchy and the relative powerlessness of governments to 'stem the tide'. These concerns typically focus on the 'exceptionality' of international terrorism, serial killing, 'crimes of passion', stabbings and shootings, and child abduction, along with a more 'mundane' range of behaviours considered to reduce the 'quality of life' and to increase fear, which are referred to variously as 'anti-social behaviour' or 'incivilities'.

The purpose of this introductory chapter is to provide some means whereby such understandings of what constitutes 'crime' can be subjected to critical interrogation. In particular, three questions are addressed:

1   How have criminology and criminal justice traditionally framed an understanding of 'crime' and the 'criminal'?

2   What are the implications of broadening an understanding of 'crime' to take account of a wide range of social problems and social harms that may victimise individuals, social groups or whole societies and countries, but are rarely, if ever, considered to be central criminological or law and order issues?

3   How is an understanding of crime significantly altered by exploring the ways in which it is recognised and responded to, not just in individual nation states but in broader international and global contexts?

Section 2 of this chapter examines how 'crime' is typically understood in Western societies as a violation of criminal law. It explores how such societies have arrived at this particular understanding, and how this has been underpinned by relationships of power and influence. Section 3 looks at how some aspects of criminology as an academic discipline have attempted to overcome the limitations of governmental and legal definitions of crime by extending the analytic inquiry to incorporate a broader context of social problems, violences, social harms and injurious practices. Such an approach necessitates moving 'beyond the borders' not only of 'everyday' understandings of the 'crime problem', but also of individual nation states' definitions of crime. In order to do this, Section 4 considers how far the concepts of harm, violence and power intersect with that of 'crime' and can be utilised to reach a deeper and critical interrogation. Two case studies – on violence against children and on 'natural' disasters – are presented to illustrate the implications of moving beyond the boundaries of nation-state-specific criminal law and the traditional concerns of criminology.

The aims of this chapter are to:

- encourage critical reflection on 'everyday' understandings of what constitutes the 'problem of crime'

- untangle the historical, legal and social complexities of 'crime'

- explore the implications of taking a global approach to understanding crime and, in particular, what this means for the constitution of criminological studies

- consider how notions of harm, violence and power intersect with crime and criminality.

2   The construction of 'crime' in Western societies

This section and Section 3 explore some of the complexities of 'crime' and the way in which it is typically framed within legal, political and academic discourses. The purpose is to reveal that 'crime' is not an uncontested concept. Its meaning is contingent on shifting historical, political and cultural contexts.

Activity 1.1

Stop for a moment and reflect on what immediately comes to mind when the idea of 'crime' is raised. What particular behaviours does the word 'crime' suggest to you?

Comment

We might reasonably expect there to be some broad consensus about what is meant by the term 'crime'. A typical definition routinely encountered in media and political discourses might be: 'Crime is doing something forbidden by law. That could mean stealing a mobile phone, vandalism, graffiti, mugging, stealing or taking and selling drugs.' This definition was taken from the Labour Government's 'Respect' website in 2007 (Home Office, 2007). It should not be surprising, in so far as the issues mentioned affect people in their everyday lives and are prohibited by law. However, regardless of how important we might consider these crimes to be, the definition tends to focus on 'street crimes', meaning those committed, in the main, by 'youth' in urban and public contexts. Such a focus has some notable absences. For example, it does not refer to crimes committed in the home or in 'invisible spaces' against the 'powerless' – domestic violence, child abuse, slavery, trafficking – regardless of the increasing prominence of these in public awareness (Chapter 4 explores some of these 'invisible' crimes in greater depth).

Even more absent are those 'faceless' crimes committed by the powerful as a product of corporate activity. Insider trading, environmental pollution, illegal arms dealings, and so on, are, broadly speaking, prohibited by domestic law in many countries, yet are rarely discussed as 'crime' except in some very high-profile cases. In addition, they are even more rarely prosecuted successfully. Importantly, the 'global' or international nature of such crimes also challenges 'everyday' thinking about what crime is and how to control it. Such 'crimes of the powerful' (as they are known within criminology) are discussed in detail in Chapters 5, 6 and 7. The understanding of crime, as provided by government and much media discourse, typically reflects those events and behaviours that appear to most threaten safety and security, particularly in public places. However, it tends to omit a series of potentially more harmful behaviours and events that, directly or indirectly, might cause greater pain and loss: environmental devastation or the loss of pension funds, for example.

2.1 Crime as a construction of the law

In 1933, lawyer Jerome Michael and philosopher Mortimer Adler authored a report in the USA in which they argued that an act can be a crime only when it violates the prevailing legal code of the jurisdiction in which it occurs. In their view the most precise and least ambiguous definition of crime is: 'behaviour which is prohibited by the criminal code' (Michael and Adler, 1933, p. 2). A legal definition is presented as the only possible definition because it appears to avoid moral vagueness and imprecision. Such logic was expressed again in Paul Tappan's (1947, p. 100) argument that 'Crime is an intentional act in violation of criminal law (statutory and case law), committed without defence or excuse and penalised by the state as a felony or misdemeanour'. Taking such an argument to its logical conclusion, in numerous jurisdictions a number of conditions must also be met before an act can be defined legally as a crime:

- The act must be legally prohibited at the time it is committed.

- The perpetrator must have criminal intent (*mens rea*).

- The perpetrator must have acted voluntarily (*actus reus*).

- There must be some legally prescribed punishment for committal of the act.

Three important consequences flow from such formulations of crime as law violation:

1 Definitions of crime depend on the prior formulation of criminal law sanctions. No behaviour can be considered criminal unless a formal sanction exists to prohibit it.

2 There can be no official recognition of an individual offence until an offender has been proven guilty in a court of law. No behaviour or individual can be considered criminal until formally decided as such by the criminal justice system.

3 By focusing on certain behaviours, criminal law tends to concentrate on identifying individual offenders, rather than offences committed by state or corporate organisations.

Criminal law therefore tends to individualise crime. Take, for example, the illicit international trade in cultural artefacts. The state and corporate plunder of cultural antiquities from countries in transition, or those devastated by war and civil conflict, creates a multimillion pound illegal market each year. Reputable auction houses and prestigious antique traders occupying elite residences in major cities throughout the world sell stolen ancient relics to the highest bidder in violation of international law (Mackenzie, 2005). Yet the theft of people's culture for corporate gain remains an area in which it is difficult to secure prosecutions. For example, the UK Government passed the Dealing in Cultural Objects (Offences) Act in 2003, but up to the time of writing in 2008 there had been no convictions. Individuals and corporations with vested interests are able to dictate the terms of the legislation, rendering an effective prosecution almost impossible, while at the same time ensuring that the level of illegal market regulation is determined by the traders themselves (Mackenzie and Green, 2008). Such powerful elites achieve this through lobbying politicians, funding influential think tanks and negotiating the needs and terms of regulation. The theft and sale of cultural artefacts therefore provide an excellent example of the way in which the powerful can avoid the 'criminal label' by shaping and escaping the processes of criminal justice. How the powerful both define and evade the law globally is a major theme that runs throughout this book.

2.2 Beyond legal constructions

In this section we illustrate some of the limitations of uncritical acceptance of legal definitions of crime. Understandings of what constitutes crime are often context specific and therefore open to change and dispute.

Activity 1.2

Consider the following list of behaviours and events:

■ abortion

■ taking the life of another

■ slavery

■ global warming

■ anti-social behaviour

■ keeping money found in the street

■ wearing a suit of armour in the UK Houses of Parliament.

Which do you think would be considered by legal definition to be 'criminal'?

Comment

As you might have anticipated, no straightforward 'yes' or 'no' response can be made to this question. A first obvious observation to make is that what is defined legally as criminal depends on where in the world it is committed. Abortion, for example, while legal within prescribed limits in many Western jurisdictions, is considered a criminal act in many others, whatever the circumstances. At the time of writing, women who become pregnant and whose lives might be endangered as a result are banned from having abortions in Nicaragua, Chile and El Salvador. Sixty-six other countries, such as Ireland and Portugal, ban abortion but make an exception if the mother's life is at risk. Others, such as Malaysia, allow abortion on the grounds of protecting a woman's mental health. Socio-economic reasons can be cited in the UK and India for having an abortion, while in fifty-six other countries there are no restrictions at all on the reasons that can be given to terminate a pregnancy. What is a 'crime' in one country is a 'right' in another. So, one factor to take into consideration is that a country's history and social mores may produce very different kinds of laws and thereby different kinds of crimes. It is obvious that where a country or a state is heavily influenced by particular religions, such as Catholicism, we might expect abortion to be severely proscribed.

Reponses to particular acts also depend on the social and political context in which they occur. Murder, homicide and manslaughter are widely perceived as particularly heinous, yet in certain situations, such as war, taking another's life is not only expected but encouraged. Variations are also to be found in the taking of life by the state as a form of punishment (capital punishment). Despite broad movements towards its abolition, over sixty countries, including the USA and China, still retain powers of capital punishment, usually for acts of murder, but also, in some countries, for homosexuality, adultery or treason. Homosexuals in Iran, for example, may be executed, and women who drive cars in urban areas of Saudi Arabia may be arrested. In many Western societies such activities are not generally subject to criminal law sanction; indeed, social movements have long campaigned for the decriminalisation of people's sexual choices and for women's rights. However, it is also worth remembering that, up to 1967 in the UK, homosexuality was considered both criminal and punishable by imprisonment. Conceptions of crime are both historically and culturally specific – contested and changeable.

Issues of power play a large part in the formation of law and the mobilisation of powers of enforcement. This can be seen very clearly in the examples of slavery, global warming and anti-social behaviour. Although no state currently legitimises the coerced ownership of one person by another purely for commercial gain, slavery remains widespread throughout the world, particularly in the form of child labour and human trafficking (see Section 4.1 of this chapter; also Chapter 4). The power of certain commercial enterprises and organised crime to evade prosecution is critical here.

In the case of global warming, the causes continue to be disputed but, increasingly, it is recognised as being driven by human activity. Yet the over-production of carbon emissions in the pursuit and use of natural resources is not a criminal offence (as yet) and is dealt with mainly through international agreements noted to be unenforceable and inadequate. In 2007, BP (British Petroleum) announced plans for oil exploration in the wilderness of Northern Canada. Environmentalists described this as 'the "biggest global warming crime" in history' (quoted in Milmo, 2007).

Anti-social behaviour (ASB) was defined by the UK Labour Government's 'Respect' website in 2008 as 'a wide range of selfish and unacceptable activity that can blight the quality of community life' (Home Office, 2008a). Examples of ASB cited by the website are 'Nuisance neighbours'; 'Yobbish behaviour and intimidating groups taking over public spaces'; 'Vandalism, graffiti and fly-posting'; 'People dealing and buying drugs on the street'; 'People dumping rubbish and abandoned cars'; 'Begging and anti-social drinking'; and 'The misuse of fireworks' (Home Office, 2008a). The choice of examples is revealing because it tends to refer to behaviour committed, in the main, by young people (Fergusson and Muncie, 2008) and those who are socially marginalised, and leaves out 'selfish and unacceptable activity' committed by wealthier and more powerful sections of society. While ASB is not specifically a criminal offence (although some activities, such as vandalism, might be punishable through the law as criminal damage), a breach of any Order made against anti-social behaviour is punishable through criminal law.

Figure 1.1
Contesting crime

In contrast, keeping money found in the street and wearing a suit of armour in the UK Houses of Parliament provide clear examples of specified criminal offences in the UK, even though keeping money found in the street (technically theft) is rarely prosecuted and we can assume that the prohibition – dating from 1313 – on wearing armour has long fallen into disuse! It is sometimes the case that while laws remain on the statute books, they are not enforced because of changing practices, values and norms.

What is defined as a crime is, therefore, in a constant process of negotiation and struggle over time and dependent on specific contexts. Yet it is evident that what we view as a crime also depends on who has the power both to define what a crime is and to mobilise powers of enforcement against those deemed to have committed such a violation of the law. Historically, the development of criminal law in the West was slow until its acceleration in the eighteenth century, as particular groups sought to protect their own interests and property. As Jerome Hall (1952, p. 34) notes, it was not until then that such crimes as receiving stolen property, obtaining goods by false pretences and embezzlement were first legally recognised. Many explanations of the origins of criminal law have illustrated such a relationship between economic power and the forging of new legislation suited to protect the unique interests of dominant groups. For example, the extension of property rights, particularly from the eighteenth century, had the effect of criminalising many activities, such as hunting or the gathering of wood and food, that took place on 'common land' (land that was free to all) (Lea, 2002). Hence a strong relationship can also be found between social relations of power and criminalisation.

So far this chapter has examined how the law has been central to definitions of *what* is considered to be criminal. A further key question relates to *who* is considered to be criminal. As philosopher Michel Foucault (1970 [1966]) observed, the development of specific 'scientific' disciplines (such as psychology), which purported to be able to define the 'dysfunctional' human, has been central to the development of the social understanding of 'problem people' as well as to the development of systems of social control. This is no less true of the role of criminology in developing theories of crime and criminality. The next section examines some of the key contestations within criminology itself and how they throw light on the definition and construction of 'crime' and the 'criminal'.

3   Criminology and the criminal

The term 'criminology' was first coined by the French anthropologist Paul Topinard in 1879 and defined as the 'science of understanding the criminal' (Mannheim, 1960). It arose at a time when the study of criminal behaviour was emerging as a positivist science and it was used to harness the existing sciences of 'criminal biology', 'criminal anthropology' and 'criminal psychology' (Garland, 1988).

Criminal science was first developed by an Italian school of criminologists in the late nineteenth century and was based on the principle that the causes of criminal behaviour could be explained empirically through a 'scientific' exploration of identified differences between the criminal and the non-criminal. The 'criminal' was to become the object of a distinct examination, and criminology was the science for explaining the causes of criminal behaviour. This position rejected earlier notions of free will, arguing that individuals were propelled into criminal lifestyles by a diversity of determining factors, such as 'bad blood', dysfunctional personality and material deprivation (Walters and Bradley, 2005).The earliest criminologists were concerned principally with the identification of the criminal, or what was referred to by Cesare Lombroso in 1876 as 'anatomy and crime'. That is, the criminal and the non-criminal could be identified by certain physical features.

Activity 1.3

Is it possible to tell who the 'criminals' are in society? Think about the following two examples – one from medieval England and one from the present day.

Example 1 Medieval guilt

'A Law in medieval England stated that: If two persons fell under suspicion of crime, the uglier or more deformed was to be regarded as more probably guilty.'

(Ellis, 1890, Chapter 1).

Example 2 A bus driver's blog

The Glasgow Ned (Non Educated Delinquent). Also known as the Chav or the Townie. These urban cavemen are relatively harmless on their own but can become very dangerous when they come on the bus in large groups.

Their gang (or *Young Team*) provide a sense of belonging of which their dysfunctional home life has left them bereft. For some neds this involves nothing more than getting drunk and 'goin' aboot.' However, other neds indulge in petty crime (and some not so petty) in order to validate their place within their Young Team. On a bus, this usually means: smoking, drinking, shouting, swearing, picking fights, smashing windows, seat slashing and extensive graffiti.

The neds' drink of choice is Buckfast –a fortified wine made by Roman Catholic Benedictine monks in Devon. The drink is known to make some people go crazy and act violently. When you consider that Red Bull is marketed as an 'energy drink' due to its massive caffeine content of 32mg per 100ml, Buckfast on the other hand is marketed as a 'red wine based aperitif' but packs a colossal 37.5mg of caffeine per 100ml. Rocket fuel.

(bloodbus.com, undated)

Comment

The second example is taken from one of many spoof websites that track and describe what have variously been called 'Neds' (Scottish) or Chavs (English): working-class youth who are marginalised and 'delinquent'. However, regardless of their ironic presentation, the serious point is that, like earlier forms of thinking, the descriptors of the Neds aim to show that delinquency can be observed through certain group characteristics and behaviours. This kind of thinking has embedded itself in both criminology and policy making, albeit in a less ironic fashion. Criminology, particularly as it emerged into a positivist 'science', has attempted to investigate the causes of crime, whether these are driven by, for example, 'faulty' biology, economic marginalisation, poverty, poor upbringing or peer influence. In all such cases positivist criminology focuses on particular groups that are believed, as a result of these determining factors, to be particularly prone to crime (Talbot and Mooney, 2009). The categorisation and classification of groups as 'social problems' has, as Foucault (1970 [1966]) argued, been a feature of modernity. Such groups have typically been seen as 'requiring expert intervention and knowledge' (Lea, 2002, p. 41) in the form of psychiatry, social work and the criminal justice system in general.

In contemporary policy across many Western jurisdictions, the attempt to identify social and behavioural factors that suggest that certain individuals and groups may be at risk of committing crime and anti-social behaviour has become common practice.

Activity 1.4

Read the risk factors given in Extract 1.1, which were identified by the UK Home Office in 2008 and purport to explain predispositions towards anti-social behaviour. To whom do you think these descriptors apply and where do you think these people are to be found?

Extract 1.1

Family environment

Risk factors include:

- poor parental discipline and supervision
- family conflict (between parents or between parents and children)
- family history of problem behaviour
- parental involvement/attitudes condoning problem behaviour

Schooling & educational attainment

Risk factors include:

- aggressive behaviour (e.g. bullying)
- lack of commitment to school
- school disorganisation
- school exclusion and truancy patterns
- low achievement at school

Community life/accommodation/employment

Risk factors include:

- community disorganisation and neglect
- the availability of drugs and alcohol

- lack of neighbourhood attachment
- growing up in a deprived area within low income families, high rates of unemployment and a high turnover of population
- areas where there are high levels of vandalism

Personal and individual factors

Risk factors include:

- alienation and lack of social commitment
- early involvement in problem behaviour
- attitudes that condone problem behaviour
- for young people, a high proportion of unsupervised time spent with peers and friends or peers involved in problem behaviour
- mental illness
- early involvement in the use of illegal drugs and crime

Source: Home Office, 2008b

Comment

Some of the risk factors listed concern individual psychological and behavioural characteristics and problems. It is important to observe, though, that some factors refer to issues of economic marginalisation and place, specifically to places where there is a lack of employment and public facilities and a high proportion of people living in poverty (see Chapter 2). Nowhere is it indicated that excessive wealth might also lead to a predisposition to personal exploitation or incivility towards others (behaviours that might also be considered anti-social). In a very 'broad-brush' fashion, therefore, the poor, living in deprived areas, are seen as being prone to anti-social behaviour (as both perpetrators and victims) more than any other group and are targeted as requiring a range of social policy and criminal justice interventions (**Drake, 2010**).

While such policy analyses and identification of what constitutes crime and criminals are not entirely fictional (and anyone living in deprived areas would recognise these kinds of social problems), such deterministic thinking, where cause A leads to behaviour B, assumes both that crime and problem behaviour have a fixed and ahistoric quality and that near-universal agreement can be reached on the nature and cause of social problems. Further, it creates damaging perceptions of particular 'problem' social groups that may further promote their demonisation and marginalisation. Chapter 2 will continue this discussion on the harmful nature of social segregation in cities in so far as it mobilises fears and anxieties about difference. Here, Sections, 3.1 and 3.2 below examine some critical criminological theories that have sought to question deterministic accounts of crime.

3.1 Crime as a social construct

A vast array of behaviours have been (or can be) deemed 'deviant' or 'criminal' because they violate legal, normative or human rights prescriptions, as we have already seen. But there is no common behavioural denominator that ties all of these acts together. A social constructionist perspective argues that interpretations of reality (including crime and deviance) are learned through the ways in which people perceive and react, either positively or negatively, to the behaviours of others. It accords a central role to processes of producing and circulating meanings. Within this perspective, reality is always mediated by meaning (Berger and Luckmann, 1966). How people and events are named, identified and placed within a 'map' of the social order has profound consequences for social reaction. There cannot be 'social problems' that are not the products of processes of social construction – naming, labelling, defining and mapping them into a place – through which we can 'make sense' of them.

With regard to crime, a social constructionist position would argue that crime does not exist 'out there' waiting to be discovered, but is only brought into existence through a negotiated process that involves the rule violator, the police, the courts, lawyers and the law makers who define a person's behaviour as criminal. Behaviour may be labelled 'criminal', but it is not this behaviour in itself that constitutes crime. Rather, behaviour is criminalised by a process of social perception and reaction and by the ascription of particular meanings, and their interpretation, by agents of the law. It is not what people do, but how they are perceived and evaluated by others, that constitutes crime. Much of this argument was first formulated by the American sociologist Howard Becker (1963). According to Becker, the social construct argument is concerned not so much with locating the causes of crime and deviance in individual behaviours, social factors or social situations, but with establishing that 'deviance is not a quality of the act a person commits, but rather a consequence of the application by others of rules and sanctions to an "offender". The deviant is one to whom that label has been successfully applied; deviant behaviour is behaviour that people so label' (Becker, 1963, p. 9). The identification of deviance involves the exercise of judgement by social actors, located in social institutions, applying social norms. Moreover, deviance is context specific rather than universal. As a result, Becker argued, it is incorrect to pursue the explanation of crime and deviance in terms of discovering the 'deviant characteristics' of the 'deviant' person, when deviance is a product of a process of labelling some behaviours as deviant and others as not.

This social constructionist position was further underlined by Leslie Wilkins's observation that 'there are no absolute standards. At some time or another, some form of society or another has defined almost all forms of behaviour that we now call "criminal" as desirable for the functioning of that form of society' (Wilkins, 1964, p. 46). The temporal and cultural relativity of 'crime' ensures that 'there is no one behavioural entity which we can call crime, there is no behaviour which is always and everywhere criminal' (Phillipson, 1971, p. 5). Such a view has also been advanced more recently from within anthropology by Laura Nader (2003). Nader notes that the ethnocentric nature of dominant Western conceptions of 'crime as law violation' holds no relevance for understanding how conflicts and disputes are understood and responded to in other societies. She reminds us again of the political nature of the identification of crime and of a fundamental lack of consensus of what constitutes 'the criminal' both locally and globally.

These insights are important in alerting us to the 'constantly problematic changing and contested nature of crime and social problems' (Young, 1999, p. 40), but are also in constant tension with those who argue that crime cannot be viewed simply as a 'construction' and that the very real and harmful consequences of some behaviours and events must be acknowledged. Social constructionism does often appear to be turning common sense on its head. Surely crime is a self-evident behavioural problem? How can crime be created by those very forces that are designed for its control? Reversing conventional logic, however, was crucial in radicalising the discipline of criminology that had, up to the 1960s, appeared to be largely an adjunct of, and in collusion with, prevailing relations of power. Labelling was a critical first step in understanding why and how it is that only certain troubling behaviours, acts and sections of the population are subject to criminalisation and why a host of other more serious social harms appear to be routinely practised with impunity (Section 4 looks at the concept of social harm in greater depth). Indeed, in some instances (e.g. domestic violence, human rights abuses) it is arguably a lack of labelling, negative social reaction or intolerance that provides a climate for their continuation.

3.2 Crime as the mobilisation of political power

Raising such issues inevitably leads to consideration of the political role of criminal law and to a different set of questions about the power to define what is criminal and processes of criminalisation. Such issues were first raised by the American criminologist Edwin Sutherland in the 1940s. In particular, Sutherland's work on 'white-collar crime' noted that many of these offences were processed as regulatory violations rather than as crimes. Sutherland (1940) opened up a new line of inquiry, which proposed an expanded definition capable of taking in regulatory offences as well as those identified in criminal law and of recognising the extent of criminal behaviour across the social spectrum, rather than being restricted to the traditional gaze on the working classes. In the 1970s, Jeffrey Reiman (2007) noted, in his classic text *The Rich Get Richer and the Poor Get Prison*, how events such as avoidable deaths from injury in the workplace, medical malpractice, pollution and poverty never enter dominant discourses of crime. The label of 'crime' seems reserved for the 'dangerous actions of the poor'. Herman and Julia Schwendinger (1970) expanded this list of potentially injurious practices to include the systematic violation of basic human rights. Working within a theoretical tradition that maintained that capitalist and imperialist social orders (and their state practices) contain their own criminogenic tendencies, they promoted a definition of crime based on a conception of the denial of basic fundamental human rights (analysed further in Chapter 7). This made it possible to begin analysing imperialism, racism, sexism, poverty, and so on, within a critical criminological framework.

The key questions this raised included whether defining 'crime' could be the preserve only of those with the power to construct criminal law, and whether criminology – as the study of crime – was being seriously undermined by having its subject matter defined by political and legal elites. In response, Richard Quinney (1970, pp. 15–16) argued that the identification and delineation of 'crime' is an inherently political process. Law (and thus crime) is created and applied by those who have the power to translate their own interests into public policy. Criminal law is coercive and partial, its political neutrality a myth. Developing this line of argument, Willem de Haan maintains that 'crime' is an ideological concept that justifies inequality and distracts public attention from more serious problems, harms and injustices (de Haan, 1990).

By the 1990s a whole range of 'injurious practices' or 'non-crimes' had been 'claimed' by a criminological agenda and had begun to be taken seriously by some academic criminologists. These include the failure to enforce health and safety standards at work; manufacturers deliberately marketing products known to be faulty; the 'culpable negligence' of

Figure 1.2
Migrant workers in
Trafalgar Square,
London, in May 2007
demand recognition of
their contribution to
the UK economy and
an end to their
deportation.

tobacco and food companies knowingly promoting unsafe and life-threatening substances; the international dumping of toxic waste; the abuse involved in the transportation of live animals; and the systematic flaunting of export controls to certain countries by arms manufacturers. Some of these issues will be explored further in Chapters 5 and 6.

These critical issues pose core dilemmas for any attempt to delimit the boundaries of crime, the legal and criminal justice process and criminology itself. The inherent problems of identifying social causation, and the historically and politically constructed nature of crime, law and criminology, suggest a need for an approach that goes beyond these definitional, legal and disciplinary boundaries. In the remainder of this chapter, we will explore conceptual approaches that attempt to go beyond borders by reframing the idea of crime as being embedded in a range of social problems. In doing so, we will look more closely at the concepts of harm, violence and power within a global context.

4   Beyond borders: utilising the concepts of harm, violence and power

The previous section explored some of the limitations of legal definitions both of crime and of criminology as an emergent scientific academic discipline. To tackle the partiality of these definitions, some authors, such as Stuart Henry and Mark Lanier (1998), have placed 'crime' within a broader context of social harm in which the visible and

Figure 1.3
The greater crime? The dumping of toxic waste into the sea off the Ivory Coast from an Estonian cargo vessel, and an illegal waste dump in New Orleans.

the obscured, the legally recognised and the legally sanctioned can be included in a comprehensive and integrated vision of criminal and harmful acts. This does not imply that everyday understandings and experience of 'crimes' are not real enough, but places them in the context of a wide range of potentially or actually more harmful practices. Moreover, if we are to grasp the significance of 'crime' on a global scale, it would appear to be necessary to move beyond conceptions that are, by definition, specific to individual nation states. The Latin origin of the word 'crime', *crimen*, reveals that it was very much packaged within notions of harm: *crimen* was used historically to describe acts that brought scandal, dishonour, harm, blame and insult – and not just to refer to those who violated state laws (see Pavlich, 2000; Walters and Bradley, 2005). From this, it can be seen that the meanings of words are not to be found solely in the static confines of dictionary definitions, but also in the social contexts in which terms evolve and are constructed. Thus, crime is a continually developing concept that must capture socio-cultural discourses – to confine it to legal parameters is to contain (and constrain) criminological interrogation within state-defined boundaries.

Some criminologists (Tifft, 1995; Hillyard et al., 2004) have developed a 'social harm approach' to facilitate understanding both of those social problems and injurious practices that are the typical remit and focus of criminal justice and of those that are not. Paddy Hillyard and Steve Tombs (2007) present four interrelated theses, all of which involve expanding the traditional boundaries of criminology. We will consider the first two together.

1   *Social harms are greater and more differentially distributed than criminal law allows.*

2   *The concept of harm incorporates notions of financial/economic, emotional and cultural harms as well as physical harms.*

Criminal law (and some forms of criminological thinking), as we have already seen, tends to view harm narrowly as either interpersonal violence or violation of property ownership. To some degree, criminal law (in some jurisdictions) does prosecute other types of harm. These may include workplace or industrial accidents; or war crimes such as torture, deliberate targeting of civilians, and human rights abuses. However, such prosecutions depend on particular circumstances: for example, whether an individual can be found to be responsible in the case of industrial accidents; whether states are inclined to pursue other states for war crimes or human rights abuses (a political issue, in the main); whether there is sufficient exposure of the issues in the global media; or whether there are sufficient resources for prosecution. Criminal law may target types of financial crime, such as fraud or the mis-selling of financial products, but again differentially and depending on circumstance. Moreover, in all of these latter cases, such prosecutions typically result in a fine (although there are occasional exceptions: see Chapter 5).

Hillyard and Tombs (2007) also point out that there are other types of harm, ranging from multiple harms (and social problems) arising from poverty and emotional and psychological abuse, to cultural exclusion from the benefits of advanced society, such as a good education. Yet these are only tangentially considered in crime control policy and, moreover, never to the point of attempting to eliminate them. So why are different types of crime treated differently and why are some harms seen to be more important than others? The proponents of the social harm approach argue that this is because of the relevance of power in the formation of discourses of crime and practices of crime control. This brings us to the third and fourth theses.

3   *The ability to define harm as a crime through the criminal law and justice system derives from social power.*

4   *Utilising the idea of harm allows for a concept of justice that is not simply focused on acknowledging the responsibility of, and punishing, the individual wrongdoer, but also incorporates the responsibility of corporations, governments and economic systems.*

Within criminological discourse, as we have already examined, there has been a tendency to define the problem of crime as one of interpersonal violence or of a property crime; to understand crime through the definitions of criminal law; and to view crime as caused by individual or group dysfunctionality, whether this is biological or psychological in origin or a function of the deviant behaviours brought about by social or spatial marginalisation (discussed further in Chapter 2). The range of harms caused by corporate or governmental bodies has been of lesser concern, partly, it has been argued, because business and government have been substantially involved in making criminal law to protect themselves and their own property (Whyte, 2009). The influence of the powerful in the formation of criminal law can also be felt if we look at who is the object of crime control and criminal justice. Criminal law focuses primarily on punishing crimes committed by individuals against individuals. Attempts to extend the notion of criminal responsibility to mass organisations have proved problematic because proving intent to commit a criminal act is hard within complex organisational structures. As a result, Hillyard and Tombs (2007) argue that the concept of social harm, utilised instead of the narrower, legal definition of crime, allows for the development of policy around wider considerations of responsibility for economic and geographical inequalities, and forces acknowledgement of the role of government and corporations in the perpetration of harms.

Consider the following. Illegal, unregulated and unreported (IUU) fishing by commercial operations is in contravention of controls imposed by various international agreements, but imported fish is worth between £4 billion and £9 billion to the UK per annum. By conservative estimates, more than 12,000 tonnes originate from illegal fishing in the offshore waters of poor countries, an activity that decimates the industry and food supply of debt-stricken countries in West Africa, while destroying marine biology. Yet unregistered pirate vessels enter British ports unchecked and the stolen fish are sold at London markets without question (Environmental Justice Foundation, 2007). Illegal actions on one side of the world – in this case, fishing off the West African coast – become normal commercial transactions thousands of miles away in London. Yet the devastation of African marine life and the social, political and cultural harm caused to the livelihoods of West African peoples already living in poverty are not accounted for or even recognised by the UK criminal justice system. Can a social harm approach help us to understand the actions and consequences of multinational corporations that escape domestic law?

Similar issues arise with the concept of violence. As far as the criminal justice system is concerned, violence is normally associated with direct physical or interpersonal harm, between either individuals or groups (Hillyard and Tombs, 2007). However, violence is a much broader phenomenon. As Jamil Salmi (2004, p. 56) points out: 'Violence is often narrowly equated with images of war (as in Afghanistan and Iraq), murders (as in Washington DC), or riots (as in Indonesia); by definition, however, violence is any act that threatens a person's physical or psychological integrity.' Salmi developed a typology of violence that stretches the boundaries of both common understanding and that operating within criminal justice. Included in this typology, alongside direct interpersonal violence or intentional harm, are indirect violence, repressive violence and alienating violence.

Indirect violence can consist either of 'violence by omission', whereby a failure to assist by individuals or government, as in the examples of the Holocaust or the ethnic violence in Rwanda, can result in the perpetration of violence, or of 'mediated violence', where there are delayed effects resulting from human interventions. An example of this might be environmental pollutants, such as asbestos, which may result in death or disease. In each case, responsibility for the violent act may lie with both the perpetrators and those who failed to act to prevent it.

Repressive violence, normally perpetrated by states or political groups, can involve a vast variety of human or civil rights violations. In Libya, Gambia and India, for example, human rights activists have been arrested by their respective governments; and those promoting democracy and free speech in Iran, Georgia and Kosovo have reportedly been imprisoned or beaten by repressive governmental regimes (Amnesty International, 2008). Consider the situation in Tibet. Since

1949 the Chinese government has devastated Tibetan culture and fails to recognise it as a separate nation. China has released nuclear explosions in Tibet, confiscated lands and subjected Tibetan people to ongoing brutality and humiliation in what has been called an act of 'cultural genocide' (Amnesty International, 2008).

Lastly, Salmi includes the category of alienating violence, which occurs when people are denied the right to 'psychological, emotional, cultural or intellectual integrity' (Salmi, 2004, p. 59); for example, when governments either permit conditions to exist that cause insecurity, or deny cultural expression. In the case of repressive and alienating violence the impact is psychological, in the main, although human and civil rights violations and the denial of cultural expression may also consist of physical violence, as in the case of torture (see Chapter 7).

As with the concept of harm, the constitution of violence can therefore extend beyond the narrow definitions operating within the criminal justice and legal professions. Indeed, loosening the conceptual framework of each in this way allows us to reinterrogate the relative harm embodied in different types of crime and violence. Understanding how harm, violence and power intersect with crime is critical to acknowledging the weaknesses of conventional understandings of crime and of the operation of criminal law and criminal justice. This is not to argue that criminal justice systems, whether nationally or internationally, can be expected to resolve and encompass the full multitude of harms. Rather, it is to demonstrate that harms of equal severity are treated differently and that this is a product of inequalities of power, whether historically or contemporarily derived.

We will now turn to two examples – youth violence and 'natural' disasters – to examine these complex interactions in more detail. When reading these two cases, think about the ambiguities of the concepts of harm and violence and how both intersect with issues of power.

4.1 Violence, children and youth

Activity 1.5

Consider the newspaper headlines reproduced below. What do they tell you about the current state of young people?

Vile Lawless Teenagers Terrorising the Streets

Source: *Daily Express*, UK, 2002

Young Criminals Show No Mercy: 'Superpredators' Leave a Trail of Ruthless Violence

Source: *Washington Times*, USA, 2000

Hardcore Child Supercrooks are Bringing Fear to Britain's Streets

Source: *Daily Star*, UK, 1992

Teen Knife Violence Surge

Source: *Sunday Age*, Melbourne, Australia, 2007

Youth Violence Behind Call for After-School Program Funds

Source: *Japan Times*, 2003

We're Witnessing the Downward Spiral of Britain. Decent Members of the Public are Being Murdered by Feral Youths on our Streets

Source: *The Sun*, UK, 2008

Comment

Youth violence seems automatically assured to be placed at the top of law and order agendas. These headlines come from newspapers in Australia, the USA, Japan and the UK dating from 1992. In some respects, their precise location in time and place is of secondary interest. They all readily equate young people with (usually perceived increases in) violence. And in some respects this appears to be justified. In 1999 at Columbine High School, in Colorado, USA, two students shot and killed twelve other students and a teacher, as well as wounding twenty-three others, before committing suicide. A student shot his classmates and teacher, killing two and injuring five, at Monash University, Melbourne, Australia in 2002. In 2007, a student shot nine dead in a school at Tuusula, Finland. In the same year in Liverpool, UK, an 11-year-old was killed in an apparently accidental shooting by a teenager; it was assumed to be symptomatic of youth gang warfare burgeoning in the major cities of the UK.

The prevailing international message is one of 'youth out of control'. These particular images of youth, crime and violence have indeed come to be institutionalised, sedimented and 'taken for granted' as objective knowledge. All of these events were certainly newsworthy and deserving of criminological attention. However, they raised key unanswered questions. What did they represent? Were they indicative of a significant new trend or were they isolated, unrelated tragedies? Were these concerns over youth violence at all new? Were they warranted? Or did they simply reproduce populist images of violence and youth and disguise other serious violence and its perpetrators?

Violence committed by young people, especially if against other young people, seems to hit a crucial moral nerve. It evokes a familiar series of responses. On the one hand, governments are blamed for not 'doing enough'; on the other, parents (usually inner city and/or minority ethnic parents) are accused of failing to bring up their children responsibly. Beyond this lies a series of alarms over 'copycatting' violent films, rap music and video games. Typically, media and political discourses, nationally and internationally, declare these rare and exceptional events to be indicative of some national malaise and use them as metaphors for the state of modern youth and of societies that are on the verge of 'anarchy'.

Critical interrogation of this youth/violence relationship often begins by noting that the vast majority of criminological research has focused almost exclusively on young people as offenders rather than victims. Significantly, too, when children (defined by the United Nations, [1989], as under the age of 18) are in conflict with the law, political and popular discourses tend to recast them as 'juveniles' or 'youth'; their 'child' status is lost and with it all that implies for their protection. The term 'child' is, however, typically retained to refer to those who are deemed 'victims'. And such victimisation does indeed appear to be extensive. In the UK, children under one year old are more at risk of being murdered than any other age group, with forty-six deaths per million of population compared with a national average of sixteen per million; parents are the principal suspects in 78 per cent of all child homicides (NSPCC, 2003). The extent of domestic child abuse remains largely unknown, although research by the NSPCC (2002) in the UK estimated that one in ten young adults has suffered serious abuse or neglect during childhood; 600 children are added to child protection registers every week. UNICEF (2006) has estimated that up to 275 million children worldwide are routinely exposed to domestic violence, including over 900,000 in the UK and 2.7 million in the USA. While child and youth victimisation was recognised as long ago as the late nineteenth century, it has generally been clouded by a discourse of cruelty and neglect, rather than being placed within a discourse of criminality. Criminological research has concentrated either on the degree to which parental abuse and neglect 'causes' future delinquency or on the relationship between delinquent activity and the risk of victimisation. Within criminology little has been done to expose the routine of violence – from slapping to serious assault – endured by young people in their own homes. The corporal punishment of children is widespread and often justified in the name of discipline and the prevention of delinquency. For example, attempts to outlaw corporal punishment in the UK have always floundered because of accusations of 'nanny state' interference. Since Sweden banned smacking in the 1990s, it has been claimed that child deaths at the hands of parents there have fallen to zero (Ahmed, 2003).

In general, the concentration on young people as the perpetrators of crime has negated consideration of the extent of their relative powerlessness. This has always placed youth at potential risk of victimisation by adults. Nowhere is this more evident than in modern 'child slavery'. In India, several thousand children 'disappear' each year. It is widely believed that these children are sold for slavery or for adoption in Western countries, including the UK (Chamberlain, 2008).

According to Save the Children UK (2007b, p. 1), around the world 218 million children aged 5–17 work as child labourers; they are forced to endure long hours for no or little pay and are left vulnerable to 'extreme harm, violence and rape'. Children are treated as commodities across all continents and in myriad ways, as the statistics given in Extract 1.2 show.

Figure 1.4
An Indian mother in South Delhi attempts to find her son who was 14 when he disappeared from home.

Extract 1.2

Child trafficking:

1.2 million children and babies are trafficked every year, including into Western Europe, the Americas and the Caribbean, and the number is increasing.

Child prostitution:

At any one time across the world, around 1.8 million children are being abused through prostitution, child pornography and sex tourism.

In the UK there are 5000 child prostitutes. 75 per cent of them are girls.

Bonded child labour:

Millions of children are forced to work away their childhood in horrific conditions to pay off debt, or simply the interest on it.

In India alone, estimates suggest up to 15 million children could be enslaved by somebody else's debt, many involved in illegal, hazardous and dangerous work.

Forced work in mines:

One million children are risking their lives in mines and quarries in more than 50 African, Asian and South American countries.

In the Sahel region of Africa, 200,000 children are daily risking their lives in gold and mineral mines.

Agricultural labour:

[More than] 132 million children under 15 are trapped working in agriculture, often exposed to pesticides, heavy machinery, machetes and axes.

In Kazakhstan, children work in cotton and tobacco fields and factories for up to 12 hours a day, seven days a week.

Child soldiers:

[More than] 300,000 children under 15 are involved with fighting forces, including government armies. Boys and girls in at least 13 countries are being actively recruited as child soldiers or as army 'wives'.

Around 11,000 children in Democratic Republic of Congo are currently being held by fighting groups.

Forced child marriage:

Child marriage, which often includes mail order and internet brides, is one of the most widespread – yet hidden – forms of slavery. Girls as young as four are forced to live and have sex with their husband, and are often kept trapped indoors.

Girls under 15 are five times more likely to die during pregnancy and childbirth than women over 20. In Afghanistan more than half of all girls are married before they are 16.

Domestic slavery:

Millions of children across the world, some as young as six, are forced to work up to 15 hour days as domestic workers. Many are beaten, starved and sexually abused.

There are 200,000 child domestic workers in Kenya, 550,000 in Brazil and 264,000 in Pakistan.

Source: Save the Children, 2007a

Adult justice:

In the USA in 2004 over 7000 juveniles were held in adult jails. Over 2000 had been sentenced to life without hope of parole.

In England and Wales the age of criminal responsibility is 10; in Scotland it is 8. These are the lowest in Europe and some of the lowest in the world.

Source: Muncie, 2009

The United Nations General Assembly study on *Violence against Children* (2006) found that such violence exists in every country of the world, cutting across culture, class, education, income and ethnic origin. The majority of violent acts experienced by children tend to be perpetrated by immediate acquaintances: parents, schoolfriends, teachers, employers, boyfriends or girlfriends, spouses and partners. But, most significantly, in virtually all nation states and in contradiction of human rights obligations and children's developmental needs, violence against children appears to be socially approved. It is often legal and is frequently state authorised.

Within law and order discourses, violence perpetrated by children is presented as a major harm to society and redefined as 'youth violence'. It is widely assumed that if unruly or disorderly behaviours are not controlled by various policy initiatives in criminal law and policing, young people will become out of control (particularly those in other 'at risk' locations, as we saw in Section 3). However, such discourse disguises the way in which young people are exposed to harm from adults globally – whether this is through physical threat or economic exploitation – because of their relative powerlessness. As such, we might view young people (if redefined as 'children') as being more in need of protection and support than law and order. Further examples of the ambiguity with which children and young people are treated are discussed in Chapter 2.

4.2 'Natural' disasters

How can a naturally occurring disaster, such as an earthquake, a hurricane, a tsunami or a tidal wave, or something like climate change, possibly be linked to crime and criminology? The United Nations International Strategy for Disaster Reduction (UNISDR) identifies that Asia continues to be the region hardest hit by natural disasters. In 2007 alone there were 399 occurrences of disaster worldwide, as defined by UNISDR. These caused an estimated death toll of 16,517 – a further 197 million people were affected by disasters. Damage was estimated at US$ 62.5 billion. Bangladesh continues to be the worst affected country: over 5000 people were killed in 2007 as a result of cyclones and flooding

(UNISDR, 2008). However, as the United Nations Educational, Scientific and Cultural Organisation reports, 'natural' disasters frequently involve non-natural or human input (UNESCO, 2008). In other words, what we consider to be a naturally occurring phenomenon is influenced by human activity. As UNESCO (2008) put it: 'natural disasters are not entirely "natural", for people are agents of disasters. ... severe flooding may be exacerbated by deforestation'. Massive concentration of populations in hazard-prone areas 'or in cities and settlements where houses and infrastructures are not safely built and where land-use is poorly planned [lead] to disastrous effects after an earthquake'.

It is also widely recognised that the devastation caused by climate change and 'natural' disasters is more widely felt by the world's poor than those living in richer countries. The affluent developed countries often emit the pollution that contributes to climate change. In other words, revising the title of Reiman's book from which we quoted in Section 3.2, 'the rich get richer, while the poor get natural disasters'. The *World Disasters Report* (International Federation of Red Cross, 2007) identified that devastating landslides are frequently caused by the illegal logging of native woodlands and forests; flooding by the increasing industrialisation and pollution of large developed nations; and collapsing buildings after earthquakes by deficient engineering. All are exacerbated by failure of corrupt and negligent governments to plan or implement disaster relief. Often it is the poorest people of the poorest countries who lose their lives and suffer the greatest harm (this is discussed further in Chapters 5 and 6).

Let us look at Bangladesh, one of the poorest nations in Asia. It is often reported as a sinking country and 'the worst sufferer of global warming' (Independent Bangladesh, 2008). As mentioned at the beginning of this section, more people in Bangladesh die each year as a result of natural disasters (notably from cyclones, tsunamis and flooding) than in any other country. Tsunamis also wash up hazardous waste illegally dumped at sea by Western corporations. South Asia is recognised as the biggest dumping ground on earth for hazardous and toxic chemicals. While the Basel Convention prohibits the transportation of dangerous waste to developing nations, such transportation continues to occur with regularity. Corporations flout international law and deliberately release toxic waste substances into the waters of Bangladesh. When cyclones and tsunamis cause flooding, the radioactive waste of other countries is washed ashore on the coastline, causing skin disease and blindness among Bangladeshi children (Independent Bangladesh, 2008).

Rising seas levels, caused by climate change, have resulted in the routine flooding of Bangladeshi streets. Thousands of people die each year from disease or drowning or are crushed under fallen buildings, as a result of poor defences against natural disasters and a lack of satisfactory infrastructure to provide sanitation and waste collection ('Bangladesh: The Drowning Country', *Unreported World*, 2009). Figure 1.6 shows a typical scene confronting coastal Bangladeshi people and a common occurrence in the nation's capital. What the picture doesn't show is the rotting carcasses of animals, the floating debris of human and municipal waste or the polluting effluent from local factories, all of which create perilous conditions for human survival.

There are fifty-seven main rivers and waterways in Bangladesh. Upstream deforestation, soil erosion and rising seas cause these rivers to swell rapidly, which in turn causes flash flooding. Thousands of fishermen died in 2007 as unexpected seas emerged in the Bay of Bengal. It is anticipated that 20 per cent of Bangladesh will be permanently covered in water within two years. Its agriculture continues to be decimated, precious biodiversity is vanishing and food security is an ongoing national crisis. Much of the flooding and unpredictable weather is caused by climate change that is not of Bangladesh's doing and is not within the budget of this poor country to prevent. Bangladesh's annual carbon dioxide emission is a minuscule 172 Kg per capita, compared to the USA's 21 tons per capita (Huggler, 2007). Moreover, the average

Figure 1.5
People walk through flood waters in Bangladesh after mudslides triggered by monsoon rains in 2007 left at least 87 people dead.

person in the UK produces forty-eight times more carbon dioxide than a person living in Bangladesh (Khaleque, 2006).

Bangladesh also faces the natural disaster of arsenic pollution in its water, which places 80 million people at risk. Arsenic is naturally occurring in pyrite bedrock under West Bengal. When the governments of Bangladesh and India began to deep pump much-needed fresh-water from underground reservoirs, they exposed arsenic-bearing pyrite to the atmosphere with catastrophic consequences. Over 18 million people in Bangladesh are affected by arsenic poisoning. A naturally occurring geological process has been turned into a human catastrophe by human intervention. Domestic endeavours in Bangladesh to rectify the problem are under-resourced and ineffective and the international community has offered no answers to the problem (Garelick et al., 2009).

The relevance of criminological frameworks to the phenomena of natural disasters has been developed by Penny Green and Tony Ward (2004), who argue that the victims of natural disasters are also the victims of human rights abuses, through various forms of what they call 'organisational deviance'. This term refers to states that are 'willing to commit human rights violations' and that are 'uniformly disinterested in protecting their citizenry against the potential catastrophe of a natural disaster' (Green and Ward, 2004, p. 55). For example, consider the state corruption that permits tax revenues to be exploited for private and commercial gain – at the expense of poverty reduction, health care service and housing – and thereby prevents the building of the infrastructures necessary to minimise harm during and after a natural disaster.

Green and Ward (2004, p. 67) argue that 'the devastating consequences of so-called natural disasters' can be exposed 'not as the inevitable products of geophysical disruption but as the direct consequence of state deviance'. On one level, this example is relevant because it demonstrates that what is often presented as a natural harm is actually one produced by humans, and, more specifically, by an inadequate (and, some might say, criminally negligent) response by governments and businesses. As such, 'green criminology', which will be examined further in Chapter 6, often makes the case for corporate activities that affect the environment (and therefore people) to be criminalised. On another level, it also illustrates how power intersects with harms, so that a population that is relatively powerless, due to poverty or a democratic deficit, is more likely to suffer negatively as a result of so-called 'natural' disasters.

5 Conclusion

Part of the problem in establishing the reality and meaning of crime does seem to lie in the concept of 'crime' itself. The term implies a unity to what is a vast array of diverse behaviours, events and legal sanctions. It is constrained by the legal definitions differentially employed in different jurisdictions (Aas, 2007). This chapter has explored how the elusive nature of 'crime' can begin to be captured by revealing how the concept of crime becomes active through the variable meanings attached to it in specific political and socio-historical contexts and through the diverse 'voices' of the media, the public, criminal justice professionals, politicians, victims and pressure groups. 'Crime' clearly takes on different meanings for different social audiences. Interrogation of the concept of crime remains important in alerting us to relations of power embedded in social orders that generate a whole series of social problems for their populations, but of which only a selected few are considered worthy of criminal sanction. As such, it might be argued that a conception of crime without a conception of power is meaningless (Muncie, 2001). It is important to recognise how structures of power render certain harmful acts visible and define them as 'crime', while maintaining the invisibility of others (or defining them as beyond criminal sanction). As well as offering some protection for members of society, criminal law also seems to immunise those with power and influence, who generate the most serious social harms from legal sanction. Notions of 'crime' do seem to provide a peculiarly blinkered vision of the dangers, harms, risks and injuries that are a routine part of everyday life. If the criminological intent is to reveal such risks and harms, the concept of 'crime' has to be either rejected or substantially expanded and equitably applied (Muncie, 2000). Many incidents (such as petty theft, shoplifting, recreational drug use, vandalism, brawls, anti-social behaviour) that are commonly accepted as criminal would not seem to score particularly high on a scale of serious widespread harm. And yet it is often these 'minor' events that take up much of the time and preoccupation of law enforcement agencies and criminal justice systems. Equally, the chance of suffering many of those crimes defined by many states as 'serious', such as murder, abduction and armed robbery, would seem negligible compared to such everyday risks as workplace injury and avoidable disease (Hillyard and Tombs, 2007).

This chapter has also suggested that some of the most serious social, environmental and economic harms operate beyond the borders of the nation state. Hence, we have the spectacle of Western companies embedding themselves in countries where low wages are backed by human rights violations (as in Burma, at the time of writing) or where companies are protected by the law even when they have committed devastating violations and caused thousands of deaths (as in the industrial 'accident' by the US company Union Carbide in Bhopal, India). Such a perspective necessitates a shift from a local to a global focus in assessing how harm, violence and power intersect with and extend the concept of crime.

Because the term 'crime' is of such emotive and political value and is by necessity tied to the criminal justice apparatus of particular nation states, some (e.g. Hulsman, 1986) have argued for its replacement by more sensitising notions, such as social injury and social harm. However, this also assumes universal agreement as to what those harms consist of, and indeed implicates the problem of power. So, for example, we might view the exploitation of child labour as a harm or an injury, yet it is supported by some of those we regard as the 'powerful' (governments and companies), which perceive low wages and child exploitation as essential to maintaining consumer economies. Similarly, arguments have been made for the 'export' of human rights and civil justice agendas to countries merely for the purpose of challenging other powers (e.g. human rights violations in Africa and Burma and the Western resistance to and resentment of Chinese expansionism). Hence, rights-based agendas, principles that might be universally expressed, are also caught up in systems of conflict and violence.

These complex relations between crime, power, violence and harm are explored in more detail in the following chapters through the diverse sites of the city, cyberspace, the human body, the corporation, the environment and the state. What is clear at the present is that, if we are to fully appreciate the nature and extent of 'crime' on a global scale, the particular understandings offered by criminal law and by individual nation states are partial and insufficient.

References

Aas, F.K. (2007) *Globalisation and Crime*, London, Sage.

Ahmed, K. (2003) 'Should it be a crime to hit your child?', *The Observer*, 4 May [online], www.guardian.co.uk/society/2003/may/04/ childrensservices.childprotection (Accessed 27 March 2009).

Amnesty International (2008) 'Real lives', *Amnesty Magazine*, issue 148, pp. 34–5.

'Bangladesh: The Drowning Country', *Unreported World*, (Channel 4), Friday 7 March 2009.

Becker, H. (1963) *Outsiders: Studies in the Sociology of Deviance*, New York, Free Press.

Berger, P. and Luckmann, T. (1966) *The Social Construction of Reality*, New York, Doubleday.

bloodbus.com (undated) *Glasgow Neds* [online], http://bloodbus.com/about_neds.php (Accessed 6 January 2009).

Chamberlain, G. (2008) 'Sold for £20: just two of India's million stolen children', *The Observer*, 7 September [online], www.guardian.co.uk/world/2008/sep/07/india.humantrafficking (Accessed 6 January 2009).

de Haan, W. (1990) *The Politics of Redress*, London, Unwin Hyman.

Drake, D. (2010) 'Punitiveness and cultures of control' in Drake, D., Muncie, J. and Westmarland, L. (eds) *Criminal Justice: Local and Global*, Cullompton, Willan Publishing/Milton Keynes, The Open University.

Ellis, H. (1890) *The Criminal*, London, Walter Scott.

Environmental Justice Foundation (2007) *Save the Sea: Defending Oceans* [online], www.ejfoundation.org/page357.html (Accessed 6 March 2009).

Fergusson, R. and Muncie, J. (2008) 'Criminalising conduct' in Cochrane, A. and Talbot, D. (eds) *Security: Welfare, Crime and Society*, Maidenhead, Open University Press/Milton Keynes, The Open University.

Foucault, M. (1970 [1966]) *The Order of Things* (trans.) New York, Pantheon.

Garelick, H., Jones, H., Dybowska, A. and Valsami-Jones, E. (2009) 'Arsenic Pollution Sources' in Whitacre, E. (ed.) *Reviews of Environmental Contamination. International Perspectives on Arsenic Pollution and Remediation*, New York, Springer.

Garland, D. (1988) 'British criminology before 1935', *British Journal of Criminology*, vol. 28, no. 2, pp. 1–17.

Green, P. and Ward, T. (2004) *State Crime: Governments, Violence and Corruption*, London, Pluto Press.

Hall, J. (1952) *Theft, Law and Society*, Indianapolis, IN, Bobs-Merrill.

Henry, S. and Lanier, M.M. (1998) 'The prism of crime; arguments for an integrated definition of crime', *Justice Quarterly*, vol. 15, no. 4, pp. 609–27.

Hillyard, P., Pantazis, C., Tombs, S. and Gordon, D. (eds) (2004) *Beyond Criminology: Taking Harm Seriously*, London, Pluto Press.

Hillyard, P. and Tombs, S. (2007) 'From "crime" to social harm?', *Crime, Law and Social Change*, vol. 48, nos. 1–2, pp. 9–25.

Home Office (2007) *Tackling Anti-social Behaviour and Its Causes* [online], www.respect.gov.uk/article.aspx?id=10086 (Accessed 17 August 2008).

Home Office (2008a) *What is Anti-social Behaviour?* [online], www.respect.gov.uk/article.aspx?id=9066 (Accessed 17 August 2008).

Home Office (2008b) *What is ASB?* [online], www.homeoffice.gov.uk/anti-social-behaviour/what-is-asb/?version=1 (Accessed 27 June 2008).

Huggler, J. (2007) 'Bangladesh: at the mercy of climate change', *Independent*, 19 February [online], www.independent.co.uk/environment/climate-change/bangladesh-at-the-mercy-of-climate-change-436950.html (Accessed 6 January 2009).

Hulsman, L. (1986) 'Critical criminology and the concept of crime', *Contemporary Crises*, vol. 10, no. 1, pp. 63–80.

Independent Bangladesh (2008) 'Bangladesh to be worst sufferer of global warming', in collaboration with *Daily Commercial Times*, 11 March [online], www.bcas.net/Env.Features/ClimateChange/2008/March2008/1%20to%2015.htm#5 (Accessed 6 January 2009).

International Federation of Red Cross (2007) *The World Disasters Report* [online], www.ifrc.org/publicat/wdr2007/summaries.asp (Accessed 6 March 2009).

Khaleque, V. (2006) 'Bangladesh is paying a cruel price for the west's excesses', *The Guardian*, 7 December [online], www.guardian.co.uk/commentisfree/2006/dec/07/comment.christmasappeal2006 (Accessed 6 January 2009).

Lea, J. (2002) *Crime and Modernity: Continuities in Left Realist Criminology*, London, Sage.

Lombroso, C. (2006 [1876]) *The Criminal Man*, (trans. M. Gibson and N. Rafter) Durham, NC, Duke University press.

Mackenzie, S.R.M. (2005) *Going, Going, Gone: Regulating the Market in Illicit Antiquities*, Leicester, Institute of Art and Law.

Mackenzie, S. and Green, P. (2008) 'Performative regulation: a case study in how powerful people avoid criminal labels', *British Journal of Criminology*, vol. 48, no. 2, pp. 138–53.

Mannheim, H. (1960) *Pioneers in Criminology*, London, Stevens.

Michael, J. and Adler, M. (1933) *Crime, Law and Social Science*, New York, Harcourt Brace Jovanovich.

Milmo, C. (2007) 'The biggest environmental crime in history', *The Independent*, 10 December [online], www.independent.co.uk/environment/the-biggest-environmental-crime-in-history-764102.html (Accessed 6 March 2009).

Muncie, J. (2000) 'Decriminalising criminology' in Lewis, G., Gewirtz, S. and Clarke, J. (eds) *Rethinking Social Policy*, London, Sage/Milton Keynes, The Open University.

Muncie, J. (2001) 'The construction and deconstruction of crime' in Muncie, J. and McLaughlin, E. (eds) *The Problem of Crime*, London, Sage/Milton Keynes, The Open University.

Muncie, J. (2009) *Youth and Crime*, (3rd edn), London, Sage.

Nader, L. (2003) 'Crime as category – domestic and globalised' in Parnell, P.C. and Kane, S. (eds) *Crime's Power: Anthropologists and the Ethnography of Crime*, London, Palgrave Macmillan.

National Society for the Prevention of Cruelty to Children (NSPCC) (2002) *Child Abuse in Britain*, London, NSPCC.

National Society for the Prevention of Cruelty to Children (NSPCC) (2003) *Child Killings in England and Wales*, London, NSPCC.

Pavlich, G. (2000) *Critique and Radical Discourses on Crime*, London, Ashgate.

Phillipson, M. (1971) *Sociological Aspects of Crime and Delinquency*, London, Routledge & Kegan Paul.

Quinney, R. (1970) *The Social Reality of Crime*, Boston, MA, Little, Brown.

Reiman, J. (2007) *The Rich Get Richer and the Poor Get Prison* (8th edn), New York, Wiley.

Salmi, J. (2004) 'Violence in democratic societies: towards an analytic framework' in Hillyard, P., Pantazis, C., Tombs, S. and Gordon, D. (eds) *Beyond Criminology: Taking Harm Seriously*, London, Pluto Press.

Save the Children UK (2007a) *Most Widespread Forms of Child Slavery Revealed by New Save the Children Report* [online], www.savethechildren.org.uk/en/41_522.htm (Accessed 6 March 2009).

Save the Children UK (2007b) *The Small Hands of Slavery*, London, Save the Children UK.

Schwendinger, H. and Schwendinger, J. (1970) 'Defenders of order or guardians of human rights?', *Issues in Criminology*, no. 7, pp. 72–81.

Sutherland, E.H. (1940) 'White-collar criminality', *American Sociological Review*, vol. 5, no. 1, pp. 1–12.

Talbot, D. and Mooney, J. (Forthcoming) *Rediscovering Criminology*, Harlow, Pearson/Longman.

Tappan, P.R. (1947) 'Who is the criminal?', *American Sociological Review*, vol. 12, no. 1, pp. 96–102.

Tifft, L. (1995) 'Social harm definitions of crime', *The Critical Criminologist*, vol. 7, no. 1, pp. 9–13.

United Nations (1989) *The United Nations Convention on the Rights of the Child*, New York, United Nations.

United Nations Children's Fund (UNICEF) (2006) *Behind Closed Doors: The Impact of Domestic Violence on Children*, New York, UNICEF.

United Nations Educational, Scientific and Cultural Organisation (UNESCO) (2008) *Disaster Risk Reduction* [online], http://portal.unesco.org/science/en/ev.php-URL_ID=6003&URL_DO=DO_TOPIC&URL_SECTION=201.html (Accessed 6 March 2009).

United Nations General Assembly (2006) *Report of the Independent Expert for the United Nations on Violence against Children, 61st Session*, A/61/299, Geneva, United Nations.

United Nations International Strategy for Disaster Reduction (UNISDR) (2008) *Disaster Figures for 2007. Asia Continues to Be Hit Hardest by Disasters*, UN/ISDR 2008/01, 18 January [online], www.unisdr.org/eng/media-room/press-release/2008/pr-2000-01-disaster-figures-2007.pdf (Accessed 6 January 2009).

Walters, R. and Bradley, T. (2005) *Introduction to Criminological Thought*, Albany, NY, Longman.

Whyte, D. (2009) *Crimes of the Powerful – A Reader*, Maidenhead, Open University Press.

Wilkins, L. (1964) *Social Deviance*, London, Tavistock.

Young, J. (1999) *The Exclusive Society*, London, Sage.

Chapter 2
Global cities, segregation and transgression

Gerry Mooney and Deborah Talbot

Contents

1   Introduction

This chapter explores how crime, thinking about crime, and the relationship between crime and social control have a spatial or geographical dimension. It also considers the implications this might have for furthering our understanding of processes of harm, power and violence.

Historically, attention has focused on the idea of the urban, or the city, as having a specific causal role in crime and violence. For example, the eighteenth-century magistrate and author Henry Fielding (1751) railed against the crime, vice and pursuit of pleasure emerging in the 'common' classes of London, while the Victorian journalist Henry Mayhew (2008 [1895]) published an influential text exploring 'the culture of poverty and the criminal classes' in hidden corners of London in the mid to late nineteenth century. Similarly, some of the sociologists of the Chicago School, writing in the rapidly expanding Chicago of the 1920s, argued that particular areas of the city – which they referred to as 'zones in transition' – were so fast changing, transient and neglected, that they allowed crime and vice to become dominant social forms (Burgess, 1967 [1925]; Reckless, 1926) along with other transgressions and enticements offered by the anonymity of the city. In these analyses the city was typically viewed as a social and moral problem, a repository for advanced civilisation and accomplishment not offered by rural society, but also an inducement to transgression. Such examples immediately draw attention to a long history of concerns, specifically around the problem of the 'urban'.

Cities of the twenty-first century offer up an array of very different representations and problems, and indeed are shrouded in ambiguities. One core difference is that, compared to previous centuries, cities are fast becoming the dominant form of living for people globally. By 2008, more than half the human population – 3.3 billion people – was living in urban areas. This is expected to increase to almost 5 billion by 2030 (UNFPA, 2007). As Deyan Sudjic (2008) highlights, while in 1900 only sixteen cities had a population of 1 million or more, the number is now over 400. Representations of the city as a source of social fear must necessarily change when the city is the dominant social form. In the contemporary imagination, cities are more fragmented places, with some zones representing the 'badlands' of crime and disorder – for instance, 'inner city' districts or the marginal areas of some suburbs or large council estates. In others, the more (broadly) affluent have attempted to shore up a sense of security and belonging by creating 'urban villages' (e.g. areas such as Primrose Hill and Stoke Newington in London) (Mooney, 1999).

Contemporary video games reflect the imagery of cities not only as fragmented, but as dangerously so. Zones of crime and disorder are also typically represented as repositories for those who are economically and ethnically marginalised. Two of the most popular games in the *Grand Theft Auto* series in 2008, *San Andreas* (2004) and *Vice City* (2002), relied heavily on black and Latino characters, notably Cuban drug dealers. Gangs of Latino and black men feature prominently, robbing, rampaging and shooting their way across the digital city. Elsewhere, the Arab as terrorist features in many video war games (typified by *Conflict: Desert Storm II: Back to Baghdad, 2004*). It is not incidental that these representations also reflect fears of whole countries or continents succumbing to forms of religious or political extremism.

This chapter utilises the concept of segregation to explore these fragmenting realities of urban life and how they impact on crime and other transgressive behaviour. Segregation broadly means the various ways in which people (and also places) are separated from one another, and implies that they are separated according to some system of classification or differentiation. One common way in which segregation has been understood has been through categories of 'race'. In the late nineteenth century, southern states in the USA passed legislation that was known as the Jim Crow laws, which separated black people from white people in transport, schools, housing, jobs and public spaces. Racial segregation implied economic, social and spatial segregation; that is, black people and white people existing in separate spaces in all areas of life. This system was also reflected in South Africa during the period of apartheid: the rigidly enforced segregation of black people and white people (Robinson, 1999). Although those systems of segregation no longer exist in law, some sociologists and geographers have advanced the idea that many contemporary cities have created new spatial segregations that either reflect differential access to wealth and cultural goods or, intertwined with this, have continued with systems of

Figure 2.1

Images from *Grand Theft Auto: San Andreas* – representing urban 'disorders' discrimination that marginalise particular social groups spatially (Davis, 1998, 2006a; Wacquant, 2008). The chapter explores these ideas further and, in particular, aims to:

■ understand what urban segregation is and why it is an important concept for criminology

■ examine how, why and, indeed, whether segregation has become a key dynamic in urban contexts

■ consider some of the ways in which ideas of segregation come to inform dominant understandings of, and the management of, crime and criminal populations

■ appreciate the social as well as spatial consequences of segregation, with respect to crime and transgression

■ understand the relevance of power to the concept of segregation.

Section 2 explores how relationships between spatial segregation and crime, and transgression and crime control, have been represented through processes of mapping. Mapping has influenced thinking about crime since the late nineteenth and early twentieth centuries and more recently has become a dominant tool in crime prevention and detection through the application of Geographical Information Systems (GIS) computer packages. Section 3 then looks at critical sociological ideas about the origin and impact of segregation in urban contexts. Finally, in Sections 4 and 5, two case studies are presented – slums and gated communities – which, in different ways, express the economic, social, cultural and policy manifestations of segregation.

2 Mapping crime, fear and security

Mapping is one of the ways in which the social sciences classify and demarcate social and city life. However, mapping within social science is not an objective or technical process, as one might see in the various *A to Z*s of UK and other European cities; it is a way in which social phenomena and social problems can be understood as geographically patterned or distributed. In this sense, mapping presents 'idealised' versions of actual space. In this section we look at various forms of mapping that express particular constructions and representations of the relationship between crime and place, which are prevalent within social science thinking.

The first idealised mapping we consider has been called 'the most famous diagram in social science' (quoted in Davis, 1995) – that created by Ernest Burgess from the Department of Sociology in the University of Chicago in the 1920s, although mapping as a way of classifying populations had begun much earlier. Early studies of the development and growth of cities, such as Chicago at the end of the nineteenth and beginning of the twentieth centuries, indicate that they were highly differentiated along the demarcations of class and ethnicity, so that working populations, and newly arrived immigrants from Europe in particular, found themselves living in over-populated 'slum' tenements (Addams, 1895; Abbott, 1936). Burgess (1967 [1925]) developed this work into a conceptual map (see Figure 2.2) that would assist in understanding the city as subject to natural processes of competition and survival in the same way that we might understand the ecology of plant life.

In Burgess's theory, the consistent expansion of the central business district in Zone I ('the Loop'), as shown in Figure 2.2, meant that Zone II (the 'zone in transition'), which was primarily a residential zone, was unstable. This was because property owners in these districts might, for

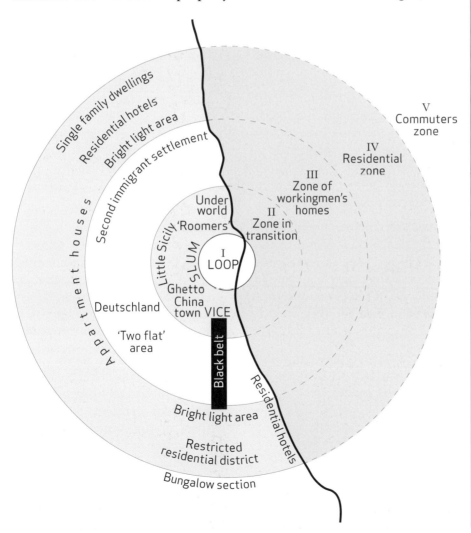

Figure 2.2
Ernest Burgess's model of 'concentric zones', 1925: mapping the segregated city? (Source: Burgess, 1967 [1925], p. 55, Chart II)

example, wait for their property to accrue higher values as a result of city speculation. In the interim, they would cease to maintain their property or develop stable residences, turning instead to short-term tenancy. This would tend to create a high turnover of populations, as those who had the means would seek to move on to more stable residential districts. This area also contained a high proportion of newly arrived immigrants, whether from Europe or from rural areas, attracted because of the ease of finding accommodation and the possibility that they might encounter less hostility towards immigrants and outsiders (Burgess, 1973 [1928]). The 'zone in transition' was an area of high crime, vice and youth delinquency, attributed to a lack of social control by residents and institutions such as the family, the church and voluntary organisations. What is also significant about this map is its representation of concentrations of nationalities and ethnicities in particular areas – for example, the 'black belt', which consisted of African Americans; the Jewish 'Ghetto'; China Town; and Little Sicily – all of which had specific cultures that distinguished them from other areas: a different style or 'moral order', as Robert Park (1967 [1925]) described it (Talbot and Mooney, forthcoming).

It is possible to see such patterns, albeit configured differently, in many cities in the West. It is important to be aware, however, that Burgess's map was a construction, an ideal, typical way of conceptualising both the city of Chicago of the 1920s and other cities. Burgess depicted such spatial patterning or segregation as evolving from natural or biological competition rather than from a social process (e.g. the reversible decisions of policy makers, big business or the wealthy). As US social commentator Mike Davis argues:

> Burgess's dartboard represents the spatial hierarchy into which the struggle for the survival of the urban fittest supposedly sorts social classes and their respective housing types. As imagined by academic Social Darwinism, it portrays a 'human ecology' organized by the 'biological' forces of concentration, centralisation, segregation, invasion, and succession.
>
> (Davis, 1998, p. 364)

By contrast, Davis presents a very different way of thinking about mapping the city. Rather than seeing city segregation as being created by a natural process, for Davis, social, economic, political and psychological factors are highly significant. Specifically, his map represents how fear of crime and of racial difference, especially from among those living in largely white suburbs, shapes the security structure, and therefore the physical layout, of cities, in this case Los Angeles (see Figure 2.3; see also Macek, 2006). The map depicts the various securitisation measures in place that have organised the architecture of Los Angeles to insulate affluent and business zones from the crime, disorder and urban unrest of the poor. This includes the development of gated communities, Neighbourhood Watch schemes and other kinds of policing mechanisms. Securitisation is also reflected in other ways, including high security walls and fences, increasing use of closed-circuit television (CCTV), tightly controlled shopping centres and the use of sports utility vehicles (SUVs or 4x4s) and other 'secure' forms of transport to traverse dangerous zones. (We highlight this also in the context of Managua in Section 4.)

Figure 2.3
Mike Davis's 'Ecology of Fear' (Source: Davis, 1998, p. 534)

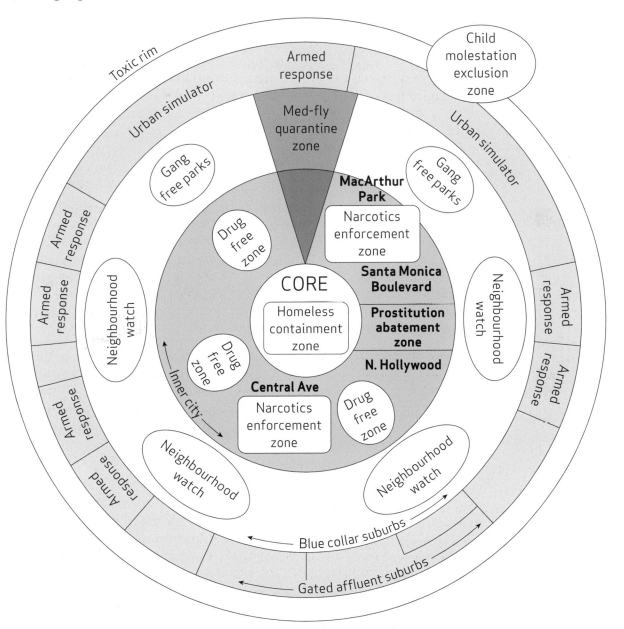

Activity 2.1

Davis's map obviously represents some security measures specific to Los Angeles. However, security measures put in place to deal with the homeless, drug dealers and users, prostitutes and other 'folk devils' of the urban landscape have become familiar in particular cities across the world, as have the ways in which people try to protect themselves against these 'threatening urban types'. Look at a map of your own town or city or one you know well. Try to sketch some of the security measures in place in different parts of that town or city. At whom do you think they are aimed?

Comment

Davis's concentric patterns represent a dangerous inner city, with a concentration of security measures, and an affluent outer suburb in which residents seek protection by living in gated communities. You may find your own map is patterned differently, but many cities appear to have areas that are regarded as 'dangerous' and against which security or anti-crime measures are directed. Generally (but not always) these areas are associated with poverty and economic marginalisation. It is also the case that the more affluent have a range of measures by which they seek to protect themselves against perceived threats by separating themselves from others. They may create security barriers through the use of gates, CCTV or private guards; they may be able to mobilise greater public resources to initiate these or similar measures; or they may simply live in geographically isolated areas.

Anti-crime measures are also put in place according to the perceived spatial distribution of crime. We will now turn to a third form of mapping, which has been used to identify 'hot spots' of particular types of criminal activity. Influenced both by situational crime-prevention thinking, which stated that criminal activity was more likely to be opportunist than planned, and by context rather than those deemed to be criminal (**Drake and Muncie, 2010**; Talbot and Mooney, forthcoming), statistical data, such as reported crime figures, were fed into a computer package (GIS) that mapped the distribution of crime geographically. We have included an example of this in Figure 2.4.

The map shown in Figure 2.4 provides a context for understanding Davis's 'ecology of fear' map. The identification of particular areas that are, according to statistics, prone to concentrations of criminal activity demarcates these areas as 'problem places' with 'problem people' (Mooney, 2008). Such areas are typically viewed as requiring heightened security measures; that is, they are, in effect, criminalised. Such thinking has sparked a series of policy and crime control initiatives aimed at

High

Above average

Average

Below average

Low or no crime

securing space through the architectural design of housing and public spaces. CCTV dominates the landscape of UK cities, while new building projects in England and Wales are influenced by strategies such as Secured by Design, organised through the Association of Chief Police Officers (ACPO). This project aims to identify changes to physical space and design that will deter the opportunistic criminal and reduce the scope for crime (see Secured by Design, undated). Such changes might include taking out hidden walkways in estates; cutting off entry and exit routes; increasing 'natural surveillance' (basically, increasing the visibility of spaces to people); installing security gates and locks; planting spiky plants around buildings; and so on. Measures such as these can be combined with more direct methods of social control; for example, mass 'stop and searches' for knives, as occurred in London and other major cities in 2008, or blanket curfews for those aged under 16 in 'risky' areas. While it is argued that these heightened security measures are necessary to control the threats that face society, from terrorism to stabbings and shootings, it is nevertheless the case that, as the map by Davis shows, many cities are being redefined by a fear of crime and disorder and the need for security (Cochrane and Talbot, 2008).

Figure 2.4

Mapping crime: GIS map of distribution of motor vehicle thefts in London at borough level, 2008 (Source: Adapted from http://maps.met.police.uk/)

In many ways, it would seem to be self-evident that dangers within society exist and that people will seek to protect themselves against them; segregation and security in urban spaces stand as one contemporary example of this. However, critical social science thinking has tried to unpack these processes further and to examine the dynamics that underpin segregation, as well as the social harms associated with it. In the following section we explore some of the ways in which ideas of separation and segregation have been used in criminological and social science discourses.

3   Boundaries, difference and spatial segregation in the urban context

Much positivist criminology is concerned with borders and boundaries. In thinking about the causes of crime, criminology has conventionally attempted to assert, in a variety of different ways, a distinction or differentiation between the 'normal', law-abiding citizen and the 'pathological' criminal. It has, in its history, attempted to break society down into distinctions based on biological characteristics – the 'born criminal' (Lombroso, 2006 [1876]) – or group differences, such as those based on class, ethnicity, age and gender. As a result, the perceived 'criminal type' is young, male, deprived and, in the inner city, possibly locatable in one or other minority ethnic group. In so far as governments over time have sought solutions to crime, they have done so in the philosophy and practice of separation. Whether this has been the committal of the 'criminally insane' in psychiatric hospitals, the punishment of law breakers through transportation or prison, the control of suspected 'terrorists' through electronic tagging and control orders, or the control of the behaviour of young people through Anti-social Behaviour Orders (ASBOs) (which prescribe where, when and how they should comport themselves), the practices of crime control and other systems of ordering have created practical and spatial distinctions between the law-abiding 'normal' citizen and the rule-breaking deviant 'other'. This process, what David Sibley (1995) calls 'casting out', may also take many other forms; for example, genocide, where an entire population can be excluded through the mechanism of mass murder.

Sibley, influenced by psychoanalytic theory, argues that the tendency to develop a simplistic view of good and bad, and the need to purify the self of bad elements, is part of human development. Taken to extremes, such separation or splitting is pathological. However, even within normal development such categorisations are possible, and Sibley argues that the tendency to separate the 'good' or normal self and the 'bad' or abnormal 'other' is embedded within Western society. For Sibley, the purification process underpins spatial exclusions, as society aims both to identify and to exclude its 'bad' elements. One of the ways of understanding how this works at the social level is through ideas such as nineteenth-century sociologist Emile Durkheim's (1982 [1895]) notion of the 'collective conscience', where moral issues are mobilised in order to sustain a notion of group identity. Another way of thinking about this process is through the idea of the 'moral panic'.

Stanley Cohen first advanced the notion of a moral panic in 1973, with the publication of his research thesis examining the mobilisation of moral censure against youth subcultural groups, the 'Mods' and the 'Rockers', in the 1960s. Sociologists, such as Howard Becker in the USA, had also conducted similar work to explore the idea that deviancy results from social reaction (Becker, 1963; see also Chapter 1). The minor skirmishes of these subcultural groups in English seaside towns were depicted within the discourses of the media, magistrates, the police and politicians as reflecting a generalised moral decline in society. In the post-1945 era, youth was perceived to be too affluent, too free and too anti-authority, and 'right-minded people' were fearful of where such attitudes might lead. According to Cohen, such fears emerged in a campaign to clamp down on the activities of young people, leading to calls for new laws and more enforcement. The point was that these public campaigns against youth were about the need to 'define the contours of normality and to eliminate difference' (Sibley, 1995, p. 40).

The social phenomenon of boundary creation suggests, therefore, that the encounter of difference or 'otherness' is a problem for society. Claude Lévi-Strauss, an anthropologist, argued in his text *Tristes Tropiques* (1991 [1955]) that two strategies were generally employed in human history to deal with otherness. One of these he called 'anthropoemic' – the vomiting or spitting out of others who were seen as alien, through murder, incarceration, expulsion, isolation or, latterly, spatial segregation in 'urban ghettos', where there is 'selective access to spaces and selective barring from using them' (cited in Bauman, 2000, p. 101). The second was 'althropophagic' – absorbing alienness through enforced assimilation or through practices such as cannibalism. As Zygmunt Bauman argues, 'If the first strategy was aimed at the annihilation of the others, the second was aimed at the suspension or annihilation of their otherness' (Bauman, 2000, p. 101). As Jock Young (1999, 2007) has argued, with the onset of modernity, both strategies were in evidence, although, in the post-1945 period, societies in the West favoured assimilation, whereas in late modern societies a complex array of mechanisms exists, which both include and exclude. Young describes this situation as bulimic (a reference to the eating disorder in which large quantities of food are ingested and then expelled). In particular, he argues that, as the boundaries between classes, ethnic communities, and so on, become increasingly blurred and porous, the need – and the failure – to shore up moral norms and differences between social groups become more intense, as exemplified in the daily regurgitation of moral panics in the news. For example, the move from the segregation of women in the home to their inclusion in the workplace and in public society more generally has been accompanied by considerable anxieties about 'binge drinking', infertility, late motherhood and neglect of children. Here, the annihilation of women's 'otherness' produces new crime and control fears in which women figure as perpetrators rather than as victims. It also weakens the regulation of harms and violence perpetrated against women. In the UK rape convictions have fallen and there is little control over the mainstreaming of sexual exploitation, such as easily accessible images on the internet (see Chapter 3) and the growth of high street lap-dancing clubs.

So how does the idea of boundaries interact with the concept of spatial segregation? In the perspectives and examples we have just examined, it is argued that systems of exclusion and segregation (of varying degrees) have traditionally been relied on to order society; but in late modern society those systems of ordering have broken down – a necessary and progressive change, but one that creates anxiety. In the face of this anxiety, Young (2007) has argued that society can become prey to a cultural and policy 'vindictiveness', whether by attempting to halt greater equality for women through strategies of discrimination and violence (see Chapter 4) or through policies that seek to punish and exclude 'problematic' social groups. Such vindictiveness, however, does not lead to closure but to the creation of new anxieties. One example of the latter is that of young people.

Activity 2.2

In Chapter 1, it was argued that Western societies in particular are dominated by discourses about youth violence and the need to control 'feral' youth, thereby neglecting the reality of the degree to which young people are victims of violence, abuse and exploitation. Read the following newspaper article, which describes and debates a device introduced to repel young people from certain public spaces in the UK. Try to identify what the various responses indicate about attitudes towards young people in public spaces.

Extract 2.1

We are not pigeons

Louisa Barnett

A gadget which emits a high frequency noise audible only to young people could be the latest weapon in the fight against anti-social behaviour in Hertsmere.

The Mosquito alarm, which releases a high-pitched noise that only people under the age of 25 can hear due to its frequency range, is set to be piloted in Borehamwood and Radlett in a bid to combat youths who loiter in large groups, causing nuisance to shops and residents.

The device, which costs around £500, works by emitting an ultrasonic tone which becomes so annoying, it encourages the youngsters to move away from an area and disperse.

The closer one gets to it, the more effective it is.

Trials in other parts of the country so far have shown teenagers are acutely aware of the Mosquito and move away from an area in just a couple of minutes.

Charlotte Weston, leader of Elstree and Borehamwood Youth Council, said the devices would discriminate against everyone under 25.

She said: 'I think it's awful. They are branding us as animals. I'd love to meet the person who came up with this idea. I am shocked. They can only install it if they put one in for over-25s as well, I'm dead against it we are not pigeons.'

But Hertsmere crime prevention officer Chrissy Barclay has high hopes for the device, which has undergone months of health, safety and technical trials.

'There's only so much you can do to deter nuisance youths from hanging round causing trouble on the streets,' she said. 'This is a completely new and pioneering piece of equipment and one which will hopefully help our police and police community support officers tackle the problems associated with anti-social behaviour from noise nuisance to drug-taking.

'It's unlike anything we've ever used before. It's another tool in our armoury.'

The Hertsmere crime and disorder reduction partnership (CDRP) will fund and oversee the running of the alarms, which will be tested over a three-month period. The borough council will now carry out extensive risk assessments in hotspots across the borough prior to installing the alarms to ensure they do not cause any problems to residents living nearby.

Chairman of the CDRP, Councillor Morris Bright, said: 'This is a unique way of dealing with some of the problems of nuisance caused by young people.

'However, let's make no mistake that not all anti-social behaviour is caused by young people and I want to ensure that youths aren't stigmatised by the behaviour of a few.

'Nevertheless, I do welcome any moves that sensibly cut down on low-level crime in our towns and communities.'

Source: *Borehamwood & Elstree Times*,
9 March 2006

Comment

The Mosquito alarm is part of a raft of policies and new technologies aimed at preventing crime and disorder; that is, ordering public spaces and private residences in such a way that behaviours are managed before any crime or anti-social behaviour has been committed (**Drake and Muncie, 2010**). Young people have been disproportionately cited by politicians, policy makers and sections of the public as being a major cause of 'intimidating' and anti-social behaviour. The main aim of such crime prevention measures, from this device to the power of the police to disperse teenagers hanging around in groups of more than two, is to prevent young people from congregating in public areas. Sibley (1995) argues that one of the key problems around the attempts to enforce borders and boundaries is where they are perceived to be porous, as we saw in the discussion above. He argues that this is exemplified in the case of social fears around young people, who inhabit an unclear boundary between childhood and adulthood. For example, teenagers are manifestly present in public space. Like adults, they are unsupervised, but they do not behave like adults (they behave in fact like children). This creates anxieties because their behaviour is not predictable or consistent with boundary creation.

Figure 2.5
Urban youths:
intimidating and
anti-social?

At the same time, however, the use of such devices as the Mosquito alarm causes considerable concern. As the leader of the Elstree and Borehamwood Youth Council stated in the article above, the alarm, similar to those on sale to deter cats, foxes and pigeons, treats young people like 'animals'. A report by Joost Beunderman et al., published in 2007 for the independent think tank Demos, questioned the criminalising of young people in public spaces as being detrimental to their development. Intrinsic to child development, they argue, is play, and play needs space. Being denied access to space, whether due to fears about their behaviour and their safety, or a lack of accessible areas, causes young people – and future society – considerable harm. It is also the case that urban regeneration strategies have often written out of development or policy any play not based around consumption. The Demos report argued that:

> This disempowerment is clear in the increasingly narrow definition of acceptable public behaviour; as the function of spaces becomes more narrowly circumscribed, and more clearly targeted, so do expectations of what activities can happen in them. Many public places are subject to limits on noise, skateboarding, loitering, drinking and now smoking. Many of these restrictions are for valid reasons but, arguably, they also have the unintended consequence of edging out the 'playful' or the unexpected from our cities. And such conceptions of desirable and undesirable behaviour help to explain why children and young people – the least monied, those with the greatest tendency to simply 'hang about' – have been called the 'unacknowledged outsiders' (Spencer and Woolley, 2000) in the planning and management of our places, and have effectively been written out of the urban renaissance script.
>
> (Beunderman et al., 2007, p. 69)

Being denied access to public spaces may eventually result in young people being unable to communicate and integrate with others unlike themselves (Bauman, 2000). Indeed, these kinds of exclusions, according to the study by Beunderman et al. (2007), may actually exacerbate anti-social behaviour, along with other symptoms of isolation, such as lack of intellectual development and obesity. While society may seek to exclude certain troublesome social groups, there is also considerable anxiety from government and communities about the impact of that segregation, notable in discussions about gang culture, fundamentalist religions and social and economic marginalisation on estates. Hence, the treatment of young people also represents society's ambiguous relation to them in their 'otherness' in that youth policy, whether expressed through welfare strategies or crime control, is unclear about whether it wants to exclude, segregate and punish, or assimilate or reform (see also the discussion in Chapter 1, Section 4.1). Indeed, a key contradiction in public policy is that, while it frequently adopts an attitude of exclusion and segregation, at the same time it professes anxiety about the outcomes of segregation, because segregation is perceived to cause greater insecurity (Cochrane and Talbot, 2008).

Let us summarise the issues we have explored so far. First, we have suggested that embedded within what we might call social structures in general – but the control and ordering of social problems in particular – societies (and we have focused mainly on Western society) have tended to adopt strategies of segregation. However, far-reaching social changes have created more fluid boundaries. Second, we have argued that, for many, this fluidity has manifested in anxiety and unsettlement, often leading to (vindictive) demands for greater control and exclusion or to exploitation and violence in the case of women. This is reflected in the increasing call for the management and regulation of those considered unruly or disorderly. However, third, strategies of segregation, such as those directed against young people, can lead to more social harm, such as marginalisation, violence and alienation, and therefore the potential for more anxiety and more segregation.

In the following two sections, we will explore theses paradoxes in more detail by looking at two examples of urban segregation. In Section 4, we will look at the global phenomenon of slums, in which the global poor are increasingly 'warehoused'. In Section 5, we will look at the same issues from a different standpoint: the segregation of the affluent. In each case, we will look at the social problems – specifically the harms of crime and violence – experienced by these communities.

4   Slums, segregation and violence

Slums epitomise in many ways what sociologist Manuel Castells has called 'the Fourth World' 'of multiple black holes of social exclusion throughout the planet' (Castells, 1998, p. 164). A 'slum' is defined by the United Nations Human Settlements Programme (UN-HABITAT) as:

> ... an area that combines, to various extents, the following characteristics (restricted to the physical and legal characteristics of the settlement, and excluding the more difficult social dimensions):
>
> ■ inadequate access to safe water;
> ■ inadequate access to sanitation and other infrastructure;
> ■ poor structural quality of housing;
> ■ overcrowding;
> ■ insecure residential status.
>
> (UN-HABITAT, 2003, p. 12)

Slums accommodate around one billion people today – with some projections that this will double by the middle of the twenty-first century (Davis, 2006a; UN-HABITAT, 2006). This is approximately one-sixth of the world's population. According to estimates produced by UN-HABITAT, an additional 400 million people will be living in slums across the world by 2020 – some 1.4 billion people in total (UN-HABITAT, 2006; see also Davis, 2006a; Martinez et al., 2008). Davis (2006a, p. 26) has estimated that there are more than 200,000 slums across the world.

At the start of this chapter, we referred to the phenomenon of global urbanisation, and the growing prevalence of slum conditions is one manifestation of this. It is estimated that around 180,000 to 200,000 people migrate to urban areas every day. The world is becoming increasingly urbanised. This is reflected in the rapid growth of so-called 'mega-cities' such as Tokyo, Mexico City, São Paulo, Mumbai and Jakarta. Since the late 1970s, for example, over 200 million Chinese citizens have moved from rural to urban areas – with a further 300 million projected to follow in another 'peasant flood' over the next few decades (Davis, 2006a, p. 11). Mumbai is projected to gain an additional 33 million people in the near future (Davis, 2006a, p. 5). In Brazil, urbanisation has been accompanied by 'favelisation'; that is, an exponential increase in the numbers of people living in *favelas*, or slum areas, in cities such as São Paulo and Rio de Janeiro. In Delhi, in India, it is estimated that of the 500,000 people who migrate to the city each year, 400,000 end up living in slums. One Indian planning expert has commented that 'If such a trend continues unabated, we will have only slums and no cities'

Figure 2.6
A world of slums?

(quoted in Davis, 2006a, p. 18). In addition to mega-cities, then, for some commentators we are now witnessing the emergence of 'mega-slums'.

Slums have long been a concern of policy makers, politicians and researchers: one that has been manifested in different ways. First, the elimination of slum living is held to be an important aspect of progressive social reform; thus in the UK during the twentieth century, for example, so-called slum areas – old red-brick Victorian houses – were bulldozed to make way for tower blocks. Second, slums are also equated with crime, violence and disorder. The language and image of 'the slum', mobilised in academic research, the cinema, literature and countless documentaries, hardly requires much elaboration here, so powerful is the imagery of such locales as centres of crime and places of disorder and disease. Films that have received widespread international acclaim – such as *City of God* (dir. Fernando Meirelles, 2002), based around conflicts between gangs and the police in the *favelas* of Rio de Janeiro, or *Tsotsi* (dir. Gavin Hood, 2006), based in the Soweto township near Johannesburg and which also focuses on gangs – have, for some commentators, propelled the developing world slum to a position of global media stardom (Dasgupta, 2006).

Both policy concerns relate to what Davis (2006a) has referred to as a critical factor in the nature of slum, and urban, living, and what Loïc Wacquant (2008) has described as 'advanced marginality': the prevalence of a surplus population that is either unemployed or under-employed, as rapid urbanisation has become detached from industrialisation. However, in recent years, particularly through the United Nations' 'human security' agenda (UNCHS, 2003), marginalisation and poverty have not only been seen as producing crime and violence. The opposite is also the case in that the insecurity caused by crime and violence – and the stigma attached to such 'problem places' – in turn reproduces conditions of marginalisation and poverty (Koonings and Kruijt, 2007). A critical policy initiative, then, would be to eliminate the sources of insecurity.

Slums therefore represent, in the policy imagination, segregated places that produce the social harms of poverty, crime and violence. They represent in many ways the contradictions explored in Section 3 of this chapter – on the one hand, places where groups of people have been 'warehoused' or 'excluded' and, on the other hand, a source of anxiety precisely because of the exclusion of these groups. As we also discussed in Section 3, however, life within segregated spaces cannot be so clearly defined, nor can the boundaries between areas be seen as rigid. Robert Neuwirth (2006), for example, has argued in his book *Shadow Cities* that slums contain many different and diverse communities with their particular histories and contemporary realities. People who live in slums and shanty towns are still people, struggling to build lives and to survive. These can be ordinary places, home to people with ordinary lives – in often extraordinary circumstances. In other words, slums are shaped by heterogeneity and diversity. This is reflected in the rich and diverse forms of social organisation to be found there, and in the widely varying slum economies and ways of surviving and coping. Slum economies not only serve to reproduce slums and slum populations, they are often central to the wider economic functioning of particular cities and urban areas – and, indeed, to national and transnational economies – by producing goods and services (the 'humorous' email images of the shack dweller in a distant city at the end of the line answering computing queries may not be entirely misplaced).

Representing 'the slum poor' as a homogeneous mass of hopeless, deficient and criminally orientated people – as a 'surplus population' – works to obscure the complex interrelations between different forms of economic activity: that it is the slum dwellers who service the rich and powerful. This in turn obscures the unequal relations between rich and poor, which are reflected in the increasingly segregated and polarised urban landscapes of a growing number of cities across the world. As Davis and many others have highlighted, while slums may be viewed as centres in which an 'informal' (meaning illegal) economy can flourish, the labour of the 'stealth workforce' is often central to the activities of multinational corporations (Davis, 2006a, p. 178).

Slums are more complex and fluid places than we might at first imagine them to be. They are tied to other city areas and economic activities in ways that suggest that segregation does not preclude movement across boundaries. They contain a myriad of housing conditions and a wide heterogeneity of people, engaged in diverse activities, who contribute, in ways that perhaps few fully appreciate, to the daily rhythms not only of slum but of urban life itself. But how is this reality of social and economic diversity related to the prevalence of crime and violence?

Activity 2.3

Read the two short extracts from interviews that New York investigative reporter Robert Neuwirth conducted with some residents in the Rocinha *favela* in Rio de Janeiro. How do these begin to disrupt the dominant understanding and representation of slums as criminal enclaves?

Extract 2.2

Valéria Cristina, who owns a jewellery and eyeglasses emporium, came to Rocinha because of the guys with guns. She used to live and work in Rio's glitzy Flamengo neighbourhood. But after armed robbers assaulted her store and cleaned out her entire inventory, she closed up shop and relocated to the favela. Valéria Cristina was frank about the reason she left the legal city, 'I wanted a more secure location,' she said cheerfully ... In the rest of the city being assaulted was always a risk, she explained ... But in the squatter communities things are different. 'If someone broke in or tried to rob this store,' she said, smiling broadly, 'they would die.'

Source: Neuwirth, 2006, p. 256

Extract 2.3

Washington Gonçalves Miranda Ferreira, a teenager who has spent half his life in Rocinha, also understands the trade-off. He has witnessed shoot-outs. He has seen the smugglers – his word for drug traffickers – beat a man, douse him with gasoline, and dump his burning body onto the highway near Rocinha at the height of the rush hour. Washington is extremely moral. He has never used drugs and refuses to participate in the illegal economy – he won't even buy a pirated CD. Yet he insists that he feels most comfortable in the favela ... 'I feel safe here,' Washington said. 'I only feel scared when I go to the rest of the city. You can't fight in Rocinha. If you have a fight, you can get, well, not necessarily killed, but hurt. Because if you fight you might bring the police. And the smugglers don't want that. If you leave your knapsack somewhere, people will return it. If you leave a bucket of money, if you leave your wallet in a restaurant, people will return it to you. If you lose your wallet in Copacabana, forget about ever seeing it again: it's gone.'

Source: Neuwirth, 2006, pp. 258–9

Comment

While perhaps Washington Ferreira's claims can be interpreted as unrepresentative of those who live in the slum, uncritical and perhaps even romanticised, nonetheless his views and those of Valéria Cristina raise important questions about the nature of the association between crime and the slum and of the dominant representation of slums, in this case here the *favelas* of Rio, as places of crime and violence. For both, there is some sense of rules, of a particular way of behaving, of order that characterises *favela* life, even if the threat of violence is never far away. Criminal enterprises are often central to the reproduction of slum life – with such enterprises being seen as a legitimate part of the ways in which slums are organised. Inhabitants may have to pay off drug dealers, gangsters and criminals – or they may have to pay off the police and other law enforcement agencies. As Neuwirth comments:

> I tell these stories of crime and corruption because they are part of life in these communities. It is also true that they exist everywhere. In Nairobi, the legal neighbourhood of Eastleigh is the centre of gun dealing and is more dangerous than many squatter areas. In Brazil … things can be much more dangerous in the legal city than in the illegal one. Squatter communities may be illegal, but that doesn't make them criminal.
>
> (Neuwirth, 2006, p. 280)

The boundaries between legal and illegal, between the licit and the illicit, are entangled in complex ways in such localities – as they are in the wider organisation of the city. It may be the drug dealers and the gangs who support community and residential associations, contribute to church funds and protect people from the police and military – from state violence and state crimes (see Koonings and Kruijt, 2007, p. 3). In other words, such areas may be marked by a form of social order, albeit a different one from 'normal' society: a form of social order that is established as the state withdraws from providing both security (due either to police corruption or to its increasing militarisation, which results in more social violence) and social support. Alternative economies in marginalised areas are not always easily demarcated as criminal, however. Studies of 'racial ghettos' demonstrate that economic marginalisation can produce economic innovation in the form of small business; indeed, the economic and cultural diversity such activity produces can become the basis for gentrification, as in the case of Harlem in New York (Maurrasse, 2006) and 'Southview' (a pseudonym) in south London (Talbot, 2007). Importantly, however, the integration of marginalised spaces can interact painfully with the exclusion of the existing population and the 'colonisation' of these diverse places by the affluent (Talbot, 2007).

The designation of slums as segregated spaces that express a variety of social harms, from poverty and marginalisation to crime and violence, neglects the complexity of social relations in these areas as well as their dynamic relationship to 'normal' spaces. Social harms might also be produced through the stigmatisation of slums and the economic and security measures designed to 'improve' and 'control' them.

Figure 2.7
Slums as places of
normality and order:
a slum shop

So far, we have looked at the segregation of the poor. However, other forms of segregation are evident in urban contexts. In the context of insecurities and anxieties produced by crime, violence and disorder – viewed as manifesting from the urban slums – the affluent have sought to segregate themselves from the rest of society. It is important to note here how these different forms of segregation (driven by both the affluent and the organised gangs of the slums) interact and coexist. Social anthropologist Dennis Rodgers has explored processes of urban segregation in the Nicaraguan capital, Managua (Rodgers, 2007, 2008). Like many other cities in Latin America and elsewhere, Managua has undergone significant and rapid change in recent decades: change that reflects Nicaragua's political turmoil, violence and revolution. Managua has long been a highly divided and unequal city, but Rodgers claims that new forms of urban segregation have emerged in recent times, unlike other experiments in the segregation of the affluent. As he notes:

> Partly because of the small size of the Managua elite, what has emerged instead of gated communities and closed condominiums is a 'fortified network', which has been constituted through the selective and purposeful construction of high-speed roads connecting the spaces of the city elites within the city: their homes, offices, clubs, bars, restaurants, shopping malls and the internal airport. The poor are excluded from these locations by private security, but also from the connecting roads, which are cruised at breakneck speeds by expensive 4x4 cars. ... a whole 'layer' of Managua's urban fabric has

been 'ripped out' of the metropolis for the exclusive use of the city elites, thereby profoundly altering the cityscape and the relations between social groups within it.

(Rodgers, 2007, pp. 71–2)

Rodgers also draws our attention to other forms of segregation: to segregation 'from below'. In the poor Managuan district, Barrio Luis Fanor Hernández, for example, Rodgers explores the ways in which drug dealing in this barrio contributed not only to new forms of economic activity, which are reflected in the conspicuous consumption of a barrio elite, but also to new patterns of inequality, to a new hierarchy of power where drug gangs enjoyed and deployed their monopoly of violence.

For Rodgers, parallel but interrelated processes of segregation are taking place here: elites seek to reshape the city in ways not only that offer some form of security in Managua, but which also work to secure the position of elites in Nicaragua. The barrios fracture into ganglands, wherein violence and insecurity grip large sections of the population and where social order and regulation are achieved only through violence or the threat of violence. The example of Managua illustrates different processes of segregation, where zones or 'layers' of the city reserved for a powerful elite coexist alongside what might be termed 'zones of exclusion' where the marginalised poor attempt to survive as best they can. Urban insecurity, violence and fear feature as everyday issues in both the slum and 'non-slum' areas and this is reflected in the cityscape and the built environment. Indeed, such segregations appear to be mutually reinforcing, producing a society that is, as Bauman (2000) has argued, unable to communicate across the social divide.

In the following section we focus more on affluent spaces of segregation, highlighting the social harms associated with affluent segregation and gentrification, as well as the porous boundaries of the gated enclaves of the wealthy.

5 Affluent segregation, transgression and violence

The concept of gentrification was first coined by the British sociologist Ruth Glass in the early 1960s (Glass, 1964). In general, it is taken to refer to the transformation, in whole or in part, of a working-class or derelict part of a city into a middle-class residential locale or a locale for commercial and, increasingly, leisure, retail and consumption activities. Gentrification can involve the rebranding of particular places to expand their appeal to more affluent, middle and 'creative' classes (Florida, 2005). It has been associated either with the exclusion of less affluent existing populations, as both housing and leisure and retail facilities all become more expensive, or with the splintering of and conflict between different segregated elements of the population, divided by class, wealth or ethnicity (Foster, 1999; Talbot, 2007). The separation of the affluent can also be seen as an expression of fear: of crime or of social differences that seem threatening (Young, 1999). Phenomena such as 'gated communities' – often luxury developments protected by gates, CCTV and security guards – are but one expression of ways in which people have attempted to protect themselves against perceived and/or real external threats (Jewkes, 2008).

While segregation into 'secure' communities may be seen as an understandable response to the array of bewildering spectacles of crime and violence in urban spaces that is continually portrayed by the media, it also has some negative consequences. Bauman (2000), for example, explored a pantheon of contemporary attempts to recreate community, specifically through the mechanisms of spatial separation, which may range from the gated community already described to more natural forms where privileged communities are segregated from less privileged ones by bridges, roads or the near absence of public transport or by being located on the outskirts of towns and the tops of hills. For Bauman, the idea of community is one where we seek to be with like-minded people or those with whom we share a common identity – whether based on defined social distinctions, such as class and ethnicity, or on other distinctions, such as politics, culture or shared aspirations (Mooney and Neal, 2009). Cities, by contrast, are defined by the idea of civility, which is 'the ability to interact with strangers without holding their strangeness against them and without pressing them to surrender or renounce some or all of the traits that have made them strangers in the first place' (Bauman, 2000, pp. 104–5).

The segregation of the affluent can also, in extreme cases, be expressed in culturally unusual ways. Here the concept of transgression is relevant. Transgression is a term often utilised by cultural criminologists (Ferrell et al., 2008) who explore the relationship between late modernity, the dominance of a 'culture of consumption' and tendencies towards transgressive activity (i.e. behaviours that are outside of behavioural norms, such as thrill seeking, risk taking and instant gratification). They examine a range of behaviours, from binge drinking, graffiti and speeding to the extreme violence of terrorism (Hamm, 2007). In the following example of Dubai, in the United Arab Emirates, we will explore how the concepts of affluent segregation and transgression are interconnected.

In his study of residential segregation and 'zoned consumption' in the city state of Dubai in the Persian Gulf, Davis (2007, p. xiv) highlights what he terms the 'unprecedented spatial and moral secession of the wealthy from the rest of humanity'. The super-rich can retreat from global threats and fears in this 'dreamworld of neoliberalism', where an army of bodyguards, concierges and security guards police the city to ensure that luxurious consumption and investment in escapist megastructures (huge skyscrapers, the world's largest hotels and malls, vast theme parks, large marinas) continue untrammelled. As Davis (2006b, pp. 58, 60) states, 'Dubai actually earns its living from fear' in a 'paradise of personal security'. The 'imagineered' urbanism – the vision of a highly ordered, safe and modern city – of Dubai, then, reflects a conscious desire to attract the super-rich, to keep them secure and to keep them investing and spending money (Davis, 2006b).

J.G. Ballard (1997), in his novel *Cocaine Nights*, depicted a segregated 'ex-pat' wealthy community, on the coast of southern Spain, literally dying of boredom. The residents of this fictional gated development had eliminated both challenge and striving from their lives and, as a consequence, were increasingly unable to act or move. What created a new sense of vigour for these residents was the presence of a new individual in their midst, who organised destructive, criminal and violent acts, thus giving residents something to react against and therefore something to do. Fear, lust and violence – in other words, transgressive acts – reinstated in them a sense of being alive and of the creative possibilities associated with this.

While Ballard created in this novel a fantasy world, in many ways it depicts the way in which the idea and the impact of segregation intersect with culture, one definition of which is simply 'the symbols, images, meanings, habitual comportments, stories, and so on through which people express their experience and communicate with one another' (Young, 1990, p. 23). As we have already seen, societies globally are increasingly giving expression to forms of economic segregation, which is manifested in segregated housing (gated communities on one side, slums on the other), different habits of consumption and different lifestyles. These forms of residential, spatial and economic segregation can result, on the one hand, in an increasing lack of contact across social boundaries and, on the other, where boundaries are unclear or undefined, in a rising anxiety resulting in demands to reinstate those boundaries. However, the story that Ballard conveys is that culture – in other words, experience, creativity and communication – thrives on an encounter with the 'other'. It was the residents' encounter with the 'externality' (i.e. coming from outside their community) of the frisson of crime and violence, and their experience of their own transgressive selves, that created new social orderings and creativity. Of course, Ballard himself was keen to portray the dystopian nature of this relationship, in that the wealthy had no other recourse to recapture social experience but through brutality. It is this relationship between affluence, transgression and violence that finds its representation in some global cityscapes.

Figure 2.8
Dubai: urban paradise
or pinnacle of urban
segregation?

Activity 2.4

In this activity we will look more closely again at the example of Dubai
and how it has marketed itself as a centre for investment and the
funding of megastructures through oil revenue. As such, the nature of
social ordering in Dubai is based around:

> ... the business plan, not from a constitution, much less 'inalienable
> rights'. Al-Maktoum [the monarch] and his executives have to
> arbitrate between lineage-based power and Islamic law, on the one
> hand, and Western business culture and recreational decadence on
> the other. Their ingenious solution is a regime of what might be
> called 'modular liberties' based on the rigorous spatial segregation of
> economic functions and ethnically circumscribed social classes.

(Davis, 2006b, p. 62)

Essentially, this means that different forms of regulation and control
operate in different spheres. While press freedoms and internet access
are largely suspended throughout Dubai, within special zones dubbed
'Media City' and 'Internet City' freedom for these activities is unfettered.
This is similarly the case with leisure. While ostensibly an Islamic
country in which certain forms of transgression are prohibited, for the
global elite Dubai is a permissive country. Read the following extracts on
Dubai from Davis's essay and William G. Ridgeway's blog (posted on the
Social Affairs Unit's website) and think about how these activities can

take place in what is normally understood to be a context disapproving of alcohol consumption and the sex trade. What is the relationship and clash between culture and class that is being depicted here?

Extract 2.4

In addition to these enclaved regimes of greater media and business freedom, Dubai is also famously tolerant of Western vices, with the exception of recreational drugs. In contrast to Saudi Arabia or even Kuwait City, booze flows freely in the city's hotels and expat bars, and no one looks askance at halter tops or even string bikinis on the beach. Dubai – any of the hipper guidebooks will advise – is also the 'Bangkok of the Middle East', with thousands of Russian, Armenian, Indian and Iranian prostitutes controlled by various transnational gangs and mafias. The Russian girls at the bar are the glamorous façade of a sinister sex trade built on kidnapping, slavery and sadistic violence. Al-Maktoum and his thoroughly modern regime, of course, disavow any collusion with this burgeoning red-light industry, although insiders know that the whores are essential to keeping the 5-star hotels full of European and Arab businessmen. When expats extol Dubai's unique 'openness', it is this freedom to carouse and debauch – not to organize unions or publish critical opinions – that they are usually praising.

Source: Davis, 2006b, p. 64

Extract 2.5

Anything goes here. I mean anything. Dubai is the place where Arabs come to sin – the Bangkok of the Middle East. Sometimes unfrocking, sometimes not, Saudis, Kuwaitis, Bahrainis, Egyptians, fly in daily like a plague of locusts, buzzing into the bars and discotheques of the city. To meet the huge demand for sex, in come planes from other directions, China, Russia, Kazakhstan, packed to the rafters with gum chewing women, anxious to profit from rich Arab punters. Emirates airlines recently opened a new route to Accra, Ghana. It now does good business ferrying African prostitutes back and forth to Dubai. The city thus profits from the transport of its own service workers. Here is a business model that works.

An economist recently informed me that vice, directly and indirectly, accounts for over 30% of Dubai's money-go-round. It is big business, and there in every bar in town. Naïve tourists are often amazed to see Saudis, pint in hand, whirling around makeshift dancefloors with

Chinese prostitutes. Here on the sacred soils of Arabia, are Muslims, drinking, drugging and womanizing.

And here is the problem. Just next to Dubai, almost within hearing distance of the constant boom, boom, boom, lies Sharjah – a place that is relatively poor, pious and alcohol free. Here there is growing, ground level support for the austere Saudi cult of Wahhabism, which bans womanizing and urges the death penalty for women involved in it. (Women are routinely stoned, drowned or walled up in Saudi Arabia). Wahhabism bans alcohol and music. It does not like foreigners – infidel – on the sacred land of Arabia. For many Arabians – those not roistering in the Bangkok of the Middle East – Dubai is Sin City, and something has to be done about it.

Source: Ridgeway, 2005

Comment

From these accounts, it is possible to see some of the economic imperatives behind the vice industry. If a city or country is to attract investment and become a centre of financial trade (including money laundering), a space must be found for the permissive cultures of the global elite. Alcohol consumption and prostitution are therefore ubiquitous in wealthy enclaves, often facilitated by organised crime (see Chapter 4). However, different forms of social ordering apply to the poor. In the example given above, partly as a reaction to the open, decadent culture of the elite of Dubai and partly as a form of policing, the relatively poor area of Sharjah is controlled by a form of fundamentalist Islam. The case of Dubai and Sharjah illustrates not only that dual standards apply in Dubai, but that they apply at two levels. They are evident at one level in official prohibition and unofficial permissiveness and at another in the way in which different norms and laws apply to the wealthy global elite, on the one hand, and to the poor, on the other. From this it can therefore also be seen that segregation and transgression intersect with power.

However, it would be easy to assume from this example that gated communities, gentrified enclaves and the homes of the super-rich mark the complete segregation of the affluent from those areas of the city inhabited by the poor, and which surround them. In the case of the slums, while these might be geographically isolated from areas of wealth and affluence and from business districts, this is by no means always or everywhere the case. It is important to grasp the interdependence between these localities and their populations. To some extent, this point has been signalled already, in Section 4: that is, that slums and shanty towns are home to workers and a vast range of economic activities that support 'formal' economic activity across the world. Places connect in other ways too. Young (2007), for example, highlights the extent of the global penetration of Western culture in particular through the media (television, the internet, and so on), which intersects painfully with systems of economic deprivation. 'Cultural globalisation' raises aspirations that are never possible to realise in the economic structures of a global marketplace that creates extremes of wealth and poverty, fuelling resentment on the one hand and fear on the other.

As such, segregation is rarely complete and so-called segregated localities connect and link in many different and complex ways to other places and activities, relations and experiences across the city and across the world. Differentiated places connect in different, uneven and unequal ways. Here we are reminded of the ever-important question of inequality and power. Segregation, in whatever shape or form, relates to and is shaped by unequal relations of power. And this also underpins the mutual interdependence between different groups in cities. As Frank Webster (1995) states of Los Angeles in the USA:

> Illustrations of this are easy to find. One the one hand, maids are an essential element of the professionals' lifestyles, to cook, to clean, to look after children, to prepare for the dinner parties held in the gaps found in frenetic work schedules of those deep into careers in law, corporate affairs, trading and brokerage. The maids, generally Hispanics, ride the infamously inadequate public transit buses to points in the city where their employers may pick them up in their car to bring them home to clean up breakfast and take the children off to school ... In spite of this dependence, which obviously involves a good deal of personal interaction, the lives of the two groups are very far apart. Of course this is largely because they occupy markedly different territories, with members of the poor venturing out only to service the affluent on their terms as waiters, valets, shop assistants and the like; the underclass also inhabit areas which the well-to-do have no reason (or desire) to visit.
>
> (Webster, 1995, pp. 205–6)

Global chains of care and other forms of work tie both segregated and excluded places and populations into economies in different, although all too often very vulnerable and volatile, ways. Boundaries continue to be crossed; they are porous, contested and fought over.

6 Conclusion

In this chapter we have utilised the concept of segregation to demonstrate how processes of harm, violence and power are played out in urban spaces. Cities are becoming the dominant social form globally, in which insecurities and fears about crime, violence and social change are enacted in different ways. Within contemporary urban contexts, places are zoned (and in Section 2 we demonstrated how this was represented by mapping) through a variety of economic, cultural and policy processes. For some people some places represent areas of safety, where they have been able to mobilise personal resources to insulate themselves from 'dangers': as this chapter has shown in the examples of affluent urban areas or gated communities. Other spaces, normally areas of deprivation, neglect and violence, represent places of danger; these segregated or marginalised spaces are a source of anxiety for society and policy makers alike.

In the case studies of global slums and gated communities we looked at two forms of segregation: segregation of the (presumed) economically marginalised poor and segregation of the affluent. By comparing these two cases, it is possible to interrogate ideas of harm. Slum areas represent (and in many cases are) places of despair, crime and violence, and hence depict, for many, the harms of a voracious global economy as well as the parasitic nature of organised crime such as the drugs trade. Yet, they are also places where people survive and innovate if left to their own devices long enough for stable economic and cultural activity to develop. Gated communities, and other ways in which the affluent segregate themselves, are sought as a means to provide security, yet can also become zones where manifold social harms are enacted, such as economic and sexual exploitation. Harms are not just distributed in different ways across different types of segregated spaces. Segregation itself, as Bauman (2000) argues, also contains an intrinsic harm of mutual misunderstanding and miscommunication among people who inhabit different spaces, creating a fear of encountering others who are perceived to be different.

It is also the case that urban segregation represents the differential distribution of power. Although, as we demonstrated through the two case studies, harms are to be found in both types of area, it is rarely the case that society, or policy making, focuses on the harms of the 'powerful' – or the relatively affluent. The case study of Dubai is perhaps easy to grasp here from the perspective of writing in a Western country – it is an extreme example of the mobilisation of wealth and power: one that has transformed the landscape of a city into a playground for affluence. Yet, we perhaps rarely consider how similar processes are present in UK or other 'Western' cities. The case study also demonstrates, of course, the critical point that it is not possible to insulate affluence. Boundaries between different populations are by nature porous, and are crossed in the course of daily life, cultural exchange and economic activity, fuelling new dilemmas and problems of harm, violence and power.

References

Abbott, E. (1936) *The Tenements of Chicago 1908–1935*, Chicago, IL, University of Chicago Press.

Addams, J. (1895) *The Settlement as a Factor in the Labour Movement*, Hull-House Maps and Papers, New York, Thomas Y. Crowell.

Ballard, J.G. (1997) *Cocaine Nights*, London, Flamingo.

Bauman, Z. (2000) *Liquid Modernity*, Oxford, Polity.

Becker, H. (1963) *Outsiders: Studies in the Sociology of Deviance*, New York, Free Press.

Beunderman, J., Hannon, C. and Bradwell, P. (2007) *Seen and Heard: Reclaiming the Public Realm with Children and Young People*, London, Demos.

Burgess, E.W. (1967 [1925]) 'The growth of the city: an introduction to a research project' in Park, R.E., Burgess, E.W. and McKenzie, R.D. (eds) *The City*, Chicago, IL, University of Chicago Press.

Burgess. E.W. (1973 [1928]) 'Residential segregation in American cities' in Cottrell, L.S. Jr, Hunter, A. and Short, J.F. Jr (eds) *Ernest W. Burgess on Community, Family and Delinquency: Selected Writings*, Chicago, IL, University of Chicago Press.

Castells, M. (1998) *End of Millennium*, Vol. 3 of *The Information Age*, Oxford, Blackwell.

City of God, film, directed by Fernando Meirelles, co-directed by Kátia Lund, Miramax Films, 2002.

Cochrane, A. and Talbot, D. (eds) (2008) *Security: Welfare, Crime and Society*, Maidenhead, Open University Press/Milton Keynes, The Open University.

Cohen, S. (1973) *Folk Devils and Moral Panics: The Creation of Mods and Rockers*, St Albans, Paladin.

Conflict: Desert Storm II: Back to Baghdad [US title, released in rest of world as *Conflict: Desert Storm II*], console game, released by Gotham Games, 2004.

Dasgupta, R. (2006) 'Maximum cities', *New Statesman*, 27 March [online], www.newstatesman.com/200603270031 (Accessed 6 March 2009).

Davis, M. (1995) *Beyond Blade Runner: Urban Control (1). The Ecology of Fear* [online], www.mediamatic.net/page/6147/en (Accessed 6 March 2009).

Davis, M. (1998) *Ecology of Fear*, London, Picador.

Davis, M. (2006a) *Planet of Slums*, London, Verso.

Davis, M. (2006b) 'Fear and money in Dubai', *New Left Review*, Vol. 41, Sept–Oct, pp. 47–68.

Davis, M. (2007) 'Sand, fear, and money in Dubai' in Davis, M. and Monk, D.B. (eds) *Evil Paradises: Dreamworlds of Neoliberalism*, New York, The New Press.

Drake, D. and Muncie, J. (2010) 'Risk prediction, assessment and management' in Drake, D., Muncie, J. and Westmarland, L. (eds) *Criminal Justice: Local and Global*, Cullompton, Willan Publishing/Milton Keynes, The Open University.

Durkheim, E. (1982 [1895]) *Rules of Sociological Method*, London, Macmillan.

Ferrell, J., Hayward, K. and Young, J. (2008) *Cultural Criminology: An Invitation*, London, Sage.

Fielding, H. (1751) *An Enquiry into the Causes of the Late Increase in Robberies with some Proposals for Remedying this Growing Evil*, London, A. Miller.

Florida, R. (2005) *Cities and the Creative Classes*, London, Routledge.

Foster, J. (1999) *Docklands: Cultures in Conflict, Worlds in Collision*, London, UCL Press.

Glass, R. (1964) *London: Aspects of Change*, London, MacGibbon & Kee.

Grand Theft Auto: San Andreas, console game, released by Rockstar Games, 2004.

Grand Theft Auto: Vice City, console game, released by Rockstar Games, 2002.

Hamm, M.S. (2007) *Terrorism as Crime*, New York, New York University Press.

Jewkes, Y. (2008) 'Insecurity, fear and social retreat' in Cochrane, A. and Talbot, D. (eds) (2008) *Security: Welfare, Crime and Society*, Maidenhead, Open University Press/Milton Keynes, The Open University.

Koonings, K. and Kruijt, D. (eds) (2007) *Fractured Cities*, London, Zed Books.

Lévi-Strauss, C. (1991 [1955]) *Tristes Tropiques* (trans. J. Weightman and D. Weightman, 1973), London, Penguin.

Lombroso, C. (2006 [1876]) *Criminal Man*, Durham, NC, Duke University Press.

Macek, S. (2006) *Urban Nightmares*, Minneapolis, MN, University of Minnesota Press.

Martinez, J., Mboup, G., Sliuzas, R. and Stein, A. (2008) 'Trends in urban and slum indicators across developing world cities, 1990–2003', *Habitat International*, vol. 32, no. 1, pp. 86–108.

Maurrasse, D.J. (2006) *Listening to Harlem: Gentrification, Community, and Business*, London, Routledge.

Mayhew, H. (2008 [1895]) *London Labour and the London Poor*, London, Penguin.

Mooney, G. (1999) 'Urban "disorders"' in Pile, S., Brook, C. and Mooney, G. (eds) *Unruly Cities?*, London, Routledge.

Mooney, G. (2008) '"Problem" populations, "problem" places' in Newman, J. and Yeates, N. (eds) *Social Justice: Welfare Crime and Society*, Maidenhead, Open University Press/Milton Keynes, The Open University.

Mooney, G. and Neal, S. (eds) 2009) *Community: Welfare, Crime and Society*, Maidenhead, Open University Press/Milton Keynes, The Open University.

Neuwirth, R. (2006) *Shadow Cities*, London, Routledge.

Park, R.E. (1967 [1925]) 'The city: suggestion for the investigation of human behaviour in the urban environment' in Park, R.E., Burgess, E.W. and McKenzie, R.D. (eds) *The City*, Chicago, IL, University of Chicago Press.

Reckless, W.C. (1926) 'The distribution of commercialised vice in the city: a sociological analysis' in Burgess, E.W. (ed.) *The Urban Community: Selected Papers from the Proceedings of the American Sociological Society 1925*, Chicago, IL, University of Chicago Press.

Ridgeway, W. (2005) *Dubai, Dubai – The Scandal and the Vice*, London, Social Affairs Unit, 4 April [online], www.socialaffairsunit.org.uk/blog/archives/000345.php (Accessed 25 March 2008).

Robinson, J. (1999) 'Divisive cities: power and segregation in cities' in Pile, S., Brook, C. and Mooney, G. (eds) *Unruly Cities?*, London, Routledge.

Rodgers, D. (2007) 'Managua' in Koonings, K. and Kruijt, D. (eds) *Fractured Cities*, London, Zed Books.

Rodgers, D. (2008) 'A symptom called Managua', *New Left Review*, vol. 49, Jan–Feb, pp.103–120.

Secured by Design (undated) [online], www.securedbydesign.com (Accessed 6 January 2009).

Sibley, D. (1995) *Geographies of Exclusion: Society and Difference in the West*, London, Routledge.

Spencer, C. and Woolley, H. (2000) 'Children and the city: a summary of recent environmental psychology research', *Child Care, Health and Development*, vol. 26, no. 3, pp. 181–98.

Sudjic, D. (2008) 'Cities on the edge of chaos', *The Observer*, 9 March [online], http://www.guardian.co.uk/artanddesign/2008/mar/09/architecture.design (Accessed 6 January 2009).

Talbot, D. (2007) *Regulating the Night: Race, Culture and Exclusion in the Making of the Night-time Economy*, Aldershot, Ashgate.

Talbot, D. and Mooney, J. (Forthcoming) *Rediscovering Criminology*, Harlow, Pearson/Longman.

Tsotsi, film, directed by Gavin Hood, 2006.

United Nations Commission on Human Security (UNCHS) (2003) *Final Report of the Commission on Human Security*, New York, United Nations.

United Nations Human Settlements Programme (UN-HABITAT) (2003) *The Challenge of Slums: Global Report on Human Settlements 2003*, Nairobi, UN-HABITAT/London and Sterling, VA, Earthscan.

United Nations Human Settlements Programme (UN-HABITAT) (2006) *State of the World's Cities 2006/7, The Millennium Development Goals and Urban Sustainability: 30 Years of Shaping the Habitat Agenda*, London, Earthscan.

United Nations Population Fund (UNFPA) (2007) *State of the World Population 2007: Unleashing the Potential of Urban Growth*, New York, UNFPA.

Wacquant, L. (2008) *Urban Outcasts: A Comparative Sociology of Advanced Marginality*, Cambridge, Polity.

Webster, F. (1995) *Theories of the Information Society*, London, Routledge.

Young, I.M. (1990) *Justice and the Politics of Difference*, Princeton, NJ, University of Princeton Press.

Young, J. (1999) *The Exclusive Society: Social Exclusion, Crime and Difference in Late Modernity*, London, Sage.

Young, J. (2007) *The Vertigo of Late Modernity*, London, Sage.

Chapter 3
Cybercrime, transgression and virtual environments

Sarah Neal

Contents

1   Introduction

People tend to engage with the internet or cyber environments in very different ways. But that people do engage with the internet – and on staggering levels – is a phenomenon that is increasingly of interest to social science and particularly to criminological analysis. The combination of the strange, unique space of the internet and the sheer number of people interacting with this space raises some immediate questions. How do people behave when they are in cyber environments? Are these environments utopian spaces of freedom and anonymity or are they regulated spaces in which individual behaviours are monitored and subject to surveillance? What harms do cyber environments present to cyber users? What opportunities do cyber environments present for criminal behaviours, and, conversely, for controlling criminal behaviours? Perhaps most importantly, what is the relationship between what happens in cyberspace and what happens in the 'real' world? Does cyberspace simply facilitate new ways of committing familiar crimes, such as fraud – is it just 'old wine in new bottles' (Grabosky, cited in Yar, 2006, p. 11)? Or, does it offer an arena for completely new crimes or transgressive behaviours? In a context in which crimes occurring on and through the internet increasingly feature as part of media discussions and everyday anxieties, this chapter examines these kinds of questions.

So what does cybercrime mean and what are the particular crimes and criminal behaviours that define it?

Activity 3.1

Read the extract below, taken from the *The Guardian* newspaper. Do the criminal activities described in the report correspond with what you think of as cybercrime?

Extract 3.1

Hunt for Russia's web criminals

The Russian Business Network – which some blame for 60% of all internet crime – appears to have gone to ground. But, asks Peter Warren, has it really disappeared?

Peter Warren

A curious game of cat and mouse is being played out on the internet, as high-tech hunters close in on a group of cybercriminals known as the Russian Business Network, or RBN. The chase started a week ago when the RBN – a Russian ISP alleged to be behind much of today's web crime – slipped its internet moorings in the Baltic coastal city of St Petersburg and made for servers in China.

But the RBN's attempts nine days ago to hide there behind a hastily formed Italian front company failed. Only a day after setting up in its new home, the sites run by the RBN – which specialises in identity theft, denial of service, phishing, computer extortion and child pornography – vanished from the web. Since then sightings have been few. But does that mean the RBN has gone? And does it matter?

According to experts from Team Cymru, a research group specialising in internet crime, the Russian firm is linked to around 60 per cent of all cybercrime. But recently the RBN started to attract some unwelcome attention from bloggers and the US media, forcing it to try to vanish from view.

...

On the face of it the Russian Business Network, launched by young computer science graduates, sounds like any other high-tech company offering web hosting and other services. In the US, young entrepreneurs from similar backgrounds launched Google and eBay. But the RBN is a little darker.

Go onto Russian underworld servers and you enter an emporium of crime, with lists of looted documents, stolen identities and hijacked computers ... with almost all of it linked in some way to RBN. 'We scanned its entire netblock [i.e. internet addresses registered to the company] and we did not find one legitimate business,' says one researcher. Yet RBN was founded and is run by techies, not career criminals.

Source: *The Guardian*, 15 November 2007

Comment

Behaviours such as hacking (gaining unauthorised access to computer systems); designing viruses or Trojan Horses (disguised malicious software programmes) to 'infect' and disrupt and/or destroy computer systems and their data; phishing (using email technology to trick people into revealing their financial information); and identity theft are perhaps most immediately connected to the concept of cybercrime. However, this newspaper report also mentions computer extortion and child pornography, which are crimes that are not automatically linked with cyberspace – although in the case of the latter this is rapidly changing. In beginning to think tentatively about how to define cybercrime, it is possible to see that it can refer to crimes and harms that can only happen because of cyberspace; for example, hacking. However, it is also possible that cybercrime can refer to more 'familiar' crimes and harms that have been able to 'benefit' from, and operate more effectively through, cyber environments, as is the case with child pornography and paedophilia.

Figure 3.1

State of Crime: the home page of the online multiplayer gaming site

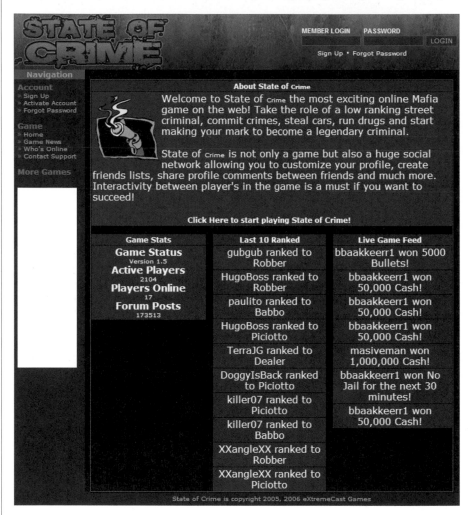

Activity 3.2

Let us now consider another, and very different, way in which a relationship between crime, harm and virtual environments may be viewed. Read the home page of the *State of Crime* website given in Figure 3.1. What is your reaction to it?

Comment

What may have struck you most immediately is the game's explicit invitation to enter a world of criminality and misdemeanour. This home page offers an example of how, in cyberspace, entertainment and ideas and/or fantasies about crime can converge. What *State of Crime* appears to offer is an online leisure site in which players adopt criminal identities, engage in criminal activities, form friendships and interact socially all at the same time. While irony and humour are in evidence here – it is a game – it is the appeal of such games, and the ways in which multimillion-pound entertainment industries have engaged with developing and packaging crime and fantasy via online and computer-based gaming, that is of interest.

This chapter suggests that the existence of this appeal means that any rounded discussions of cybercrime need to engage with the social and cultural worlds in which cyberspace and the activities that take place there are embedded.

In this context, the five main aims of this chapter are to:

■ review the debates about what cybercrime 'is' and examine how the phenomenon of cybercrime has been responded to

■ examine the strategies for the governance of cyber environments and in particular strategies for cyber harm prevention and cybercrime control

■ examine the convergences and distinctions between cybercrime, real-world crimes and fantasies of crime, and the implications of these for social relations

■ question what happens to the concepts of harm and violence in the context of cyber and virtual environments

■ explore how cyber and virtual environments further complicate attempts to grasp the meaning of crime.

Reflecting these aims, the chapter is organised into four main sections. Section 2 outlines the current ways in which cybercrime has begun to be debated and defined in criminology. Section 3 then discusses the ways in which a range of strategies that work through policing, law, technology, community and identity are emerging as means by which harmful behaviours within cyberspace can be managed or governed more effectively and thereby defined in particular ways. Section 4 applies aspects of these debates to the broader social and cultural contexts in which cyberspace and virtual environments are used, particularly in relation to the popularity of console and online gaming, which involves players adopting violent and criminal identities. It is worth noting at this point that the chapter distinguishes between defining cyberspace as an online electronic environment and virtual space as an electronic but not necessarily online environment. The final section revisits the arguments of the chapter and the implications for harm and violence in particular.

2   Ways of thinking about and defining cybercrime

This chapter began by suggesting that the term 'cybercrime' has entered everyday usage. Alongside our familiarity with the term, cybercrime is also able to evoke, at some level, a particular shudder as it taps into a wider unease and sense of precariousness that some have argued characterise late modernity (Young, 2007). The unease relates to the seemingly unregulated strangeness and possibilities of cyberspace and to its simultaneous familiarity and mundanity. For example, on the one hand it is the place where people can become someone other than who they are in the real world and communicate intimately with total strangers. On the other, it is a space of everyday convenience – where holidays can be booked, shopping ordered and film times found out. Lawrence Lessig (2006, p. 9) captures this neatly when he notes that there is a distinction between the internet and cyberspace. The internet is familiar and informative – 'a Yellow Pages on steroids' – but cyberspace is 'something more'. It provides a richer, more complex qualitative experience that can involve personal lives in extensive and engaged ways, such as spending vast amounts of time in social universes, chat rooms, playing with identities, gaming, and developing virtual support and friendship networks. Given the 'beyond-geography' and transformative and intimate opportunities of cyberspace, it is not surprising that there is anxiety about it and about the crimes and transgressions that may occur within it. As the criminologist David Wall (2007a, p. 28) comments, 'we are shocked by cybercrime but also we expect to be shocked by it because we expect it to be there'. Part of this anxiety stems from what this chapter has begun to discuss – the uncertainty that surrounds what cybercrime is and means.

Wall suggests that cybercrime could be understood in different ways. He argues that the definitive question, what he calls the 'transformation test' (Wall, 2007b, p. 398), is to ask what the relationship between a particular crime and cyberspace technologies is. In short, 'what happens to the "crime" if the Internet is removed?' (Wall, 2007b, p. 398). From asking this question, Wall proposes three models of cybercrime:

1 *Traditional cybercrime.* This category relates to immediately recognisable criminal behaviours with which the criminal justice system is familiar and which it regularly encounters. These criminal activities would still exist and would continue *without* the internet, but they have adapted to cyberspace and are able to 'benefit' from, or become more effective and widespread through, the utilisation of technology. The most obvious examples of traditional cybercrime would include violent pornography, child pornography, paedophilia, the distribution of hate materials, stalking, the sale of illegal medicines and remedies, and so forth.

2 *Hybrid cybercrime.* This category refers to those criminal activities that, like 'traditional cybercrime', can also exist 'offline'. Hybrid cybercrime is also similar to traditional cybercrime in that it works with the global scope that cyber environments offer. Unlike traditional cybercrime, however, hybrid cybercrime has not simply benefited from the opportunities of cyberspace. Rather, it integrates cyber technology and in doing so offers scope for new forms of crime. Among the most obvious examples of hybrid cybercrime would be large-scale fraud and identity fraud and activities such as phishing, entrapment scams (stories that offer money in exchange for 'permission' to 'use' a personal bank account) and piracy of intellectual property rights (this relates to the illegal copying and distribution of music, film, television and software material).

3 *True cybercrime.* This category refers to those criminal behaviours that are wholly contained within and by cyberspace. In other words, if the internet were to be removed, the 'crime' could not take place. Hacking and spamming – bulk emailing that advertises, and which invites recipients to enter into various schemes and can 'put recipients at risk if they [the emails] are responded to' (Wall, 2007a, p. 230) – are obvious true cybercrime examples and both have become, if not completely successfully, the focus for legislation in the USA (Section 3.1 discusses cyber legislation further). Another emerging example of true cybercrime is the theft of virtual property or virtual goods that people have purchased in cyber worlds such as Second Life (see Section 3 for extended discussion of Second Life). The case detailed in Extract 3.2 below provides an example of true cybercrime.

Extract 3.2

Police arrest teenager over virtual theft

Bobbie Johnson

Police in the Netherlands have arrested a teenager suspected of stealing virtual objects inside a popular social networking site, it has emerged.

The 17-year-old, who has not been named, is alleged to have tricked players of 3D cartoon world Habbo Hotel before removing a number of virtual items they had bought. It is believed to be the first time European officers have arrested someone for stealing virtual property.

'The accused lured victims into handing over their Habbo passwords by creating fake Habbo websites,' said a spokesman for Sulake, the Finnish company that runs Habbo. 'As in many other virtual worlds, scamming for other people's personal information such as user names has been problematic for quite a while.'

The website, which has around 6 million users each month, is popular among teenagers and younger web surfers around the world. Users of the site are able to create and dress characters, or decorate their virtual hotel rooms with items and furniture bought using real money.

Police in Amsterdam confirmed that five other teenagers were being questioned over the theft, which is believed to have netted items worth around €4,000 (£2,800).

The sale of virtual goods for internet games and online worlds is a boom industry, with the market currently valued at around £750m a year. Despite the popularity of virtual environments such as World of Warcraft and Second Life, virtual property laws remain untested in most parts of the world.

Police in China have been tackling cases of virtual theft for years, including instances of organised gangs engaging in online robbery. Last year officers in the southern city of Shenzhen arrested more than 40 suspects who were accused of stealing up to 700,000 yuan (£45,500) worth of virtual items from users of one popular website, QQ.

Source: *The Guardian*, 15 November 2007

It is sensible to emphasise that most criminal activities that involve cyberspace are likely to incorporate elements of these three positions – they are not necessarily one or the other – but Wall's definitions are useful because they present a broad typology *and* highlight the diversity and multiplicity that defines the crime and cyberspace relationship.

Activity 3.3

How useful is this typology in terms of thinking through the concepts of harm and violence? Look again at each of the types of cybercrime. Do you think there are differences between them in terms of direct associations with harm and violence? If so, why?

Comment

While there is obviously no right or wrong response to this question, you may have identified the traditional crimes as the most harmful or violent – not only are these criminal behaviours ones with which we are most familiar, but in terms of child pornography and the dissemination of hate materials they are also the ones that easily translate to personal and juridical understandings of harm and violence. However, cyber theft, cyber fraud, viruses, hacking and spamming are certainly not victimless crimes. As the criminologist Sheila Brown (2003, p. 146) notes, 'it does not necessarily follow that "virtual" victimisation is less destructive in its effects; arguably they are much greater and more pervasive'. However, like white-collar crime, the distance with which the crimes take place from their victims, and the fact that they are likely to involve many individuals rather than one single individual, may shape our perception of these behaviours as low-impact crimes and minimise our association of them as violent and harmful. It is also the case that these crimes may be committed by many people and often portrayed as a form of resistance against big business. Majid Yar (2006, pp. 68–9), for example, makes the point that in relation to piracy and copyright theft, 'Far from being confined to a small class of "professional criminals", "piracy" activity appears to be socially widespread, and undertaken on a regular basis by individuals who would otherwise consider themselves "law-abiding citizens"'.

Crimes that only exist virtually, such as virtual theft, even though virtual goods are paid for by real currency – pounds, euros, dollars, yen, rand – demonstrate the mystification and uncertainty surrounding cybercrime. Can true cybercrime be harmful when the harms are experienced only at a virtual level and when internet-based activities anyway have well-known and accepted risks? This uncertainty means that some cybercrimes are viewed in a different way from those that are currently recognised within sovereign nations' criminal justice systems and are a focus of mainstream policing activities. These perceptions of cybercrime are perhaps reflected most obviously in the under-reporting of cybercrime by victims and in the very low trial and conviction rates for cybercrime. As Wall (2007b, p. 401) notes, despite widespread anxiety about cybercrime, 'In the UK during the first decade following the Computer Misuse Act 1990 there were only about a 100 or so prosecutions against hackers and even fewer convictions.'

The diversity in the forms of cybercrime and the uneven association of cybercrimes with harm and violence are reflected in the ways in which cybercrimes are responded to and cyberspace is regulated. It is this that the next section now considers.

3 Regulating cyberspace and policing cybercrime: managing harm and violence

As we have already begun to establish, cyberspace presents a unique environment and a corresponding set of unique challenges in terms of how it is regulated, how order is maintained within it and how it is understood. As Brown (2003, p. 172) notes, 'Cyberspace cannot be treated as a neutral space, or as a definitively different space but neither can it be grasped by existing notions of crime and the law.' The challenges are constituted in multiple ways, not least because of the vast scale of cyber worlds: that they are transnational, 'beyond-geography' spaces. The predominantly sovereign or nationally organised criminal justice and juridical systems do not necessarily map directly or straightforwardly on to the global structures of cyberspace. The absence of national/political and geographical structures, the diversity of the forms of cybercrime and the uneven relationship between cybercrime and harm and violence have meant that it is possible to identify the emergence of multiple strategies for countering crime and for protecting people when they visit and use cyberspace. These multiple strategies involve a range of organisations and approaches, including, for example, conventional policing; specialised policing; criminal law; technology;

Figure 3.2

Global drought: scene of a Second Life landscape with an avatar

cyber-based companies and internet service provider (ISP) security and regulatory systems; and grass-roots cyber community vigilante direct actions, such as shaming and ostracisation. Wall (2007b) has suggested that it is helpful to think of these multiple regulation and order maintenance strategies as falling into two broad categories: distal (offline) governance of cyberspace, such as conventional policing and criminal law, and proximal (online) governance of cyberspace, such as technology and vigilante approaches. This section examines the various techniques through which harm and violence within cyberspace are regulated.

Activity 3.4

Read Extract 3.3, taken from the monthly magazine *Marie Claire*. This extract comes from an article by journalist Jenny Kleeman about Second Life, an online virtual universe. Second Life has a virtual population of around 8 million; it has its own economy, currency, geography and property. Its residents are three-dimensional 'avatars', which are selected/designed by the player when they enter the universe. Second Life is increasingly attracting the attention of corporations and big business as a site in which to conduct business and make profit. Make a note of why and in what ways this account from a Second Life player summons up notions of crime, harm, violence and protection.

Extract 3.3

I'm walking down a deserted street with my friends after a night out dancing. We're on our way back to my house laughing about the bizarre characters that have been trying to chat us up all night. Suddenly I realise that one of the men we saw at the club is following us. My heart thumps in my throat. I'm in a place with no police force, no CCTV and nowhere to hide. I've heard that people have been stalked here and that paedophiles use this place to trade child pornography. My immediate instinct is to run but I don't know where I can go. Fortunately this isn't real life. It's Second Life, the online virtual world where anything is possible – and where you can always just switch off your computer. It's a collective utopia constructed entirely from the imaginations of its seven million residents who each exist in the computer-generated universe as a three dimensional model known as an avatar. But while Second Life's population is nearly the size of London, it's almost entirely unregulated. Everyone operates under assumed names here, and there are no ASBOS [Anti-social Behaviour Orders], no courts, no police force. In May, a German TV programme revealed that paedophiles were buying and selling child pornography in Second Life. It also discovered that adult male avatars were paying to have virtual sex with child avatars. Linden Lab the producer and commercial owner of Second Life has since expelled a 54 year old man and a 27 year old woman as a result. Some Second Life residents say they have been left deeply traumatised after being 'raped' in-world ... I've come to Second Life to investigate why so many people are choosing to live virtual lives and to see whether residents should be wary of its darker side.

Source: Kleeman, 2007, p. 190

Comment

This short extract captures a number of key concerns in relation to the challenges regarding how to manage or govern cyberspace and counter cybercrime. You may have noted how this Second Life visitor emphasises the absence of any policing or surveillance technologies. There are no courts or ASBOs. At the same time, the sense of vulnerability and the crimes that she describes are more familiar. Child pornography and the sexual threat for a woman coming home from a night out are both very recognisable in the 'real' world. You may have agreed with this Second Life player when she points out that there is the ultimate act of safety – she can always just turn off her computer. However, as we have seen from discussion earlier in the chapter, the regulation of cyberspace is not always so straightforward and, moreover, such actions as turning off the computer may not deal with the entanglement of real and virtual selves and the sense of vulnerability that that entanglement may bring.

What Kleeman's *Marie Claire* article does effectively is highlight the governance dilemmas arising from questions of how to create and maintain social order in cyberspace. What role can conventional policing play in countering cybercrime? What role can technology play in countering cybercrime? What harm and crime prevention responsibilities do internet companies and content providers, like Second Life's Linden Lab, have and what can cyberspace users do to minimise risk? It is these questions that are considered next.

3.1 Policing and legislation

Wall argues that the relationship between public policing, internet technology and cybercrime is an uneasy one. This unease is a reflection of the reactive and conservative nature of public policing. Wall (2007a, pp. 159–61) describes this as the Peelian framing of contemporary policing – by which he means that policing continues to be dominated (as it was when Robert Peel established the first police force in the early nineteenth century) by notions of explicit dangerousness and disorder and tends to associate both of these with particular populations (see Chapters 1 and 2 of this book). This approach does not transfer effectively to the anonymity and the 'beyond-geography' nature of cyber environments. Similarly, the localised and nationally based structures of the police, and the limited financial and technical knowledge resources available to them, also impact on the ways in which cybercrime can be regulated. This historical legacy combines with other key limitations of policing: the global and networked contexts of cybercrime; the sheer size of the internet population, currently in excess of 1.8 billion and estimated to be double that by 2010 (Kohl, 2007, p. 7); geographical and resourcing limits; and factors already noted – under-reporting, bulk victimisation, low trial and conviction rates. As a consequence, conventional policing has tended to respond to cybercrime in three principal ways:

1   Through the development of specialised units. For example, in the UK the National High Tech Crime Unit was created in 2001 and later became absorbed as the e-Crime Unit into the Serious Organised Crime Agency in 2006. However, as Yar (2006, pp. 16–17) notes, while the High Tech Crime Unit comprised 80 officers with a budget of £25 million, this amounted to less than 0.1 per cent of the total number of police and less than 0.5 per cent of the overall expenditure on the 'reduction of crime' budget.

2   Through a prioritisation of resources on traditional and hybrid forms of cybercrime, especially those that relate to such issues as national security, economic security and high-level public concerns, such as terrorism, child pornography and organised illegal immigration smuggling. For example, there is an explicit recognition of cyber terrorism in the UK Terrorism Act of 2000, which makes provision for 'those that seriously interfere with or seriously disrupt an electronic system'. In the USA the 2001 PATRIOT Act (Uniting and Strengthening America by Providing Appropriate Tools Required to Intercept and Obstruct Terrorism Act), passed shortly after the 9/11 attacks in New York and Washington, included life imprisonment for convicted cyber terrorists (Yar, 2006, p. 51).

3   In recognising the 'beyond borders' nature of cybercrime, conventional policing has increasingly sought to work transnationally and through multi-agency partnerships and networks. For example, in the European Union a high-tech crime unit, the European Network and Information Security Agency (ENISA), was established in 2004 with a remit to coordinate the various police investigations of cybercrime within member countries. In the UK the National Infrastructure Security Coordination Centre (NISCC) works in multi-sector ways with law enforcement, private security and national infrastructure (e.g. water, gas, electricity) agencies (Wall, 2007a, p. 181).

The limits, constraints and challenges that are presented in terms of the policing of cyberspace are replicated in the relationship between legal systems and cyberspace. Uta Kohl (2007) argues that a difficulty at the heart of the legislative–cyber environment is the fundamental tension between:

> ... transnational Internet and national law. The law struggles with the global reach of the Internet while everyone else revels in it ... although regulators have for years struggled with rising transnationality, in the form of global trade and transnational corporations, the Internet presents an entirely new dimension to the problem of squeezing transnational activity into the national legal straightjacket.
>
> (Kohl, 2007, pp. 3–4)

Sovereign states have developed various computer- and internet-focused legislation, particularly in relation to hacking and spam. For example, the USA passed some of the earliest legislation in 1984 with the Computer Fraud and Abuse Act. This Act, which has been updated five times, includes custodial sentencing and addresses issues of unauthorised access and damage to computer systems (Yar, 2006, p. 40). In 2004, also in the USA, the CAN-SPAM (Controlling the Assault of Non-Solicited Pornography and Marketing) Act was passed. This legislation 'imposed limitations and penalties on the transmission of unsolicited commercial electronic mail via the Internet' (Wall, 2007a, p. 193). In the UK, computer protection legislation has existed since the 1990 Computer Misuse Act. This is similar to the US Computer Fraud and Abuse Act in that its provisions focus on unauthorised access and damage to computer systems. The Act includes penalties of up to five-year custodial sentences and a range of fines. However, the issues relating to working across national borders and how to enforce such legislation effectively remain. As Wall (2007a, p. 194) observes, the number of spams originating in the USA actually increased by 43 per cent in the first six months after the introduction of the 2004 CAN-SPAM Act. Similarly, Peter Maggs argues that the 2004 Act has been:

> A total failure ... less than 1% of unsolicited commercial email conforms to the Act's requirements ... . The reasons for the failure of the Act lie not in its flawed provisions introduced through industrial lobbying but in the structure of the Internet itself. Meanwhile private industry has made major strides in developing anti-spam measures.
>
> (Maggs, quoted in Kohl, 2007, p. 266)

Given the apparent limitations of conventional legislative measures in controlling cybercrime, those involved in the use and protection of computer systems – governments, non-government organisations (NGOs), ISPs, industries, institutions, individuals – have increasingly turned to technology itself as a cybercrime control and risk reduction strategy. How successful is this and what questions are raised by the deployment of technologies in this way?

3.2 Technology

In Steven Spielberg's 2002 futuristic film *Minority Report*, set in 2054, a specialist policing unit relies on the use of psychics or 'pre cogs' who are able to relay visions and details of criminal acts to virtual reality computer screens before they have taken place. With this 'future' information police officers can then intervene and arrest offenders prior to any crime actually occurring. While *Minority Report* presents a dystopian policing future in which technology, corruption, control and free will all nightmarishly collide, it also raises questions about how technology and communication systems can be mobilised effectively in crime prevention strategies. This relationship is not a new one. For example, Wall (2007a, p. 2) notes that the electric telegraph was incorporated into nineteenth-century policing immediately after it was developed.

It is not surprising that the use of technology to counter high-tech crime is seen as a key preventative solution. Using technology in this way addresses some of the challenges and difficulties that cybercrime presents to public policing that were explored above. There are a number of advantages in deploying regulatory-orientated technology within virtual environments. Most obviously and advantageously, technology works on the same 'beyond-geography' scale of cyberspace. Technology can be monitored and controlled by those developing and designing preventative systems or crime control programmes. It provides means of controlling the behaviours and actions of others and can do this in very direct and immediate ways. There are many everyday and basic examples of the application of technology to increase security and prevent risk, which are routine and familiar and include the use of passwords to individuals' online accounts and the ability of parents to 'write in' preconfigured software in order to constrain their children's access to particular online sites. Firewalls and protective software are used by companies, organisations and individuals to protect their computers and network systems against hackers, viruses and spam. Companies also aim to protect their customers through implementation of protected payment systems. All of these examples reflect an approach that aims to design crime and risk out of the internet.

Technology has also been used as a method of designing in crime control strategies. The idea that the technical architecture of the internet can provide highly effective regulatory controls and restraints is central to the work of Lessig (2006) and what he calls 'Code'. By Code,

Figure 3.3
Publicity image for the
Steven Spielberg film
Minority Report

Lessig means the laws that are put in place by governments, ISPs, law enforcement agencies, lawyers, citizens and others to police and control cyberspace and the behaviours that take place within it. Lessig (2006, p. 32) argues that far from cyberspace being a utopian world of freedom, increasingly it 'will be the most regulated space humans have ever known'. So despite the scale of the internet and the seeming anonymity of its constantly evolving architecture, it lends itself uniquely to policing and surveillance possibilities. Most obviously, these possibilities can and have been utilised to collect electronic information on individuals. This 'data mining' (Wall, 2007a, p. 189) or 'dataveillance', which is the collating and analysing of data about individuals' activities (Yar, 2006, p. 156), is undertaken by a range of state, governmental and commercial bodies.

In an example of such a relationship, Lessig (2006) suggests that Google's adaptation of its software in China in 2006 demonstrated the ways in which governments are able to control and monitor cyber and real worlds. In a specific arrangement between Google and the Chinese Government, Google agreed to block access to particular sites the Chinese Government did not want its population to see. Internet users in China would not be aware that the Google search engine had been government filtered. As Lessig argues, this case shows the ways in which commerce, state and technology are able to converge effectively in cyber environments: 'Google can build the technology the Chinese need to make China's regulation more perfectly enabled, and China can extract the talent from Google by mandating it as a condition of being in China's market' (Lessig, 2006, p. 80).

At the same time, such monitoring and the ability to trace individuals clearly hold attractions in relation to harmful behaviours. One such crime control measure is the use of 'honeynets'. Honeynets are fake websites that individuals enter if they input particular flagged words and/or images or combinations of flagged words and images into internet searches – for example, around child pornography, hate material or terrorist-related material. Honeynets request that users agree to their entry into each level of the website and, by doing so, manipulate or trick those involved into a position in which they reveal data about themselves, are then traced and possibly become subject to criminal and legal investigation.

Honeynets, data mining and information gathering, and the more general surveillance and monitoring capabilities of cyberspace, work directly as crime control strategies. But can they also work more indirectly? Despite the apparent freedoms and vastness of the cyber world, there is also an increasing perception on the part of internet users of their leaving a constant electronic 'footprint'. For cyberspace users, the continual possibility of monitoring and detection may inhibit harmful behaviours and in this way self-regulation limits criminal activities. We can see some of social theorist Michel Foucault's idea of the Panopticon in this. Foucault (1977) argued that when people believe they are being constantly monitored or subject to surveillance, they tend to discipline themselves and regulate their behaviour irrespective of whether they are actually being watched. Foucault used the idea of the Panopticon – originating in a type of prison designed in the late eighteenth century in which a central watch tower is surrounded by a building made up of individual cells into which those in the watch tower have a perfect view if they choose to look – as a metaphor for analysing how societies operated to maximise social control and regulation. While the mobilisation of technologies to design out crime and design in crime control strategies is clearly seductive in terms of their effectiveness, it also raises a series of issues. First, technology is reactive – it may be able to intercept problem behaviours and reduce risk effectively, but it does not address the social sources or causes of cybercrimes such as spam and hacking. Second, technologically driven regulatory systems also raise issues about privacy and censorship in the context of mass monitoring, data holding and the filtering of information. Third, technology-based systems that define what legitimately happens in cyber environments raise much broader political concerns about the levels of transparency and democratic accountability of those who make decisions about what gets written and instituted as Code or law in cyberspace.

3.3 Communities and cyberspace

From the discussion above it is possible to see that public policing, the law and technology do play roles in the regulation of cyberspace and the management of risk within it. However, we have also seen how all these strategies have limitations and work within constraints and how they raise political questions about democracy and civil liberties. For example, while anti-spam legislation exists in the USA and the UK, it is the technologically based anti-spam initiatives provided by ISPs and internet content providers, such as eBay, Google, Expedia and Amazon, which are more effective in containing spam (Kohl, 2007, p. 267). In this context it then becomes important to ask what values, norms and ethics are designed into ISPs' regulatory technological architectures. In other words, who is, or which organisations are, monitoring what the ISPs decide is acceptable or unacceptable cyber behaviour?

The uniqueness of cyberspace has meant that what has emerged in relation to its management or governance is an alignment of different, cross-sector partnerships and actors that cooperate both directly and indirectly in order to maximise efficacy in relation to maintaining cyber order and controlling cybercrime. Individual internet users are an integral part of these partnerships and alignments, and it is the ways in which individual cyber users act individually, and at times work collectively, that this section now examines.

We have already discussed how individual users employ technologies to minimise their risk. At the most basic level, as the Second Life user stated in her account in *Marie Claire* (see Extract 3.3 in Activity 3.4), a computer can always simply be turned off and disconnected. However, it is becoming clearer that when people are 'in' cyber environments they engage in more complex, self-appointed and socially interactive ways in their management of harmful cyber behaviours. This engagement by internet users to protect both themselves and other internet users, and to report extreme behaviours, has become part of broader notions of civic responsibility and online communities.

In many ways, the concept of community – one of the earliest social science concepts – seems a strange descriptor for the 'beyond-geography' nature of the internet and the absence of face-to-face contact experiences for internet users. Nevertheless, the concept of community has become widespread in describing how internet users develop a sense of belonging in online environments. For example, Lessig quotes from a cyberspace user who explains:

> I believe virtual communities promise to restore to Americans at the end of the 20th century what made many of us feel was lost in the decades at the beginning of [that] century – a stable sense of community, of place. Ask those who've been members of such a virtual community, and they'll tell you that what happens there is more than an exchange of electronic impulses on the wires ... people really do care for each other.
>
> (Quoted in Lessig, 2006, p. 83)

Despite the absence of geography and face-to-face contact, perhaps the mobilisation of the concept of community is not as strange as it may initially seem. First, community can be understood as something that is imagined (we feel connections) as much as something that is concrete (we actually are connected). In cyberspace, as the quotation above demonstrates, this 'feeling connected' to others, rather than having any literal social ties, particularly applies. As Gerard Delanty (2003, p. 171) has suggested, the 'Internet brings together strangers in a sociality often based on anonymity and where a "new intimacy" is found ... the exclusive aim of the virtual community is the sharing of information in a communicative context outside of which it does not always exist.' Second, community can work as a vehicle for the management and maintenance of social order and regulation as well as one through which social connections are forged and maintained (Rose, 2000; Clarke, 2008; Mooney and Neal, 2008; Neal, 2009). Increasingly, the ways in which the idea of community appears to control behaviour and deliver stability has meant that it has become the focus of attention for politicians, policy makers, practitioners and individuals, and local, regional, national, transnational and global organisations. As Graham Day argues:

> Society is deconstructed into many different kinds of communities leaving individuals to be identified according to particular networks of affiliation within which they are located. People are seen as owing

primary responsibility to these personal networks of communal ties, rather than to any sense of society as a whole. Government increasingly works by finding ways of regulating and orchestrating these relationships ... this allows key tasks to be devolved away from the centre, relieving the state of its burden ... [for example] communities are called on to play a more active part in ensuring their own safety and security, by hiring private protection or making sure they exclude criminals.

(Day, 2006, p. 243)

In virtual environments social networks of personal affiliation – or communities – are clearly identifiable. Alongside the emergence of senses of community and belonging, it is also possible to identify practices of collective action that govern online deviant and harmful behaviours. These crime preventative practices can range from individuals registering complaints with ISPs; the establishment of specific cyber risk reduction non-governmental organisations, such as Adult Sites Against Child Pornography, Association of Sites Advocating Child Protection; the Computer Emergency Response Team and Internet Watch (see Figure 3.4); and monitoring by the police or online content providers and companies, to individuals working collectively through more ad hoc and 'direct action' vigilantism. In the more explicitly community-influenced social (but non-gaming) online universes or sites, the development and sophistication of these forms of direct intervention have increased. Wall (2007b) discusses how, in virtual social universes such as Cyberworlds and Second Life, this vigilante action has taken the form of social shaming and humiliation of misbehaving users. Activity 3.5 looks at an example of this.

Figure 3.4

Symbols and logos of some of the online risk reduction organisations

Activity 3.5

The accounts given in Extract 3.4 are from two Cyberworlds users describing the efficacy of vigilante online community action. Read through what Bola and Teamdoyobi describe. Why might shaming be effective in changing behaviours? Is there anything problematic about such vigilante action?

Extract 3.4

Bola: Were punishments effective? Mostly, the offending party usually left or modified his behaviour. Why? Because the offender was often shamed into modifying his behaviour as he was often publicly ridiculed for his abusive behaviour. As soon as his behaviour stopped so did the ridicule.

Teamdoyobi: I have been to worlds [outside of Cyberworlds] where harassers have been turned into toads because of their behaviour. Banning them from the community doesn't work as they can get around the technical blocks. The only way to really make sure they stop is to make them feel small and ashamed.

Source: quoted in Wall, 2007b, p. 405

Comment

It is clear that both the Cyberworlds users do feel that the shaming and ridiculing of user misbehaviour is an effective tool and that it is more effective than ISP or online content providers' strategies of excluding or banning users. Virtual shaming draws on the same real-world complexities of social relationships. That it is effective in regulating behaviours demonstrates the extent to which online social behaviours reproduce long-standing real-world social relationships (in which shaming has long been a feature of crime control policy as well as more informal, community-based forms of control). However, virtual technologies do allow shaming and humiliation practices to take on more contemporary forms. Teamdoyobi speaks of those virtual social worlds – usually multi-user domains (MUDs) – in which systems administrators can change the user's online persona to that of a toad. Collective textual shaming of users' deviant behaviours has also been adopted as a regulatory online practice. While there may be some efficacy in vigilante tactics, there are challenges in terms of accountability. Who decides what deviant behaviour is? Who decides what shaming or ostracisation or banning punishment is appropriate? In

Cyberworlds a more organised voluntary policing presence has emerged called the Peacemakers. There is even a training academy and a Special Response Team for serious misdemeanours. The Peacemakers model is one very much based around conventional policing, although the Peacemakers have very limited sanctions. Similarly, Cyberangels – fashioned on the original Guardian Angels (volunteer citizens who patrolled New York City's subways in the 1970s and 1980s in an effort to combat crime and increase public safety) – is an informal virtual policing body of internet users who have organised themselves to protect online users and, according to Yar (2006, p. 127), receive around '500 complaints a day about cyber-stalking of which 65–100 are estimated to be legitimate'.

As with more ad hoc vigilante actions, those of the Peacemakers and Cyberangels also raise issues of accountability. Brown (2003) argues that the real-world law and the associated crime control systems disappear in cyberspace and, in many ways, we can see virtual vigilantism as part of this 'beyond-the-law' activity.

In the online environment there is always the question of identity and authenticity. In other words, online users may assume identities that are other than their real-world identities. Role playing and imposture are an integral element of online practices and this presents challenges to notions of victims and offenders and, of course, to notions of harm and violence. In order to illustrate this point a little more fully, included here is the story of Lewin Sanford, an able-bodied, conservatively inclined, Jewish, male psychiatrist whose online persona was Julia, a severely disabled atheist woman who engaged in drug taking and sexual adventures and who started a women's discussion and advice group on CompuServe. Julia was able to spot other male impostors and would warn women users in 'her' online discussion group of the real-world identities of men entering 'her' group. More generally, 'she' also advised on the dangers of false online personas and group members being other than how they presented themselves (cited in Brown, 2003, p. 150). While imposture is a key concern with regard to internet misuse, particularly in relation to paedophilia, the case of Julia raises a series of broader, although still highly pertinent, questions regarding who is the offender and who is the victim, and who is harassing whom. As Brown (2003, p. 151) notes, 'the splitting of the body and identity creates an enormous problem for conventional paradigms of harassment and assault'. Put simply, is a victim really a victim (and, likewise, is a perpetrator really a perpetrator) if we cannot be sure who they are and what their motivations are?

The case of Julia illustrates the ability of cyberspace to allow individuals to take on identities that are radically different from who they are in the real world. It is important to remember, however, that multiple identities are part of the everyday real world as well. People's identities are not fixed in stone: they are different depending on particular social and cultural contexts. However, in the real world these identity shifts tend to be gradual and incremental and still connect to the recognisable individual. In the cyber environment the possibilities to become radically different and unrecognisable are, of course, much greater. Cyberspace offers a landscape of freedom of communication and opportunities to engage in fantasy. As this chapter has already examined, the internet is not as free as we think it is; nevertheless, the invitation to play and take up personas and identities that are other than those of the everyday real world can be hard to resist. The ways in which this play intersects with criminal identities and behaviours are considered in the next section.

4 Fantasies of crime in virtual environments: playing with harm and violence

In April 2008, the pre-order demand for *Grand Theft Auto* (*GTA*) *IV* was so high that the game sold out weeks before it had even been released. The latest issue in the highly successful *Grand Theft Auto* series, *GTA IV* follows the model of its predecessors in that the player takes on a criminal identity, inhabits the post-industrial, gangster-ridden Liberty City and engages in various missions that involve often violent, and invariably criminal, tasks. We look more fully at *GTA* below, but the key point being made here concerns both the existence of the game and the extent of the market demand for it. It is in this context that the perspectives offered by cultural criminology are particularly useful. Rather than focusing on instrumental criminal behaviour (i.e. criminal acts committed for material gain), cultural criminology is much more interested in the relationship between the emotional content of criminal and deviant behaviours and the socio-cultures of late modern societies (see also Chapter 2). This means that, for cultural criminologists such as Jeff Ferrell (1999), Mike Presdee (2000) and Keith Hayward (2004), criminal and illicit behaviours – joy riding, vandalism, peer group violence, recreational drug use, and so forth – are both transgressive and excitement driven. The pleasures seemingly offered by such rule-breaking behaviours have to be analysed in terms of the interplay between these behaviours and the particular norms and values of contemporary Western societies. Because of this, Presdee argues that there is a need for a criminology:

> ... that understands that crime itself has become a valuable consumer entertainment commodity to be enjoyed and consumed daily through modern media and communication processes. We need a criminology that grapples with the question as to where acts of hurt, harm and hate come from and how such actions have permeated contemporary culture in such a 'fun' way that we are no longer ashamed of our lust for violence.
>
> (Presdee, 2000, p. 11)

For Presdee, the concern is the relationship between the rise of extreme pleasures and illicit behaviours, the commodification of some of these and the highly rationalised and regulated social environment that characterises late modern societies.

Presdee borrows from the sociologist Mikhail Bakhtin's (1984) theories of a first and a second life (Bakhtin's concept of second life should not be confused with the virtual Second Life world that was discussed earlier in the chapter). The first life refers to rational and official everyday existence, whereas second life refers to hedonistic, more minimally governed and less disciplined spheres of people's lives. Second life is where individuals are able to be transgressive and irrational. It is the cathartic counter to the restrictions and demands of the first life. Presdee argues that the more the first life is controlled and regulated, the more the second life behaviours become extreme, widespread and violent. In order to examine this thesis, Presdee considers examples such as joy riding, anti-social behaviours, sadomasochism and some music cultures. While he does note that people are able to perform or engage in second life transgression in more private worlds via the internet, he does not consider cyberspace in any particular detail. However, his arguments concerning the relationship between second life fantasy pleasures, performances of violence and criminality and commodification do transfer to computer gaming worlds.

Activity 3.6

Read the screen grab extract given in Figure 3.5, which is taken from the pre-release publicity for *GTA IV*. The extract provides details of one of the missions on which players will embark when they play the game. Niko, the identity or character that gamers adopt, is an East European migrant to Liberty City. How does the extract relate to Presdee's arguments about the convergences of fantasy, pleasure, violence and commodification?

Mission Preview #3: 'Search and Delete'

Brucie wants Niko to take out a police informant, before he is able to testify against Brucie's friends. The informant is currently in hiding, so the plan is to steal a cop car so that Niko can access the on-board computer and retrieve details of his whereabouts. If Niko struggles to locate a cop car, Brucie will send him a text message advising him to phone 911. The cops will arrive and inspect the scene, and then Niko can ambush them.

Brucie: *I need you to whack some people, in their hide.*
Niko: *How do I find it?*
Brucie: *man, you're cold! You didn't even blink! I love that! Fucking love that. You've got to steal a police car, get away from here, and give a call.*
Niko: *Alright Bruce, I'll give you a call.*
Brucie: *ICE cold man! Ice cold! Woo!*

Brucie runs a garage in Broker, close to Roman's taxi business.

Once the cop car has been stolen, Niko phones Brucie to update him on the current situation. The on-board computer lets you access a police search database which holds information on every individual in Liberty City who has a criminal record. Niko selects 'search by name/photo' and types in the name of the informant, 'Lyle Rivas'. The informants' last known whereabouts is 99 Long Road, Broker. This address is then entered into the car's GPS.

Niko: *I'm here, I have a computer.*
Brucie: *You're a bad ass, man! I love it. The Snitch is named Lyle Rivas, type it into the computer, and you should gets some 'known whereabouts' shit. I'd take 'em out myself, but when people see me coming they fucking RUN, man! Know what I'm sayin'? Cats don't wanna mess with someone packing 24-inch guns by each of their sides, baby, YEAH!*
Niko: *I'll track down Rivas.*
Brucie: *Cold, man! I'm feeling chills down the phone! Call me when it's done, bro.*

Niko approaches 99 Long Road, and knocks on the door before entering. Niko says that he has a message from Brucie, and the informant responds 'Brucie? I thought he was fucking joking. Shit!' Rivas makes an escape out of the bathroom window, and a chase begins, which eventually leads to Francis International Airport. After reaching a dead-end, Rivas attempts to escape on foot. He must be eliminated in order to complete the mission.

Figure 3.5
Pre-release online advertising for one of *GTA IV*'s 'missions'

Comment

What you may have picked out quickly is the way in which the game involves a relatively straightforward find, chase and eliminate narrative. You may also have noted the extent to which engaging in various violent acts is integral to the mission. This is obvious in the task culminating in killing the 'informer' and accessing police data, if necessary by ambushing the police. It is significant, however, that the conversational text between Niko and Brucie is included in the *GTA* advertising, because it is in this that the violent and extreme tone of the game is established – from Brucie being excitedly impressed at the unquestioning cold-blooded willingness of Niko to act as a hit man, to his constructions of himself as a figure of fear, seen in the visual of Brucie and in his claims that people 'fucking RUN' when they see him. That this is an advertising piece for the game is important to remember. There is satire and humour here, of course, but at the same time the content of this game also illustrates Presdee's arguments that the market is prepared to tap into second life fantasy and package up crime and violence and sell it back to us as pleasure, fun and excitement. We saw some of this same bundle being offered in the *State of Crime* home page at the beginning of the chapter (Figure 3.1) and it is again present in the ways in which Amazon chose to market the features of the previous (best-selling) and award-winning (Play Station 2 Game of the Year 2005) *Grand Theft Auto* game, *GTA: San Andreas*.

Product Features

- Based in the fictional state of San Andreas, featuring 3 cities
- Explore internal locations and the countryside
- Set in the 1990s
- Purchase property and *build a criminal empire*
- Improved AI, *allowing for gangs to accompany you*
- You are what you eat – gain or lose weight to affect game physics and character appearance
- New vehicles, including bicycles
- *New weapons and targeting system*

(Amazon, undated, emphasis added)

Commenting on *GTA: San Andreas*, Derek Burrill argues that, for players, the game represents 'the twin processes of anxiety and desire' as they veer in 'the crosshairs between the narrative justification for CJ's [the central character whose identity players take up] behaviour ... and the virtual excitement of thug life' (quoted in Higgin, 2006, p. 79). *GTA: San Andreas* was controversial as it included race dimensions that required gamers not only to take on a violent criminal identity, but to do so through CJ, its African American gamer character, which in itself racialised and commodified African American 'ghetto life' (Leonard, 2006). *GTA: San Andreas* was also controversial because it included explicit and violent sexual content. A 'hidden game'– known as the Hot Coffee modification – was built in, and players who discovered this hidden game could unlock graphic sex scenes involving the CJ character. This led to government involvement in the *GTA* debates, with US Senators Hilary Clinton and John Liebermann demanding stricter legislative intervention on classification of games in order to protect children by 'making sure kids can't walk into a store and buy a video game that has graphic, violent and pornographic content' (quoted in Leonard, 2006, p. 51). In the USA this led to *GTA: San Andreas* being given a higher adult certificate rating and to its withdrawal from the shelves of mainstream major retailers. A second version of *GTA: San Andreas* was then designed by Rockstar, the game's Scottish-based production company, without the Hot Coffee modification and given a younger certificate. The intensity of the political, legislative and media controversies surrounding *GTA: San Andreas* can be understood as a reflection of its dominance in Western 'youth' culture.

GTA IV, like its *GTA* predecessors, is not marketed as extreme or specialised games console software. The *GTA* series is mainstream gaming. That both *GTA: San Andreas* and *GTA: IV* were sold out before they were even released demonstrates its popularity and profitability. In many ways, *GTA* illuminates the key puzzle that Presdee (2000) sets out: the disjuncture between the structures, order and rationalism of first life and the freedoms, disorder and transgressions of second life – the more we have of the former, the more we will have of the latter. For Tanner Higgin this means that *GTA: San Andreas* offers a satirical comment on Western societies and a cathartic expression of the experience of living in them: 'Placing the character [i.e. the player] in the position of performing the violence of society's margin is cathartic but more importantly it is experiential' (Higgin, 2006, p. 79).

However, as Higgin (2006, p. 78) also notes, 'The problem, as with any form of satire, is that the audience will not get the joke or that players will feel the need to continue the joke outside of virtual space and into real space.' This is of concern for the rational first life as the darker and more transgressive elements of second life behaviours are commercialised, profited from and flow – potentially harmfully – back into first life. As the Clinton- and Liebermann-led debates cited above show, one obvious example of the ways in which this concern gets articulated is by raising questions about the effect on children and teenagers of exposure to and engagement with violent gaming. This is part of long-standing and unresolved debates about what influences social behaviours, particularly of young people – from the moral panics over rock and roll music in the 1950s and fears of imitation violence after viewing Stanley Kubrick's 1970s film *A Clockwork Orange*, to arguments as to the possible social implications of violent console gaming in the 2000s.

The controversy over *Manhunt* is a further example of these debates and concerns and their transnational status. *Manhunt*, which is also made by Rockstar (the company mentioned above that produces *GTA*), is an extreme violence console game described on Amazon as a game that explores 'the depths of human depravity in a vicious sadistic tale of urban horror' (Amazon, undated). It was withdrawn in the UK by the Dixon retail group after the game was blamed by the parents for the violent murder of their teenage son Stefan Pakeerah in Leicester in 2004 (BBC News, 2004). The controversy over *Manhunt* has continued: in June 2007 the British Board of Film Classification (BBFC) in effect banned the new release *Manhunt 2* by refusing to give it a certificate because of its 'cumulative casual sadism' and for being 'brutal and bleak' (Johnson, 2008). Rockstar reversioned the game, removing some of the more extreme and gratuitous scenes, and pursued its classification through the courts. The BBFC finally awarded *Manhunt 2* an 18 certificate (Johnson, 2008).

The intention of this chapter is not to engage in the debate about whether violent gaming influences or affects social behaviours. Rather, its concern is to note two key issues. The first relates to the intersections and tensions between the virtual gaming industry, governments, commercial retailers, classification agencies, the media and people. The second relates to the ways in which violence, harm and criminality have been packaged up and reversioned as leisure and pleasure activities in late modern societies where, at the same time, in those same societies, social fears (based on an erroneous belief that crime and criminality and social disorder are increasing) are acute. Indeed, as the cultures of control (Garland, 2002) have become increasingly dominant in the UK and the USA in particular, it is important to note linkages between the rise in social fears, demands for more punitive criminal justice systems (see, for example, Garland, 2002, p. 194) and the commercial successes of violent gaming. What is being highlighted here are the ways in which virtual environments offer satirical (or amoral?) spatial and communicative opportunities for people to fantasise and to mimic violent criminal behaviours as transgressive forms of entertainment, release and pleasure. This complex set of linkages is evidenced in the online commentary among gamers themselves. David Leonard (2006, p. 58) describes how gamers' conversations in chat rooms tend to fall into three discursive themes: that the *GTA* series is fantasy entertainment and virtual play and not socially harmful; that while children should not have access to such violent games, playing them was pleasurable and exciting; and that these games reflect a realism – this is what society is like. Whether the *GTA* series represents a satirical and cathartic space in which violence is playfully and ironically performed or whether it represents a commodified, racialised and gendered package that invites audiences to problematically engage and revel in violent and harmful virtual-based behaviours remains a key question. As Presdee argues:

> ... we know that to watch and enjoy pain, violence, cruelty and crime is transgressing in itself and produces both pleasure and guilt. A global multimedia industry enables us to consume many of these forbidden pleasures in the privacy of our own homes without questioning how these commodities came into being or whether there are victims involved.
>
> (Presdee, 2000, p. 30)

What is clear from this discussion is, first, that violent gaming in virtual and online environments cannot easily be separated from real-world social relations and, second, that violent gaming in virtual environments unsettles and disrupts normative notions of violence and harm. The frisson, the pleasures and the extent of engagement with virtual violent gaming raises questions about what constitutes violence and harmful behaviours and how this may intersect – or not – with the meanings and categorisations of harm and violence in real-world settings.

5 Conclusion

The journey that this chapter has taken through the new virtual, non-geographical landscapes of 'crime' has involved a series of encounters with a diverse range of concepts – space, identity and governance – and behaviours – harmful, illegal, violent, playful. This concluding section reviews and revisits some of these by returning to where the chapter began. The Introduction listed five principal, interrelated aims for the chapter. These were to: review the debates about what cybercrime 'is' and examine how the phenomenon of cybercrime has been responded to; examine the strategies for the governance of cyber environments and in particular strategies for cyber harm prevention and cybercrime control; examine the convergences and distinctions between cybercrime, real-world crimes and fantasies of crime, and the implications of these for social relations; question what happens to the concepts of harm and violence in the context of cyber and virtual environments; and explore how cyber and virtual environments further complicate attempts to grasp the meaning of crime.

The chapter has suggested that although cybercrime is becoming an increasingly common and familiar term, when it is viewed through the lens of harm and violence any single definition is impossible. Not only does cybercrime carry a diverse range of meanings, it works on a range of scales. For example, piracy and copyright theft tend not to be widely interpreted as serious crimes or even crimes at all. Hacking, too, tends to be perceived either as subversive or as just an anti-social activity perhaps perpetrated by a lone(ly) youth. The extent and nature of the supposed harm of theft of virtual property is similarly puzzled over. However, the connection of crime and harm with cyber environments and terrorism, theft, paedophilia and violent pornography does command widespread concern, and, as we have seen, is a particular focus of efforts to police and manage cyberspace. If we return to Wall's (2007b) typology of cybercrime, it is possible to suggest that it is traditional cybercrimes of these latter types that elicit the most intense political, policy and populist anxiety and attention; they are also the crimes that produce anxiety and attention in the 'real' world. This has been a key argument that has been threaded through the chapter: that cyberspace and virtual environments and what happens within them reflect and are constituted by the social relations of the real world.

Following this, the chapter has explored the ways in which what happens within cyberspace reflects real-world policies, particularly those of harm protection, crime control and regulation. It has suggested that there is a relation between real-world approaches to managing cyberspace and, conversely, how cyberspace is used to manage the real world; for example, state surveillance and censorship, and data mining. The controversies over the content of virtual games such as *GTA* and *Manhunt* also offer examples of the convergences – and worries about these – of virtual environments and real-world behaviours.

In terms of how virtual environments are governed by the real world – in a combination of distal and proximal (off- and online) approaches – the chapter has looked at policing and legislation, technology and cyber world inhabitants themselves. Space, identity and governance were very apparent in all three of these. Let us think through some examples. In relation to space, the chapter has detailed the difficulties and limitations of transferring real-world, territory-based policing and legislation to the 'beyond-geography' cyber world. In relation to identity, the questions and issues that are raised by the virtual possibilities of individuals becoming someone other than who they are in the real world have been discussed. There is both a transformative liberation in this potential to take on a different identity and a potential threat to others. Are people who they say they are? In what ways have they changed their identities (or aspects of these), for what reasons and are there harms attached to this?

In relation to governance, the chapter has detailed how technology and Code (the regulating architectures of cyberspace) are being increasingly drawn on as ways of tracking and authenticating cyber users and regulating and controlling behaviours. Traditional and technologically driven governance strategies work in partnerships and on global, transnational scales. These developments have meant that the older associations of freedom and anonymity within cyberspace do not accurately reflect its increasing regulating and surveillance capabilities – the example of China particularly illustrated this. The chapter has argued that the ways in which this regulation occurs and its reliance on 'cross-sector' partnerships also involves cyberspace users or inhabitants regulating themselves. The concept of community has been shown to be one that enables the building of social bonds between cyber (and virtual) users, and to be a vehicle through which the (mis)behaviour of cyber users can be managed and/or punished. The convergence of space, identity and governance presents a series of troubling questions about power, democracy and accountability in cyberspace. For example, who gets to write cyber Code? Who decides what values technologically driven cyber laws incorporate? And, who gets to enforce the Code?

The chapter has suggested that *cyber and virtual spaces further challenge, complicate and disrupt real-world notions of crime, harm and violence* and it has developed this argument by looking at the socio-cultural phenomenon of violent gaming, and of the *GTA* series in particular. Again, the ways in which space, identity and governance intersect are very apparent in this case study example. The political, media, policy and popular furore over the content and rating of violent adult gaming contributes to the anxieties of the relationship between real and virtual worlds or, more precisely, the governance of anxiety in the real world over what happens and is permitted in the virtual world. On the one hand, virtual gaming environments offer fantasy spaces of freedom and allow for the opportunity to play and take on different identities, albeit criminal and/or violent, amoral identities, and to (satirically?) behave accordingly. On the other hand, as gaming industries have recognised and responded to the adult market in virtual gaming, these environments and the identities available within them appear to commodify, reinforce and package reflections of real-world social problems, divisions and stereotypes as entertainment. What is the basis of the appeal and popularity of the *GTA* series? Is it because, as Presdee (2000, p. 152) argues, in late modern, social order- and social disorder-obsessed societies 'the option to be "violent", to use "violence", to enjoy "violence" and to watch "violence" has become more of an acceptable behaviour and has permeated society'? Or is it because, as Soraya Murray (2005, p. 59) argues, in *GTA*'s, 'Liberty City [and] ... the streets of the staggeringly expansive state of San Andreas ... [these] are boundary zones in which it becomes possible to experiment safely with extremely disorientating aspects of modern life'?

Far from trying to provide definitive answers to these questions, this chapter has used the concepts of space, identity and governance in order to invite and suggest multiple interpretations of cyberspace and cybercrime. It has argued that cybercrime is more than 'old wine in new bottles'. While the discussion has noted that real-world 'crimes', harms and violence occur within cyber worlds, it has also suggested that, within these worlds, 'crime', harm and violence can and do take different forms, have different meanings and present different challenges to our understanding. Similarly, challenges are raised in terms of understanding the particular strategies – such as policies for protection against harm and for risk reduction and crime control – that are called on for the management of social order and behaviour within cyber worlds.

References

A Clockwork Orange, film, directed by Stanley Kubrick, Warner Bros. Pictures, 1971.

Amazon (undated) www.amazon.co.uk (Accessed 28 July 2008).

Bakhtin, M. (1984) *Rabelais and His World*, Bloomington, IN, Indiana University Press.

BBC News (2004) *Manhunt Game Withdrawn by Stores*, 29 July [online], http://news.bbc.co.uk/1/hi/england/leicestershire/3936597.stm (Accessed 28 July 2008).

Brown, S. (2003) *Crime and Law in Media Culture*, Buckingham, Open University Press.

Clarke, J. (2008) 'Community, social change and social order' in Mooney, G. and Neal, S. (eds) *Community: Welfare, Crime and Society*, Maidenhead, Open University Press/Milton Keynes, The Open University.

Day, G. (2006) *Community and Everyday Life*, London, Routledge.

Delanty, G. (2003) *Community*, London, Routledge.

Ferrell, J. (1999) 'Cultural criminology', *Annual Review of Sociology*, vol. 25, pp. 395–418.

Foucault, M. (1977) *Discipline and Punish: The Birth of the Prison*, New York, Pantheon.

Garland, D. (2001) *The Culture of Control: Crime and Social Order in Contemporary Society*, Oxford, Oxford University Press.

Garrelts, N. (ed) (2006) *The Meaning and Culture of Grand Theft Auto: Critical Essays*, New York, McFarland and Co.

Grand Theft Auto: San Andreas, console game, released by Rockstar Games, 2004.

Grand Theft Auto IV, console game, released by Rockstar Games, 2008.

Hayward, K. (2004) *City Limits: Crime, Consumer Culture and the Urban Experience*, London, Glasshouse.

Higgin, T. (2006) 'Play-fighting: understanding the theft in Grand Theft Auto III' in Garrelts, N. (ed.).

Johnson, B. (2008) 'Rockstar wins *Manhunt 2* battle', *The Guardian*, 14 March [online], www.guardian.co.uk/technology/2008/mar/14/games.law (Accessed 29 July 2008).

Kleeman, J. (2007) 'Get a (new) life', *Marie Claire*, September, pp. 190–6.

Kohl, U. (2007) *Jurisdiction and the Internet: A Study of Regulatory Competence over Online Activity*, Cambridge, Cambridge University Press.

Leonard, D. (2006) 'Virtual Gangstas, coming to a suburban house near you: demonization, commodification and policing blackness' in Garrelts, N. (ed.).

Lessig, L. (2006) *Code: Version 2.0*, New York, Basic Books.

Manhunt, console game, released by Rockstar Games, 2003.

Manhunt 2, console game, released by Rockstar Games, 2007.

Minority Report, film, directed by Steven Spielberg, Twentieth Century-Fox Film Corporation, 2002.

Mooney, G. and Neal, S. (eds) (2008) *Community: Welfare, Crime and Society*, Maidenhead, Open University Press/Milton Keynes, The Open University.

Murray, S. (2005) 'High art/low life: the art of playing *Grand Theft Auto*', *PAJ: A Journal of Performance and Art*, vol. 27, no. 2, pp. 91–8.

Neal, S. (2009) *Rural Identities: Ethnicity and Community in the Contemporary English Countryside*, Aldershot, Ashgate.

Presdee, M. (2000) *Cultural Criminology and the Carnival of Crime*, London, Routledge.

Rose, N. (2000) 'Government and control', *British Journal of Criminology*, vol. 40, no. 2, pp. 321–9.

State of Crime, multiplayer gaming site [online], www.stateofcrime.com (Accessed 29 July 2008).

Wall, D. (2007a) *Cybercrime: The Transformation of Crime in the Information Age*, Cambridge, Polity.

Wall, D. (2007b) 'Policing diversity in the digital age: maintaining order in virtual communities', *Criminology and Criminal Justice*, vol. 7, no. 4, pp. 391–416.

Yar, M. (2006) *Cybercrime and Society*, London, Sage.

Young, J. (2007) *The Vertigo of Late Modernity*, London, Sage.

Chapter 4
Gender abuse and people trafficking

Louise Westmarland

Contents

1 Introduction

Throughout this book a number of 'crimes', behaviours and harms are considered, which appear to 'cross borders' and, as a result, are difficult to locate as originating in one particular jurisdiction, state or continent. This chapter explores a phenomenon that became a focus of attention around the beginning of the twenty-first century, and yet is not new; namely, the trade in and trafficking and smuggling of human beings. It is widely assumed that the opening up of global markets and mobilities has encouraged and facilitated the trade in people, particularly in women and girls for prostitution. The tensions that arise from the desire to migrate and to escape poverty and/or political oppression have become a key concern of law enforcement agencies across the world and for individual governments and agencies that attempt to help and protect women in these situations. This chapter adopts an explicitly feminist position in order to examine core issues about freedom of choice, the criminalisation of women as victims, the buying and selling of sex and whether prostitution is either abuse of women or legitimate work. It will reveal a crucial need, as some feminists have argued, for such research to be *for* women as well as being *about* women (Stanley and Wise, 1993, p. 30).

The phenomenon of people trafficking has attracted increasing amounts of attention in academic, media and policy discussions in the twenty-first century as awareness has increased in parallel with its apparent international proliferation. Despite this, both the treatment of trafficked people and the enforcement activities against traffickers remain vexed issues. Ideas of who constitutes the 'victim', the 'criminal' and the 'perpetrator' are typically confused and entangled, particularly when viewed in the context of public and governmental campaigns against asylum seekers and migration. This chapter explores questions surrounding the willingness of 'victims' to be trafficked, their complicity in the 'crimes' involved (such as illegal border crossing, sex work and associated activities such as pimping), and the violence directed towards women workers. The political and social effects of being trafficked, either for sex or for other types of work, lead to ambiguity of status. Issues of consent or coercion have always been critical in cases of violence against women, as is seen, for example, in rape cases in the UK, where how a woman dresses, or whether she was drinking at the time of the rape, can be viewed as critical in the final verdict (Walklate, 2008, p. 46). Consent and coercion are also factors in the ambiguous and powerless position of trafficked women, exacerbated by their status as both prostitutes and illegal migrants. So, for example, women in severe poverty in countries where their only apparent 'escape route' is to the West, may 'choose' to migrate and then find themselves enslaved, or may initially have been kidnapped against their will. In both cases, they may be subject to criminalisation and/or neglect because they are deemed to be illegal immigrants working in an illegitimate sex trade.

Activity 4.1

Read the following extract about 'Aleksa', a trafficked woman. As you do so, list the ways in which Aleksa has been 'victimised'.

Extract 4.1

'If I stay here in the shelter for four or five or six years, or he stays in prison, afterwards won't he come and cut my throat? I know he was crazy because of the way he was beating me up – "unprofessionally", not avoiding "damaging the goods".'

Aleksa was brought to Greece from a country in Eastern Europe. She was escaping difficulties in her life and hoped for a job that would allow her to support her family at home, she told Amnesty International.[1] A family friend put her in touch with people who 'would help her migrate'. They were traffickers. She said they forced her into prostitution, subjected her to severe physical and psychological abuse, and sold her on to different traffickers at least three times.

The police detained Aleksa because she did not have the necessary documentation to be in Greece. While in detention she found out she was pregnant – she had been forced by her traffickers to have unprotected sex with clients. She was taken to hospital where she had an abortion – no other help was offered her. Once back in detention, she suffered complications from the operation and bled for several days. The guards were apparently aware but took no action. She only received medical attention after another detainee put her in touch with a shelter for trafficked women run by a non-governmental organization (NGO) and one of their staff visited her. She was subsequently moved to the shelter.

Aleksa was offered protection by the Greek authorities only if she cooperated in bringing her traffickers to trial. 'Now I am really scared', she told Amnesty International in January 2007. She rarely ventures out of the shelter. She is so afraid of what the traffickers might do to her, she hopes the court will be lenient with them. She believes that if severely sentenced, they might take it out on her once released or through their network. She has no faith in the ability of the police to protect her and is dreading being called to testify in court. As one of the shelter workers said, 'It's like the authorities are saying: Put your lives on the line and we don't care if you're scared.'

Reference

1   Interview, Athens, January 2007.

Amnesty International, 2007, p. 1

Comment

This case study clearly illustrates not only the problematic situation in which trafficked women and girls in the sex trade may find themselves, but also their position and status in the world more generally. As a result of wanting to leave a difficult situation in her own country, Aleksa was smuggled, with her agreement, but was then exploited by people she thought would help her: first by her traffickers and then by the state authorities who were supposed to 'protect' her. Such women live in circumstances in which their economic and human rights are often compromised, and in countries where they are more likely than men to live in poverty. Although in European countries women have a number of rights guaranteed under the European Convention, in practice even in these countries men who murder prostitutes are rarely prosecuted. Violence against women is well documented (Westmarland and Gangoli, 2006, pp. 9–10). This is not to argue that in all countries women are totally powerless and without agency, or that some are not involved instrumentally in the global sex trade. However, unlike the majority of men in a similar position, their 'product' is the selling of their bodies for sex ('willingly' or otherwise).

Campaign groups, such as Amnesty International and the English Collective of Prostitutes, argue that trafficked women are treated as political pawns, as the newspaper extract reproduced below illustrates. They are convenient scapegoats and are typically used by political parties to convince electorates that the parties are 'tough' on immigration, while simultaneously claiming that they are committed to supporting victims of the sex trade.

Extract 4.2

Nightmare world of suburban sex slaves

Paul Lewis

Karry Mitchell, of the English Collective of Prostitutes, said: 'The government is prioritising deportations over protection, and using the so-called anti-trafficking campaign to increase deportations. We understand that many of the brothels they are targeting are being used by women who are actually in the country voluntarily who the Home Office wants to get rid of.'

According to Amnesty International, even those women who were brought to the country against their will are being deported if they refuse to assist with police investigations, in spite of the fact that branches of the same criminal networks who brought them into Britain await them in their country of origin.

The Guardian has learned that victims of trafficking are being allowed to remain in Britain only if they prove beneficial to the Crown Prosecution Service.

An unpublicised Home Office directive circulated in February [2006] ordered the Immigration Service to allow trafficked sex workers 'a period of leave ... until such time as the victim has been able to assist in any prosecution case'.

'The reality is that in the eyes of the law victims of trafficking are simply illegal immigrants,' said Amnesty International's UK director, Kate Allen. 'This has led to some highly vulnerable trafficked women being put into immigration detention, and even being deported.'

Source: *The Guardian*, 8 May 2006

Figure 4.1

A detention custody officer looks through a cell door observation hole at Colnbrook Immigration Removal Centre in Uxbridge, west London

Given these complicated and often theoretically competing issues, this chapter aims to:

- unpick the relationships and tensions between definitions of people 'trafficking' and people 'smuggling'

- explore certain economic and cultural factors that may encourage migration and attempts to control it

- analyse gendered conceptions of people trafficking

- explore ways in which power, violence and harm are evident when the activities surrounding people trafficking or smuggling are considered.

Specifically, this chapter addresses a series of questions about people trafficking, such as how it is defined, estimates of its extent, and the divergent interests of policy makers, criminologists and law enforcement agencies. At the same time, rather than simply 'adding in' gender to this book's discussion of the contingent and contested nature of crime, the chapter takes as its focus some wider issues about women and their position in the world. It begins, in Section 2, with some of the contested definitions surrounding migration and trafficking, before exploring, in Section 3, the recent history of and background to trafficking as a criminological 'problem'. Section 4 then explores how the trade, particularly in women and children, is defined, quantified, controlled and prevented. Section 5 looks more broadly at how people trafficking and the sex trade may fit into a wider pattern of abuse against women.

2　Smuggling or trafficking?

The 'new slave trade' and 'trafficking human beings' are emotive terms that evoke feelings of revulsion for what appears to be an appalling crime. Holding vulnerable and powerless people in conditions of servitude, while making vast profits from abusing their bodies, is clearly abhorrent to most sensibilities. Researchers have revealed, for example, how women are physically and mentally tortured, raped, beaten and then made to service up to fifty men a day, with their captors 'working them to death'. They have no prospect of escape or of repaying the 'debt' they supposedly 'owe' for their release (Lee, 2007). However, people also often migrate voluntarily within or across national boundaries, making long and hazardous journeys to reach destination countries. These 'legitimate' journeys may also involve the paying of facilitators, who may not tell the whole truth about 'job prospects' at their destination, and may not reveal how migrants will be expected to repay their 'debts' once they get there.

One of the ways in which some law enforcement agencies have distinguished between trafficking and smuggling is to argue that smuggling occurs when an individual pays to be assisted across a border illegally, but has no ongoing contact afterwards, whereas trafficked victims are those held in bondage or servitude (International Association of Chiefs of Police, 2007). The key distinguishing element is whether the individual concerned is able to exercise freedom of choice. However, even if someone agrees to be smuggled into another country, this does not mitigate their status as a victim if they are held or made to work against their will when they arrive. As this chapter will reveal, 'freedom of choice' is a gendered concept. The vulnerable rarely have the power to choose and although sex workers' campaign groups argue that it is legitimate work, other commentators ask: 'What sort of freedom is it to choose to sell your body?' (Gould, 2001, p. 445).

The Human Smuggling and Trafficking Center at the US Department of State has produced a fact sheet for the purposes of assisting law enforcement. This fact sheet highlights what it suggests are the core differences between trafficking and smuggling.

Activity 4.2

Look at Table 4.1, which has been taken from the US Department of State's fact sheet. Why do you think the distinctions are being made and what might be the limits of the classifications?

Table 4.1 Differences between human trafficking and smuggling

Trafficking	Smuggling
Must contain an element of force, fraud, or coercion (actual, perceived or implied), unless under 18 years of age involved in commercial sex acts	The person being smuggled is generally cooperating
Forced labor and/or exploitation	There is no actual or implied coercion
Persons trafficked are victims	Persons smuggled are violating the law. They are not victims
Enslaved, subjected to limited movement or isolation, or had documents confiscated	Persons are free to leave, change jobs, etc.
Need not involve the actual movement of the victim	Facilitates the illegal entry of person(s) from one country into another
No requirement to cross an international border	Smuggling always crosses an international border
Person must be involved in labor/services or commercial sex acts, i.e., must be 'working'	Person must only be in country or attempting entry illegally

Source: US Department of State, 2005

Comment

While it is obviously understandable on one level that law enforcement agencies must be able to understand who is a perpetrator and who is a victim in these circumstances, these neat and clearly defined categories belie the complexity of trafficking and smuggling because they imply that there are agreed and fixed definitions regarding criminality and the status of victims. The distinctions between smuggling and trafficking are often very subtle, but key components that will always distinguish them are the elements of fraud, force and coercion. However, under US law, if the person concerned is aged under 18 years of age and has been induced to perform a commercial sex act, this is considered trafficking, regardless of whether or not fraud, force or coercion has been involved (US Department of State, 2005).

To take one of the more problematic terms from the extract above, 'coercion', the exact extent to which this involves 'freedom of choice' is difficult to quantify. Some coercion does not rely on physical force or locked doors, but includes threats to families in countries of origin. Some cases provided by the US Department of State's fact sheet illustrate the complexity of the issues involved for law enforcement, as Extract 4.3 illustrates.

Extract 4.3

Sonia was invited to come to the United States by family friends and told that she could work for them as a housekeeper, and they would pay her $100.00 a week. Sonia was provided with fraudulent documents and departed for the United States with her new employer. She knew that this was illegal, but she needed the money, and was willing to take the risk.

Was Sonia smuggled or trafficked?

Sonia was smuggled into the United States. She left willingly with full knowledge that she was entering the United States illegally.

Upon arriving in the United States, Sonia was kept in isolation, she was given a place to sleep in the basement and told not to speak to anyone or she would be turned over to the Immigration Service. Sonia was never paid for her work and felt that she had no one to turn to for help.

Was Sonia smuggled or trafficked? At this point Sonia was restricted from leaving the house, threatened with deportation if she attempted to talk to anyone, and forced into involuntary servitude. Sonia is a victim of trafficking.

...

Local law enforcement authorities executed a search warrant at a brothel and arrested three 17-year-old girls for prostitution. The Department of Family Services notified Immigration and Customs Enforcement concerning the illegal immigration status of the three juveniles. Immigration and Customs Enforcement Agents interviewed the three juveniles and learned that they were smuggled into the United States.

Were the girls smuggled or trafficked? The girls were trafficked into the United States. All three girls were juveniles and were performing commercial sex acts. Since the girls were under 18 years of age, they would be considered victims of severe forms of trafficking, regardless of whether or not they have consented to participate or paid to be brought illegally into the US.

Source: US Department of State, 2005

As Maggy Lee suggests (2007, pp. 3–10), because human trafficking is such a broad, imprecise and contested term, we should focus less on choice and coercion and more on the processes and practices (and people) involved. She argues that there are a number of perspectives that underpin policy and academic debates which attempt to clarify the term.

Slavery. From this perspective the trafficked person may be in debt bondage, in the ownership of another person or part of the global economy of forced labour, which might include working in agriculture, domestic service or sweatshops.

Prostitution. Since the early 1900s, measures have been in place to prevent and suppress the traffic in women and children for prostitution. These measures, along with worries about the 'white slave trade', have meant that trafficking of women and children for sexual exploitation dominates research and academic discussions.

Organised crime. The 'trafficking-as-organised-crime' approach is based on anxieties around 'foreign gangsters', insecure border controls and the idea of human trafficking as big business with supposed similarities to regular, legitimate companies.

Migration. Due to controls and rules of exclusion for certain groups from certain countries, human trafficking can be seen as a means of overcoming poverty and political oppression in the context of a global market.

Figure 4.2

Trafficking routes from outside Europe (Source: SOCA/UK Human Trafficking Centre)

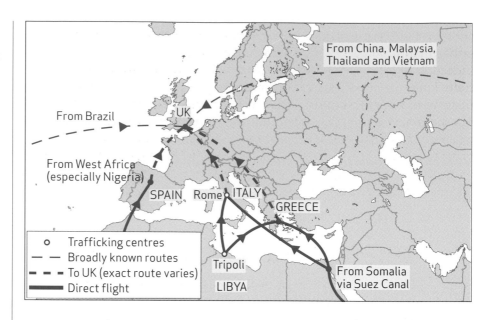

Human rights. This approach explores trafficking in terms of the degree of compliance of state policies and practices with international human rights standards and obligations.

(Adapted from Lee, 2007, pp. 3–10)

The map shown in Figure 4.2 illustrates both the way in which 'trafficking as organised crime' is assumed to operate, and the migratory flows of population. However, there is evidence that women and

Figure 4.3

A sex worker in Kompong Cham, Cambodia, waits for clients

children trafficked in Africa are often sent to neighbouring countries, rather than to Europe (US Department of Justice, 2003; Bales, 2004). Indeed, from Lee's categories listed above, it is possible to see that people trafficking – as bonded slaves or for forced prostitution, for example (the first two of Lee's categories) – may not involve any crossing of borders or international boundaries, but could happen in any town or city where women are held against their will for sex. These approaches will become evident in the consideration of the trafficking of women, and its control, as this chapter progresses. First, however, the next section begins by placing contemporary concerns within some historical context.

3 Trafficking as a 'new' phenomenon?

Historical analyses of human trafficking reveal certain patterns and methods that are still evident today. As John Picarelli (2007) has argued, since at least the eighteenth century successful slave traders have usually been entrepreneurial, small family concerns. In the colonial period they had little to fear from government intervention, because the slave trade was central to dominant market and political imperatives. Cheap labour and 'significant revenues' were viewed as pivotal in supporting the national economies of the trading countries. When the laws on slavery were tightened up in the 1800s, however, 'black marketeers' drove out the small family companies (Picarelli, 2007, pp. 40–1) and, on the surface at least, attempts were made to criminalise the trade in human slaves. The 'phenomenon of assisted cross-border, forced or exploitative migration' (Munro, 2006, p. 325) has a long history and some of its features, such as entrapment and exploitation, have not changed:

> It treats human beings as a commodity to be bought and sold, and to be put to forced labour, usually in the sex industry but also, for example, in the agricultural sector, declared or undeclared sweatshops, for a pittance or nothing at all. Most identified victims of trafficking are women but men also are sometimes victims of trafficking in human beings.
>
> (Council of Europe, 2005, p. 1)

These contemporary conditions, combined with a demand for cheap labour (mostly in the West), have increased cross-border migration. However, they can be set against various 'resistances', such as stricter criteria for migration by receiving countries and increasing resources given to enforcement agencies to prevent illegal migration. As Venessa Munro (2006) states, such situations as changing economic conditions, escape from human rights violations, and economic collapse in developing countries, have resulted in an increasing number of people

Figure 4.4

Soldiers sit outside the slave holding facility of Price, Birch & Co., a slave trading company in Alexandria, Virginia, USA, *c.*1860s

trying to migrate. But stricter enforcement regimes against legitimate migration have also led to a growth in people offering illicit routes of entry to other countries. Such pressures appear particularly significant for women, in what has been described as the 'feminization of poverty' (International Office of Migration, quoted in Munro, 2006, p. 324).

The country of Moldova is one such example. Following independence and the demise of the USSR, its economic situation was dire. Moldova has been placed between India and Honduras in terms of gross domestic product (GDP) income per capita, with US $2,672 per person, compared to US $281,590 in Belgium, a similar-sized country (Abiala, 2006, p. 92). Moldova is the poorest country in Europe – not a member of the European Union – and has a Gender Related Development rank of

113 out of 177 countries. This ranking is based on estimates of women's life expectancy, literacy rate and earned income. Although it is difficult to quantify in terms of gender, up to 25 per cent of the population is thought to have left the country. The economy is 'remittance based', with a significant proportion of the country's wealth being sent back to emigrants' families (Abiala, 2006, p. 93). Similarly, in Asian countries such as Pakistan, India, Thailand and Taiwan, where women supposedly have constitutional rights, they also suffer a range of 'economic and social hardships, including domestic violence ... and a generally inferior status in society' (Gangoli and Westmarland, 2006, pp. 9–10). Similarly, of the Moldovan women who responded to a United Nations Development Programme (UNDP) survey, 70 per cent claimed that they were not respected and that their rights were ignored. For these women, who live on the doorstep of the European Union, the opportunities presented by the possibility of a 'better' life in the West, where 'economic and job opportunities incentivize both immigration and trafficking' are much closer (Berman, 2003, p. 44). Jacqueline Berman also argues that the 'presence of trafficked East European women in Europe, in other words, indicates a boundary crisis' because anxieties about sexual behaviour and morality are mixed with fears of 'racial "otherness"', adding to a 'sense of fear and panic over "criminal networks" overrunning Europe and destroying, with lawlessness and immorality, "our" (white) way of life' (Berman, 2003, p. 54).

Consider the following story of Olena, a trafficked woman who escaped from a brothel in Sheffield, UK in 2007:

> I come from a very poor area of Ukraine. I went to Moldova with a friend who said he could help me get work, but he sold me to some Albanians. They locked me in their house, raped me and beat me regularly. I was taken to the UK, to a massage parlour in Sheffield, where I was forced to see up to 15 clients a day but could not keep any of the money. The men visited my mother and told her that if I returned home they would kill me.
>
> (Quoted in Milmo and Morris, 2008)

Activity 4.3

The following extract from a United Nations Children's Fund (UNICEF) report develops the idea that gender and poverty are intimately linked to trafficking.

Thinking about the case of Olena above and the issues discussed in the extract below, list what you think contributes to the trafficking of women and what policies could be developed that would help women in these situations.

Extract 4.4

The push factors: poverty, power and violence

Analyses of and reports on trafficking in human beings in Africa typically recognise poverty as the most visible cause for trafficking in human beings. But poverty is only one part of the picture. Another strong determinant is the particular vulnerability of women and children which makes them an easy target for traffickers. In particular, patterns of instability, oppression and discrimination may place women and children at greater risk, with social and cultural prejudices and the prevalence of gender violence presenting additional challenges to their effective protection from trafficking.

At the local level, deep-rooted practices of gender discrimination lead to a cultural climate where the practice of trafficking is perceived as morally acceptable. When these cultural attitudes and practices go hand in hand with poverty-stricken living conditions, trafficking in women and children is likely to flourish.

Trafficking of girls and women, very often under conditions of violence and deprivation, can also be connected to the high prevalence of overall violence in public and private spheres against women. In some parts of the world nearly 50 per cent of women interviewed indicate that they are regularly physically abused. In all of the three African countries (Kenya, Uganda, Zimbabwe) surveyed for a previous Innocenti study in 2000 the numbers are between 32 and 42 per cent.[1]

What is more, attitudes that consider women and girls to be inferior and weaker and, thence, objectify them, contribute to a large extent to practices of recruiting them, either by force, abduction or deception, into the most destitute living and working conditions. Poor families, unable to support their children, may be induced to sell them or hire them out – girls and young women tend to be the first to be given away for commercial exploitation and, thus, are very likely to be trafficked for this purpose. In Northern Ghana and parts of Togo, girls are 'donated' to priests, and are forced to live as 'wives' and submit sexually to the shrine priests in return for protection of the family.[2] Conclusions from the African Economic Summit 2003 also associated the use of migrant labour as another factor rendering women more vulnerable, especially in cases where families are separated for large parts of the year.[3]

In some cases traditional practices can contribute to trafficking of women and girls. The custom of early marriage is one such example. When poverty is acute, a young girl may be regarded as an economic burden and her marriage to a much older man can be a family survival strategy. In traditional societies in sub-Saharan Africa, the bride's family may receive cattle from the groom, or the groom's family, as the brideprice for their daughter. There is also a risk of trafficking linked with early marriage when men do not have the possibility to find young girls in their community (such as in the case of migrant workers).

Demand side: exploitative uses

In Africa, trafficking is driven by a demand that is multifaceted and in most cases not thoroughly analysed. With regard to the 'pull factors' which instigate trafficking in women and children... distinct areas of concern deserve our particular attention: sexual exploitation, other forms of economic exploitation, traditional practices...

Sexual exploitation – in particular, prostitution – is the most widely documented form of exploitation for women and children trafficked within and from Africa. The internal demand for such a practice is high in Africa and is present in many countries. It has been exacerbated also by a demand from foreigners, including in holiday resorts, as reported in Malawi in relation to children sexually exploited by European tourists, or sent to Europe as sex slaves.[4]

Other major areas of potential economic exploitation include the demand for domestic work, and for work in commercial agriculture and plantations. There are reports of girls from Togo trafficked far from their home countries to work as domestic workers.[5] Perceived as a cheap and always available labour source, children in West Africa are trafficked to work on tea, cotton and cocoa plantations.[6] Mining and other hazardous industries are additional sectors that sometimes use trafficking as a way to recruit labour force.

As has been noted, traditional practices, in particular forced or early marriage, contribute to the expansion of trafficking. Women and girls may be trafficked as brides for various reasons. For example, men in a migrant community may arrange for a woman to be trafficked for marriage purposes from a distant village that has national or tribal links with the migrant community. In fact, there is a growing demand by older men for young, virgin brides in times of the high risk of HIV/AIDS infection. This practice is reported in extended families in western Kenya, Zimbabwe and parts of Ghana. In these countries, girls as young as eight are selected as child brides to ensure their 'purity'.[7]

References

1   Unicef Innocenti Research Centre, *Domestic Violence against Women and Girls*, Innocenti Digest 6, Florence, 2000, p. 5.

2   Ibid., p. 6.

3   Africa Economic Summit 2003, *Empowerment of Women: How Can Women Turn the Tide against AIDS?* June 12, 2003.

4   International Organization for Migration, *Trafficking of Women and Children for Sexual Exploitation in Southern Africa*, Pretoria, April 2003.

5   Human Rights Watch, *Borderline Slavery. Child Trafficking in Togo*, April 2003.

6   Ibid.

7   Unicef Innocenti Research Centre, *Domestic Violence against Women and Girls*, Innocenti Digest 6, Florence, 2000.

Source: UNICEF, 2005, pp. 5–6, 7–8

Comment

The examples of Olena and of the women and girls in Extract 4.4 illustrate the 'feminisation of poverty' thesis with links to the feminisation of migration as an international policy concern (Kelly and Regan, 2000, p. 1). The report in Extract 4.4 identifies a series of issues to consider: discrimination and violence against women in general; traditional marriage practices; sex tourism from Europe; the widespread demand for domestic, agricultural and plantation workers; the threat of HIV/AIDS; and the demand for virgins, leading to the sexual exploitation of children. Policies that could assist women might include, for example, equal rights in employment and in the home; education regarding the source and management of HIV/AIDS; and a public discussion of traditional practices (although it should not be assumed that all traditional practices have negative outcomes for the communities that practise them). Interrelated with all of these, however, is the way in which the issue of poverty interacts with society, culture and politics to produce situations that can lead to women being made vulnerable.

So far this chapter has touched on the difficulties of placing trafficking into easily defined policy and enforcement practices. It has highlighted various aspects of the position of women within global economic, policy and enforcement systems, which heighten their vulnerability. The following section considers how national and global institutions have attempted to define, quantify and control the trafficking of women, and examines in more detail how this may contribute to their multiple victimisation.

4 Responses to the 'problem' of trafficking

There is a wide range of agencies that are interested in people trafficking, each with their own particular agendas and policy proposals. International agencies, such as the United Nations and the European Union, and national governments, often informed by law enforcement agencies such as police and customs, are most interested in law making, protocols and international cooperation. Non-governmental organisations (NGOs) tend to be more interested in rights and in support for 'victims', while campaign groups are often involved in struggles for the abolition of exploitation. Researchers and the media may have diverse aims, but knowledge about, and publicity for, the problem are often part of their agenda (although they can also influence governments and NGOs and act as campaigners). Each of these agencies begins by attempting to define and quantify the problem in order to ascertain to what extent enforcement, care and control resources are appropriate. The following sections consider these attempts.

4.1 Attempts to define trafficking

As Section 2 illustrated, attempts to distinguish 'trafficking' from 'smuggling' are problematic. This poses a problem for governments and other agencies in formulating responses or policies. For example, international legal definitions, campaigners' definitions and disagreement between agencies at a local level illustrate the contested nature of people trafficking as a 'crime' or a 'harm' (sometimes involving violence). Andrea Di Nicola (2007, p. 50) has described this as a 'never-ending story of a definition'. His argument is that legal definitions are both limiting and enabling; they usually consist of elements of recruitment, movement, deception and exploitation. They can provide some commonality across jurisdictions, facilitating the collection, sharing and comparing of data. On the other hand, using such definitions may narrow and constrain understanding because they focus too closely on state and UN definitions of what are considered to be 'deserving victims' (Kelly, 2007, p. 238). As feminist criminologists have argued, to 'deserve' justice, either as accused or as complainants, women must appear conventional, contrite and compliant (see Eaton, 1986; Kennedy, 1992; Walklate, 2001).

One attempt to define trafficking in persons can be found in the Palermo Protocol, which has been incorporated into The Council of Europe Convention on Action against Trafficking in Human Beings (Article 4a) (2005). This defines trafficking as:

a   ... the recruitment, transportation, transfer, harbouring or receipt of persons, by means of the threat of force or other forms of coercion, of abduction, of fraud, of deception, of the abuse of power or of a position of vulnerability or of giving or receiving of payments or benefits to achieve the consent of a person having control over another person, for the purpose of exploitation. Exploitation shall include, at a minimum, the exploitation of the prostitution of others or other forms of sexual exploitation, forced labour or services, slavery or practices similar to slavery, servitude or the removal of organs;

b   The consent of a victim of 'trafficking in human beings' to the intended exploitation set forth in subparagraph (a) of this article, shall be irrelevant where any of the means set forth in subparagraph (a) have been used;

c   The recruitment, transportation, transfer, harbouring or receipt of a child for the purpose of exploitation shall be considered 'trafficking in human beings' even if this does not involve any of the means set forth in subparagraph (a) of this article;

d   'Child' shall mean any person under eighteen years of age.

(Council of Europe, 2005)

Activity 4.4

Read the case of Eva in Extract 4.5. As you do so, make a list of the ways in which elements of her experience are reflected in the definitions from the Palermo Protocol given above.

Comment

In a similar way to the case of Aleksa, which was explored at the start of this chapter (see Activity 4.1), Eva initially went with her captors willingly. Once she was in their control, she became a coerced victim and was held against her will. She would also have been classed as a child victim under the Palermo Protocol. As the final line of her story illustrates, the issues of criminality and judgement tend to focus attention on women, as victims, rather than on the criminality of the traffickers. As Eva notes, although she was also 'victimised' by immigration authorities and subjected to extreme pressure and threat once she managed to escape, there was little interest from the authorities in pursuing her captor.

Extract 4.5

Profile: Eva, 18, from north London

Paul Lewis

I was 15 when he first took me from my home [in Africa]. He was a so-called friend of the family. My parents had been killed, so I was staying with a guardian who thought the friend would find me a job. Instead the man took me far from home, where he called other men who began raping me. For a year I was taken around different countries in Africa where I was made to have sex with men.

Then in 2004 – when I was 16 – he just took me to an airport. When we arrived [in London] I had no idea which country we were in. I was taken to a big house with other women trafficked from Africa. During the nights I was driven to houses where I was forced to sleep with men. I had no money, no documents. He never beat me but I was scared of him – worried he would kill me.

One night he left the car door open and I escaped. I started running. The next day I begged. Someone gave me money for a bus, and I travelled to the end of the line. There, a woman found me crying and took me to a women's refuge organisation in Kentish Town.

When I applied for asylum the security guard started shouting questions at me. Where was I staying? Why did I not have any documentation? I just broke down. They didn't believe I was 17, so I was taken to Brozefield prison. My church, Legal Action for Women and the Black Women's Rep Action Project found me legal representation and I was let out, but the Home Office still want to send me back. No-one has pursued the man.

Source: *The Guardian*, 8 May 2006

Such official definitions and identifications of people trafficking rely on women being able to 'prove' they were coerced and then being grateful to authorities who provide the opportunity to 'go home'. Without these components, women do not conform to the image of the 'innocent victim'. The crime of being poor, or of turning to sex work as a rational choice due to the lack of other marketable skills, are not regarded as 'proper' reasons for migration. In a similar way, prior to changes in the law and how it is interpreted, women who were not seen as 'deserving' of police protection – as victims of domestic violence (Westmarland, 2001) – were not given the same attention as other, more 'suitable' recipients. Until violence against women was defined as being a 'crime', such women had little chance of having their cases taken seriously by the police. In essence, therefore, establishing protocols does not necessarily reduce the incidence of female sex slavery. While it might help the police and courts put victims of trafficking into appropriate 'categories', it might not actually provide the women themselves with any assistance. Furthermore, the impossibility of the women being able to prove that they were coerced (if they present, for example, as 'experienced' prostitutes or 'returners' caught in the same country two or more times, having been returned to their country of origin on a previous occasion) further precludes any possibility of accessing help.

4.2 Attempts to quantify trafficking

The scale of trafficking is difficult to quantify, again partly because of a lack of any universally accepted definition of when it constitutes a 'crime' and who might be considered as 'deserving victims'. However, we might also ask whether quantification actually matters. Some feminists have argued that it is the experience of each individual that is important, rather than trying to decipher whether trafficking is becoming more or less of a problem generally. For those on the receiving end, it is, de facto, a serious problem (Gelsthorpe, 1990, p. 91). However, other feminists (e.g. Berman, 2003) have suggested that to dwell on women's individual histories acts only to reinforce their revictimisation and infantilisation. From another position, critical of the 'moral crusade' surrounding people trafficking, Ronald Weitzer has stated that: 'In fact, *there are no reliable statistics on the magnitude of trafficking*, and the figures can only be described as guesswork. Even ballpark estimates are dubious, given the clandestine and stigmatised nature of the sex trade' (Weitzer, 2007, p. 455).

Despite the lack of reliable data across the world, the supposed increase in trafficking of women and girls for the sex trade is causing alarm. The Council of Europe states that the scale and magnitude of 'migration' or trafficking is evident, despite its 'clandestine' nature:

> Available data on some countries suggest an estimated 200,000 women from Bangladesh have been trafficked into Pakistan over the past ten years, and trafficking continues at the rate of 200–400 women monthly. In 1994, some 2,000 women were trafficked into six cities in India. There are about 5,000–7,000 Nepalese women and girls trafficked into India annually. After India, Hong Kong is considered to be the largest market for Nepalese women.
> (Lim, writing in 1998, quoted in Commonwealth Secretariat, 2003, p. 9)

It is obvious that any statistical calculation will be uncertain, not only due to the illegal and secretive nature of the trade, but also because of the motives and agency of those involved. There are few 'crimes' or activities where the status of 'victim' and 'perpetrator' is so fluid, open to contestation and little understood. As has already been illustrated in the Introduction to this chapter, for law enforcement and campaign organisations across the world one of the critical issues is the degree of choice or coercion involved. As the Commonwealth Secretariat acknowledged:

> Trafficking is now considered the third largest source of profits for organised crime, behind only drugs and guns, generating billions of dollars annually. It is also connected to these other criminal activities, with profits from trafficking in persons being used to finance illicit arms and drugs trading. The reasons for this phenomenon are multiple and complex. However in general, this criminal activity has taken advantage of the freer flow of people, money, goods and services to extend its own international reach. It feeds on poverty, despair, war, crisis, ignorance and women's unequal status in most societies. The globalisation of the world economy has increased the movement of people beyond and across borders, legally or illegally, especially from poorer to wealthier countries.
>
> (Commonwealth Secretariat, 2003, p. 5)

From these quotations it can be seen that there appear to be at least two aspects to the trafficking debate that help to create headlines and international panic. The first is the way in which the problem can be magnified by the impossibility of obtaining accurate or verifiable statistics. Figures can be manipulated to suit any cause, such as stirring up fears over migration or moralising about the illicit sex trade. The second aspect is the link to organised crime. It cannot be denied that people trafficking is 'organised' just as any legitimate business would be, and that it may have links to other forms of existing illegal networks involved in the arms and drugs trades. Such 'foreign villains' are typically characterised as violent and dangerous, as being beyond the control of national police forces and as the main exploiters of vulnerable women and children. These aspects of the debate create powerful discourses that can be called upon by international crime control agencies to demand more resources and regulations.

4.3 Attempts to control the 'flow' of trafficking

Attempts to control the various activities that the definitions and protocols aim to categorise provide further illustration of how particular social problems are presented to the public as matters of serious concern. The problem for law enforcement agencies is that they are faced simultaneously with the 'visible' victims of the crime (i.e. the trafficked women) and the more elusive traffickers and smugglers, whom we might regard as 'criminal gangs', facilitators or entrepreneurs, depending on their specific actions, behaviour and motives. There are a number of competing interests and perspectives at play here, each with its own ideological and moral imperatives.

One of the ways in which some campaigners have suggested that the problem can be minimised is simply to suppress the demand for prostitution. This has been advocated by a number of different agencies. From a position of intra-national state law enforcement, the control of prostitution has been justified as one element in ongoing attempts to tackle the 'anti-social'. From a faith-based view, Christian charity organisations, such as Save the Children, have argued that it is simply morally wrong to sell women's or children's bodies for sex. Some feminists have argued that prostitution should be banned because it represents the oppression of women, whether or not it is entered into voluntarily (see Westmarland and Gangoli, 2006). Other 'helping' agencies (such as CARE: see Boucher, 2007) argue that men should be prosecuted for buying sex and its associated activities. By criminalising activities such as kerb crawling, in order to reduce the demand for sexual services on the street, such initiatives imitate what has become known as the 'Swedish Model', which is claimed to have reduced the incidence of people trafficking dramatically (Boucher, 2007). This approach supposedly decreases the number of women entering the country to become sex workers because the demand for them is reduced by the prosecution, and the threat of exposure, of men who cruise the streets or are caught in brothels buying the services of prostitutes. As Daniel Boucher has observed with regard to the UK:

- In reducing the market for prostitution services, it should, in turn, **reduce the number of women (generally) who are trafficked into the UK for sex**. Most trafficked women are set to work offering off-street prostitution services, e.g. in brothels, which is entirely beyond the reach of current demand provisions. As many as 81% of women working in brothels in the UK are now thought to have come from overseas (Dickson, 2004).

- It would send out a strong signal that it is not acceptable to encourage the commodification of the human body and that buying sexual services degrades and exploits. In so doing it would help build a more humane society, challenging a foundation for the distortion of the way in which men view women and vice versa.

(Boucher, 2007, p. 3, original emphasis)

According to Arthur Gould (2001, p. 453), such policy is 'Sweden's own brand of radical feminism'. In a report, published by the UK Home Office (but noted not to represent their views), Liz Kelly and Linda Regan (2000) also take the view that the legal framework should be modernised to include the creation of a crime called 'sexual exploitation' and that more severe penalties should be imposed where coerced prostitution involves a vulnerable person, such as a foreign national.

There are a number of gendered assumptions implicit in these discussions about who is trafficked and why, and who is or is not criminalised, and in the diverse attempts to define, control and regulate what is sometimes referred to as a 'growing global menace' (Berman, 2003, p. 55). As a crime 'without borders', often also without complainants or verifiable 'victims', there are very few prosecutions for trafficking and despite attempts by international organisations and supra-governmental manoeuvres to obtain agreements leading to cooperation between law enforcement agencies, trafficking has apparently increased. A supplement in 2001 to the United Nations Convention against Transnational Organized Crime declared that, in order to 'combat trafficking in persons' there must be a 'comprehensive international approach in the countries of origin, transit and destination that includes measures to prevent such trafficking, to punish the traffickers and to protect the victims of such trafficking, including protecting their internationally recognised human rights' (quoted in Commonwealth Secretariat, 2003, p. 44). Berman (2003), Laura Agustin (2007) and Ronald Weitzer (2007) have, however, criticised such an approach, arguing that it simply reinforces fears about 'strangers' and allows governments to erect borders and to criminalise 'difference'. Defining the problem as one of law enforcement also tends to cast women as passive victims, lacking human agency or common sense (Agustin, 2007).

One of the core problems of controlling the international sex trafficking trade is that the 'ambiguities' surrounding European integration, territorial boundaries and differential legislative enforcement allow for the opening up of spaces for criminal entrepreneurship. As Rob Hornsby

Figure 4.5
The 'Swedish model': criminalising kerbcrawling to reduce the demand for street prostitutes

and Dick Hobbs discovered in their study of counterfeit cigarette smuggling, criminal entrepreneurs can exploit the 'fragility of current European boundaries, and the subsequent lack of an integrated political authority' (Hornsby and Hobbs, 2007, p. 566). Control of cigarette bootlegging by governments is ineffectual, but even if it were more effective, smugglers would engage in 'commodity hopping' when the risks of capture or punishment become too high in relation to profit. Hornsby and Hobbs point out that when cigarette smuggling becomes too 'hot', smugglers move into another type of illegal or illicit trade. Similarly, situations have been created where, for some people in some places at certain times, migration or movement is a crime, whereas for others, by default – due to the absence of effective regulation and lack of agreement on the status of 'victims' and 'perpetrators' – it is blurred.

One of the agencies that has attempted to consolidate approaches to the problem of 'trafficking gangs' in the UK is the United Kingdom Human Trafficking Centre (UKHTC), described in Extract 4.6.

Extract 4.6

UKHTC is a multi agency centre that provides a central point for the development of expertise and operational co-ordination in relation to the trafficking of human beings, working together with other agencies in the UK and abroad.

It plays a key role in co-ordinating work across stakeholders and, with its partners, delivers a diverse set of programmes, including targeted campaigns to prevent and reduce the trafficking of human beings (THB). In addition, the centre conducts research, develops training packages for UK Law Enforcement partners, cascades good practice and works to deliver an improved knowledge and understanding of the way criminal enterprises associated with human trafficking operate.

The Centre will continuously develop police and law enforcement expertise and provide operational co-ordination in the UK in relation to THB, complementing and working in conjunction with the Serious Organised Crime Agency (SOCA).

The Centre promotes the development of a victim centred human rights based approach to THB. Working with Non Governmental Organisations (NGOs) and other partners, it works to improve the standard of victim care and protection and raise understanding of the complexities that attach to dealing with victim welfare in human trafficking cases in both the criminal justice and wider protection environment.

Source: UKHTC, 2007

As the aims and objectives of the UKHTC's attempts to work in 'partnerships' illustrate, continuing demand, weak political control/ agreement, loosening of border controls, and other aspects of globalisation (the internet, easier travel, communications, etc.) has led to an increase in the political will to suppress the problem and the creation of law enforcement to stop (or, some might argue, create) a 'crime' for which an agreed definition is still sought. The aims of international cooperation and control, and the involvement of the Serious Organised Crime Agency in the case of the UK, lend a prior assumption of 'criminality' to the actions it discusses.

Treating the ebb and flow of human migration as a crime, whether that migration is to escape poverty or intolerable situations or to provide a better life for children, is a reaction we might expect from agencies set up to prevent abuse and catch perpetrators. Theories and policies that inform these practices illustrate some of the points that this chapter has highlighted. By looking at such questions through a gendered lens, some understanding of why people migrate and how and why they are criminalised can be gleaned. These questions also reveal the ambiguities and ironies of the global situation in terms of migration. In some countries, an 'American dream' culture exists, which suggests that it is possible – and even admirable – to try to travel for work and to better one's life chances and standard of living. Due to the 'moral' aspect of sex work, however, women who migrate to sell sex are not considered 'welcome' citizens, even though selling sex is not usually illegal in the countries to which they wish to migrate.

To summarise, it seems, therefore, that gendered and moralised assumptions are made about women who migrate, the situations in which they find themselves and the reasons they set out to leave their own countries. Women finding themselves in the sex trade is viewed by some law enforcement agencies as unfortunate, but not unexpected. Women in this situation are caught between two identities – on the one hand, that of the 'knowing and culpable migrant' and, on the other, that of being a 'victim of trafficking' – and it is this contradiction that highlights both their enhanced vulnerability and the disagreements about enforcement and care. Such vulnerability is also compounded by the desire of law enforcement agencies to secure the role of these women as witnesses, sometimes through the threat of deportation.

5   The politics of trafficking

In this section some of the more controversial issues surrounding people trafficking are examined because, as Venessa Munro (2006) has argued, the relationship between anti-trafficking measures and anti-prostitution policy has become highly politicised. This means that disputes about definitions and legislation are occurring not only at governmental or 'high' political levels, but also at 'grass-roots' levels where campaign groups are fighting from opposing positions. This, along with the illicit nature of people trafficking and a lack of reliable data, has contributed to 'a potentially divisive conflict of interests', inhibiting an integrated strategy for a unified international response (Munro, 2006, p. 325) or an agreed and ratified UN protocol.

According to agencies (such as the UKHTC) charged with the control of this 'crime', women cannot be classed as legitimate economic migrants who want to sell sex, even in some countries in Europe where this is a legal transaction. Rather, they are typically cast as 'strangers' in the grip of dangerous 'Eastern' gangs who exploit and abuse or, by the media, as hapless, helpless victims. This is not to say that some women do not find themselves in some desperate, life-threatening situations, or that they should be made 'over-responsible for their fate' (Agustin, 2007, p.41).

Because trafficked women have conflicting roles and statuses, they are often not viewed as being 'deserving' of sympathy or help. They are 'strangers' or 'deviant others' and they are 'potentially deceptive'. But above all they are sex workers, making them morally undeserving. As Claudia Aradau argues:

> ... the situation of trafficking is represented by a specific counting of trafficked women: those who are worthy of pity and those who are not, those who are useful for legal enforcement procedures against traffickers and those who are not. Those who have experienced horrific physical suffering at the hands of their traffickers are to be deemed worthy of pity.
>
> (Aradau, 2008, p. 127)

Part of Aradau's argument is that when horrific individual stories of abuse are recounted, women are seen as 'deserving victims' and if they are prepared to help prosecute their traffickers and return 'home' when the case is over, they are politically useful. Once the individual woman's terrible circumstances are forgotten, however, her status (and that of all the other women she represents) returns to the unwelcome one of illegal immigrant and illegal worker. Hence, her moment of suffering and pain make her worthy, but only while she is of value to the media or politician. Jo Goodey argues that this is due to the '"migration–crime–security" nexus that forms the backbone of EU responses to trafficking' because migration and law enforcement approaches dominate the political agenda. This is also the case in the USA, as she outlines:

> The US Department of State, through its office to monitor and combat trafficking in persons, also plays an important global role in forming policy responses on and allocating resources to trafficking;

Figure 4.6
Sex workers march for their rights.

though it is less influential in the EU, which is governed and funded by its own stakeholders. In its annual report on trafficking in persons the Department of State assigns a 'Tier' to each country, which indicates the extent to which it is considered to be in compliance with US anti-trafficking policies (rather than taking the UN Convention against TOC [Transnational Organized Crime] and its accompanying Trafficking Protocol as the sole basis for compliance): Tier 1 indicates compliance with US anti-trafficking policies, through to Tier 3 indicating the lowest level of compliance.

> For many countries in the developing world, their placement in this tier ranking is significant, as a Tier 3 placement can mean that the government will have sanctions imposed on it by the US government; such as withholding non-humanitarian and non-trade-related foreign assistance. For this reason, the placement of countries within a particular Tier is not without its critics.
>
> (Goodey, 2008, p. 432)

The economic, social and gender inequalities that lie at the heart of trafficking mean that policies should be much more 'victim' centred and should take a human rights focus, with the needs of individual women as a priority. Goodey argues that there is some evidence of a move towards this sort of approach, but that:

> The real test of how far these initiatives are 'for' victims is whether they exist separate to conditions that stipulate that the victim should co-operate with the authorities in order to receive certain services. To this end, the continued absence of open residence permits for trafficked victims, regardless of whether they cooperate with the authorities*, is still some way off *in practice.*
>
> * The EC Temporary Residence Permit Directive (Directive 2004/81/EC, 29 April 2004), which is on the residence permit issued to third country nationals who are victims of trafficking in human beings or who have been the subject of an action to facilitate illegal immigration, *who co-operate with the authorities*, is indicative of the limited rights afforded to victims.
>
> (Goodey, 2008, p. 433, original emphasis)

6   Conclusion

As the discussion throughout this chapter has illustrated, issues surrounding people trafficking are ambiguous, not least because there is little empirical data or agreement on its constitution. Without international agreement about how many women are trafficked or smuggled, and which of them may be 'choosing' to migrate, the extent of 'criminal' activity is hard to quantify. Adding to these complications, anti-trafficking campaigns have their own agendas: namely, moral (against the selling of sex), feminist (the view of prostitution as work against the view that it is the exploitation of women's bodies) or xenophobic (political border protectionism). In some cases, more than one of these agendas operate together and, in others, it could be alleged, one campaign is used to mask another. For example, a 'moral' agenda may disguise policies that are otherwise informed by 'foreigner' and 'stranger' hatred.

The extent to which power, violence and harm are present in people trafficking or smuggling varies according to the definition and outcomes of the actions in each case. Whether or not people choose to migrate, are taken forcibly from their environment or are tricked into believing they will be free to live as they wish once they arrive in the country of destination, is an illustration of an extreme version of power to control, coerce or threaten the vulnerable. The violence described in the case studies throughout this chapter illustrates that not only the traffickers, but also the agencies set up to help the victims, can inflict harm. Harm can also be inflicted by sensational media reporting of the 'flesh trade' in headlines such as '9 YEAR OLD GIRLS SOLD FOR THE PRICE OF A TOASTER', as Joel Brinkley asserts (in Berman, 2003, p. 38), and as a result of fear that emanates from the opening up of previously 'closed' societies, such as eastern Europe. The issue of trafficking has been 'incendiarised' beyond the point at which policy could work or be devised (Berman, 2003). Berman (2003) also argues that if policies are really designed with the intention of supporting vulnerable women, the focus should be less on criminalisation and more on developing ways that might facilitate women who want to migrate to find work and support them in transit and when they arrive.

Notions of 'sex-trafficking' or 'exploitation' are also geographically and culturally contingent (which is not to say that the physical or mental coercion of women should be tolerated anywhere). Just to confuse matters, however, commentators such as Kelly and Regan (2000) argue that 'trafficking' occurs wherever coercion and exploitation take place and need not involve any crossing of national borders or travel. 'Choice' or agency is difficult to determine in migration/trafficking. Because of the diverse nature and international extent of the issues, and the way in which issues of migration, people trafficking and smuggling collide, the extent of 'criminality' and victimhood is difficult to measure.

A key concern of this chapter has been to reveal that although people trafficking and smuggling is a complicated issue, mostly it affects women and girls as a form of gender abuse. This is because there are differential power relations in societies worldwide that disadvantage women. It means that although women do not typically conform to stereotypes of the 'criminal', the desire to migrate and work in countries where they are structurally disadvantaged means that one of their most rational options is to criminalise themselves by selling sex. Social, legal and political structures (including international protocols) do not protect women from violence and harm (Walklate, 2008). Although this is true to a lesser or greater degree across the world, the countries where, ironically, women choose to go to sell their bodies, are often those that make the greater claim for female emancipation and equality of opportunity.

References

Abiala, K. (2006) 'The Republic of Moldova: Prostitution and Trafficking in Women' in Gangoli, G. and Westmarland, N. (eds) (2006).

Agustin, L.M. (2007) *Sex at the Margins. Migration, Labour Markets and the Rescue Industry*, London, Zed Books.

Amnesty International (2007) *Greece: Uphold the Rights of Women and Girls Trafficked for Sexual Exploitation* [online], http://takeaction.amnestyusa.org (Accessed 17 September 2008).

Aradau, C. (2008) *Rethinking Trafficking in Women: Politics out of Security*, Basingstoke, Palgrave Macmillan.

Bales, K. (2004) *New Slavery: A Reference Handbook*, Santa Barbara, CA, ABC-Clio, History Reference Online [online], www.historyreferenceonline.abc-clio.com (Accessed 4 January 2008).

Berman, J. (2003) '(Un)Popular strangers and crises (un)bounded: discourses of sex-trafficking, the European political community and the panicked state of the modern state', *European Journal of International Relations*, vol. 9, no. 1, pp. 37–86.

Boucher, D. (2007) *Prostitution and Human Trafficking: Tackling Demand. The Criminal Justice and Immigration Bill: A Briefing from CARE* [online], www.chaste.org.uk/public_documents/CJI_Briefing_Doc_CARE_ CHASTE_001.pdf (Accessed 10 February 2009).

Commonwealth Secretariat (2003) *Report of the Expert Group on Strategies for Combating the Trafficking of Women and Children*, London, Commonwealth Secretariat.

Council of Europe (2005) *Council of Europe Convention on Action against Trafficking in Human Beings*, Explanatory Report, Warsaw, Council of Europe [online], http://conventions.coe.int/Treaty/EN/Treaties/Html/197.htm (Accessed 14 January 2009).

Di Nicola, A. (2007) 'Researching into human trafficking: issues and problems' in Lee, M. (ed.) *Human Trafficking*, Cullompton, Willan.

Dickson, S. (2004) *Sex in the City: Mapping Commercial Sex Across London*, London, The Poppy Project.

Eaton, M. (1986) *Justice for Women? Family, Court and Social Control*, Milton Keynes, Open University Press.

Gangoli, G. and Westmarland, N. (eds) (2006) *International Approaches to Prostitution: Law and Policy in Europe and Asia*, Bristol, The Policy Press.

Gelsthorpe, L. (1990) 'Feminist methodologies in criminology: a new approach or old wine in new bottles?' in Gelsthorpe, L. and Morris, A. (eds) *Feminist Perspectives in Criminology*, Milton Keynes, Open University Press.

Goodey, J. (2008) 'Human trafficking: sketchy data and policy responses', *Criminology and Criminal Justice*, vol. 8, no. 4, pp. 421–2.

Gould, A. (2001) 'The criminalisation of buying sex: the politics of prostitution in Sweden', *Journal of Social Policy*, vol. 30, no. 3, pp. 437–56.

Hornsby, R. and Hobbs, D. (2007) 'A zone of ambiguity: the political economy of cigarette bootlegging', *British Journal of Criminology*, vol. 47, no. 4, pp. 551–71.

International Association of Chiefs of Police (2007) *The Crime of Human Trafficking: A Law Enforcement Guide to Identification and Investigation*, Washington, DC, Office on Violence Against Women, Department of Justice.

Kelly, L. (2007) 'A conducive context: trafficking of persons in Central Asia' in Lee, M. (ed.) (2007).

Kelly, L. and Regan, L. (2000) 'Stopping traffic: exploring the extent of, and response to, trafficking in women for sexual exploitation in the UK', *Police Research Series Paper 125*, London, Home Office.

Kennedy, H. (1992) *Eve Was Framed: Women and British Justice*, London, Vintage.

Lee, M. (ed.) (2007) *Human Trafficking*, Cullompton, Willan.

Milmo, C. and Morris, N. (2008) '18,000 women and children trafficked into UK sex trade', *Independent*, 3 July [online], www.independent.co.uk/news/uk/crime/18000-women-and-children-trafficked-into-uk-sex-trade-859106.html (Accessed 14 January 2009).

Munro, V.E. (2006) 'Stopping traffic?', *British Journal of Criminology*, vol. 46, no. 2, pp. 318–33.

Picarelli, J.T. (2007) 'Historical approaches to the trade in human beings' in Lee, M. (ed.) (2007).

Stanley, L. and Wise, S. (1993) *Breaking Out Again: Feminist Ontology and Epistemology*, London, Routledge.

UNICEF (2005) *Trafficking in Human Beings, Especially Women and Children, in Africa* (2nd edn) Florence, UNICEF Innocenti Research Centre.

United Kingdom Human Trafficking Centre (UKHTC) (2007) [online], http://www.ukhtc.org (Accessed 17 February 2009).

United Nations (2001) *Protocol to Prevent, Suppress and Punish Trafficking in Persons, Especially Women and Children, Supplementing the United Nations Convention against Transnational Organized Crime*, G.A. res. 55/25, annex 11, 55 U.N. GAOR Supp. (no.49) at 60, U.N. Doc. A/45/49 (Vol. 1) (2001), Geneva, United Nations.

US Department of Justice (2003) *Report to Congress from Attorney General John Ashcroft on US Government Efforts to Combat Trafficking in Persons in Fiscal Year 2003, 9*, Washington, DC, US Department of Justice.

US Department of State (2005) *Distinctions Between Human Smuggling and Human Trafficking*, US Department of State, Human Smuggling and Trafficking Center [online],
www.state.gov/g/tip/rls/fs/2005/57345.htm (Accessed 14 January 2009).

Walklate, S. (2001) *Gender, Crime and Criminal Justice*, Cullompton, Willan.

Walklate, S. (2008) 'What is to be done about violence against women? Gender, violence, cosmopolitanism and the law', *British Journal of Criminology*, vol. 48, no. 1, pp. 39–54.

Weitzer, R. (2007) 'The social construction of sex trafficking: ideology and institutionalization of a moral crusade', *Politics and Society*, vol. 35, no. 3, pp. 447–5.

Westmarland, L. (2001) *Gender and Policing: Sex, Power and Police Culture*, Cullompton, Willan.

Westmarland, N. and Gangoli, G. (2006) 'Introduction: approaches to prostitution' in Gangoli, G. and Westmarland, N. (eds) (2006).

Chapter 5
Crime, harm and corporate power

Steve Tombs and David Whyte

Contents

1   Introduction

Today, the corporation is so much a part of our everyday life it is difficult to imagine that it is a relatively recent legal and political construction. The earliest forms of the modern 'joint stock' company emerged in seventeenth-century England, established under Royal Charter to enable colonisation of the Americas and India. Those companies (such as the Virginia Company and the British East India Company) allowed the wealth of several people to be combined and brought under the name of one entity. From the end of the nineteenth century onwards, a new type of 'limited liability' company was developed in the dominant economic nations, which allowed investors to share in the profits of the company and at the same time remain exempt from its losses or liabilities. In limited liability companies, the dominant model of the modern corporation, shareholders' (or owners') losses are limited to the original sum that they invest. Corporations, then, are legal entities that give particular privileges to those who enter into business (the exchange and provision of goods and services for agreed-upon fees). The term 'corporation' is used to describe a number of different participants (investors, directors, shareholders, employees) who combine to mobilise and deliver business activities (Pearce, 2001; Glasbeek, 2002).

As a business enterprise, the number and type of corporations continue to expand. In the UK, for example, at the end of the 1970s, state provision of goods, services and employment remained widespread. Who would have imagined then that water, gas and electricity would, three decades later, all be purchased in a private marketplace; or that private provision of pensions, health care, and medical and unemployment insurance would all be the stuff of daytime advertising on television; or that the vagaries of national and international stock markets would impact directly on payments for housing or access to credit; or that most of us would rely on credit on an everyday basis for shopping and paying bills? These are truly seismic changes in the organisation of economic and social life (Tombs and Whyte, 2009).

Globally, since postcolonial states sought to industrialise, the economies of the former Soviet Union were opened up to free market capitalism and the 'communist' regime of China developed a form of market economy, the geographical scale of corporate activity has expanded rapidly. Alongside these changes, the emergence of new technologies has made the flow of information, commodities and money possible across borders at hitherto unimaginable speeds.

Corporations are key enterprises with enormous economic, political and social power, and just as enormous is the scale and potential for harm and crimes on their part. It is with a critical analysis of some of these that this chapter is concerned. In particular, the chapter aims to:

- identify ways in which corporations are a source of harms in contemporary societies

- explore the extent to which 'official' data allows us to measure corporate crimes

- examine several key national and international dimensions of corporate power and regulation.

The following section details the extent of death, injury, violence and theft that can be attributed, either directly or indirectly, to corporate activity. Some of this (such as fraud) falls within the gaze of criminal law, but many more harms (such as airborne pollution) seem to be committed with relative impunity (Passas and Goodwin, 2007). As a result, the central concern of this chapter is the exploration of the relationship between harms and crimes and the implications of applying not only greater regulation but also the criminal law to corporate harmful activity. Section 3 explores some of the difficulties faced by criminology in researching these issues, not least the processes whereby corporate harm is systematically screened out of the criminal justice system. As Section 4 outlines, the core issue here is understanding the nature and exercise of power: how corporations hold and use their power not only to evade criminalisation or regulation, but also to influence how 'crime' comes to be defined. Section 5 places these issues in a broader context of global economies and considers how far international regulatory systems can be expected to curtail corporate malpractice, harm and criminality.

2 Corporate harm

This chapter is concerned with corporate crime and corporate harm – in particular, those crimes and harms that are committed within the context of profit making and which victimise workers, consumers and the general public. As this section will demonstrate, measuring with any accuracy the scale of corporate harms is fraught with difficulty. These harms are rarely, if ever, the concern of official crime statistics or victim surveys. How, then, can we arrive at some understanding of the nature and extent of harmful corporate activity?

Activity 5.1

Choose an example of corporate harm – you will find numerous examples by scanning the Web using the search words 'corporate', 'crime', 'harm', 'violence'. Make a note of the various sources of information – beyond newspaper reports – that are available about the case you select.

To assist your search, you may wish to consider the following organisations: the Serious Fraud Office, the Financial Services Authority, the Office of Fair Trading, the Food Standards Agency, the Health and Safety Executive, the Environment Agency, or one of the hundreds of local authorities (LAs) in the UK responsible for enforcing health and safety law in over one million workplaces through their environmental health officers.

Comment

You might have found a range of data sources (further to those listed above), drawn from academic research across a range of disciplines (not just criminology) and from official data published by government bodies and non-governmental organisations (NGOs) (but almost certainly not by the Home Office). Official data sources are likely to be spread across a plethora of national and local governmental departments or 'buried' in accountancy returns – so that locating, collating and interpreting them is a time-consuming and often frustrating process. Further, the most informative data tends to be uncovered by investigative journalists, or collated by interest or campaigning groups, not least those formed by, or 'representing', victims. While these latter sources might invite the charge of being less 'objective' and reliable than information gathered or stored by official/governmental sources, they can nevertheless help us start to appreciate the scale of harm caused by corporations in the course of business activity. What follows, then, is an attempt to bring together this data in order to begin to unpack the extent of harms perpetrated by corporations.

2.1 Harms caused by theft and fraud

The general evidence available to us indicates that corporate fraud is widespread. Donald Rebovich and John Kane (2002) have estimated that 37 per cent of the US population have been victims of some form of corporate theft or fraud.

One the most prolific and well-known series of consumer thefts in the UK was the personal pensions frauds, in which as many as 2.4 million victims lost their pensions after being persuaded to replace their occupational pension schemes with high-risk private schemes by a number of high street firms between 1988 and 1994 (Financial Services Authority, 1999; Slapper and Tombs, 1999). To this can be added the endowment mortgage frauds of the 1990s, which, through mis-selling a particularly risky mortgage product to high-risk customers, created victims in perhaps as many as 5 million cases (Consumers' Association, undated; Fooks, 2003). It is estimated that losses due to the endowment mortgage frauds could total £130 billion (see Whyte, 2004a).

Corporate price fixing (the illegal agreement between parties to keep prices artificially high) – for example, in the electrical goods, car and construction sectors – has become routine activity for many of the largest and most respected corporations (Slapper and Tombs, 1999; Croall, 2001). News of this surfaces intermittently in reports of 'findings' by the Office of Fair Trading or the European Competition Commission (see, for example, Office of Fair Trading, 2007; Walsh, 2007; and European Competition Commission, 2008). It is often very difficult, if not impossible, to distinguish what and how much fraud is produced by corporations. The evidence cited above, however, is focused unequivocally on corporate fraud, not least by a host of well-known, high street names.

2.2 Harms caused by working

Death, injury and disease caused by working are global, routine phenomena. The International Labour Organization (ILO), a United Nations (UN) agency, has estimated that 2.2 million people die as a result of work-related injuries or diseases every year (i.e. 3.9 per cent of global deaths per annum). Further, there are around 270 million occupational injuries and 160 million victims of work-related illnesses annually (International Labour Organization, 2005).

This victimisation is distributed truly globally. Of the 345,000 workers estimated by the ILO to have died in incidents (as opposed to dying from occupational diseases and exposures) at the workplace in 2002, by far the greatest number, almost 220,000, were in Asia. China had the highest number of deaths of any one Asian country (73,595), India the second highest (48,176). In Europe, workers in the states of the former Soviet Union, which joined the EU from 2004, are three times as likely to die at work than those in the 'EU-15', the states that made up the EU up to 2004 (Woolfson, 2005).

In the UK, there are 1200–1500 work-related fatal injuries each year (Tombs and Whyte, 2008). And in terms of fatal disease, an annual total of some 50,000 deaths to workers in the UK has been estimated by Rory O'Neill et al. (2007). This conservative figure still excludes some major

Figure 5.1
Injuries occur in
various workplace
settings

categories of disease, but includes cancers, respiratory illnesses and heart diseases.

In this category of harms there is therefore some degree of certainty that the overwhelming majority of deaths caused by work occur in the context of corporate or profit-making business activities of some type (Tombs and Whyte, 2007).

2.3 Harms caused by air pollution

Air, land and water pollutants are a further key cause of death and disease; the focus here is on exposure to airborne pollutants. In global terms, a recent estimate of the scale of death and disease as a result of outdoor air pollution concluded that ambient air pollution causes about 800,000 (1.2 per cent of the total) premature deaths (Cohen et al., 2005): a figure supported by the World Bank (Vidal, 2005) and the World Health Organization (Global Atmospheric Pollution Forum, undated). And as with the global distribution of work-related deaths, the effects of air pollution too are predominantly located in those states that are the least able in terms of resources either to prevent or respond to such harms – namely, the developing world. An estimated 65 per cent of deaths from air pollution are in Asia (Cohen et al., 2005).

In the UK, according to Department of Health estimates, the deaths of at least 24,000 people every year can be attributed to poisoning by various forms of environmental air pollution – and this is certainly an underestimation (Department of Health Committee on the Medical Effects of Air Pollutants, 2001).

Separating the corporate from individual sources of environmental pollution (the key example of the latter being personal vehicle use) is not an easy task. However, official data available does indicate that the largest known killers are nitrogen oxide, fine particles emissions and sulphur dioxides (Whyte, 2004b). The source of those major killers can be identified as having commercial origins (Whyte, 2004b). Without underestimating the extent of the harm caused by motor vehicles, it can be assumed with confidence that most deadly environmental pollution is caused directly by corporations.

2.4 Harms caused by food poisoning

A further sphere of possible corporate harm relates to the responsibility that corporations might have for large numbers of food-related illnesses and deaths. The full scale of food poisoning-related deaths remains unknown, partly because of a lack of official figures, but also because of the complex way in which food infection affects human health. So, although between 100 and 200 people in the UK die directly as a result of salmonella and campylobacter every year, this does not quite capture the full extent of food poisoning-related deaths. Food poisoning cases are known to have lasting and complex effects on health. For example, it has been estimated that salmonella and campylobacter triple the average person's chances of dying from any other disease or condition within a year (Helms et al., 2003).

Figure 5.2
Living with chronic air
pollution

However, government estimates do indicate that around half of all food poisoning cases in the UK can be attributed to food consumed outside the home (UK Parliament, 2003). The actual figures, though, may be much higher: the fourth Food Standards Agency *Consumer Attitudes to Food Standards* survey recorded self-reported incidence of food poisoning at 16 per cent of the sample population, 82 per cent of these claiming that the source was outside the home (TNS, 2004). Although it is likely that the majority of those cases were caused by food sold by outlets owned or franchised by large corporations, there is no data that allows us to quantify those cases precisely.

Consider the case given in Box 5.1.

Box 5.1 Cadbury's and salmonella

In January 2006, the confectioner Cadbury's became aware of salmonella in products at one of its UK factories in Herefordshire. On discovering the contamination and its source, Cadbury's did not inform relevant authorities such as the Food Standards Agency and the Health Protection Agency. Six months later, in June, the Health Protection Agency became concerned about an unusual rise in human cases of *Salmonella montevideo* (Smithers, 2007). The Food Standards Agency then requested Cadbury's to withdraw seven infected products; Cadbury's took two days to comply with the request (Smithers, 2007). Two of these brands, the Dairy Milk Buttons Easter Egg and the 10p Freddo bar (Food Standards Agency, 2006), are marketed specifically at children, and in the period between recognising the presence of salmonella and product recall, Easter had come and gone. Over one million items of chocolate were recalled from retailers (Smithers, 2007). The outbreak of *Salmonella montevideo* led to three people being treated in hospital (Elliot, 2007) and 'dozens of people became ill with food poisoning' (Smithers, 2007), 'including babies and children under 10' (Elliott, 2007).

There followed a long and complex investigation, which was undertaken by Birmingham City Council and Herefordshire District Council, funded by a grant from the Food Standards Agency of 'an estimated £50,000, in cash and in the form of "back-up" experts' (Smithers, 2007). The company apologised for concern caused, but did not admit liability and was expected to plead not guilty (Smithers, 2007). The investigation uncovered another unreported outbreak of salmonella at Cadbury's Herefordshire plant in 2002. Cadbury's eventually admitted nine charges brought by Herefordshire and Birmingham councils (BBC, 2007) and was fined an 'unprecedented' £1 million (Elliott, 2007). The court had been told that Cadbury's had 'changed its testing procedures on chocolate in 2003 to save money and waste' (Elliott, 2007). The self-declared 'world's largest confectionery company', Cadbury Schweppes' annual revenue for 2007 was £7,971 million (Cadbury Schweppes, 2008). The combined fine plus costs – £1,152,000 (Elliott, 2007) – represents 0.0145 per cent of revenue. To put it another way, this is equivalent to a fine of £4.35 for someone earning, in 2007, what was the UK average gross income of £30,000.

In Cadbury Schweppes' *Corporate and Social Responsibility Report*, the product recall merited two paragraphs, in which the company noted that 'it had acted in good faith throughout' and guaranteed to modify production and quality assurance processes, concluding that 'We will continue, as we always have, to recall products if necessary. Consumers are at the heart of our decision-making' (Cadbury Schweppes, 2006, p. 42).

You will have seen from even this brief review of a small subset of harms that it is difficult, if not impossible, to quantify the scale of corporate harm either within the UK or internationally. Nonetheless, on the basis of the data that is available, two unequivocal conclusions can be reached:

1   People are killed globally each year on a huge scale by corporate activity.

2   Even on the basis of a small number of 'known' corporate frauds and thefts, the extent – in terms of numbers of people affected and total economic losses – of such harms is vast.

It is important to be clear here and to note that the chapter thus far has focused more on harm than on crime. But the data introduced to this point does indicate a clear conclusion: that the numbers of people who have been victims of corporate harms dwarf those forms of theft and violence with which we are more familiar. It is to a consideration of how far corporate theft, fraud and violence can be clearly defined within the category of crime that the chapter now turns.

3 From corporate harm to corporate crime?

If it is difficult to measure the extent to which each of the categories of deaths, injuries, illnesses, exposures and financial losses, outlined in Section 2, is the result of corporate activities, it is similarly difficult to estimate the extent to which each is the consequence of corporate *criminal* activities. In effect, two somewhat separate questions are posed here:

1   How can corporate harm be defined as crime?

2   How can corporate crime be measured?

These will be dealt with in turn in this section.

3.1 Crime without (criminal) law?

The origins of the study of corporate crime are generally traced back to the pioneering work of Edwin Sutherland and his attempt to determine a concept of 'white-collar crime' as 'a crime committed by a person of respectability and high social status in the course of his occupation' (Sutherland, 1983, p. 7). Sutherland recognised that powerful business and professional men routinely committed crimes and that, in so doing, they were aided by the power of their class to influence the implementation and administration of the law (Sutherland, 1983).

Sutherland also sought to produce a more encompassing definition of crime than that delineated by criminal law. Crime requires the 'legal description of an act as socially injurious and legal provision of a penalty for the act' (Sutherland, 1945, p. 132). This definition recognises that many laws that are enforced by administrative bodies regulate actions that both cause harm to specific individuals and undermine social institutions. It also recognises that there is a range of formal legal responses other than criminal prosecution.

Sutherland's definition of 'white-collar crime' has a number of significant theoretical and empirical implications. On the basis of such an inclusive definition, one would find that:

■ the common image of typical crimes and typical criminality, and the general acceptance of these by criminology, is inaccurate – crime occurs throughout society

■ a criminology that explains criminal behaviour solely in terms of the pathology of lower-class individuals or their families is inadequate

■ the scope of criminology needs to be extended to take account of a wider range of conduct and the political processes that define a particular event or behaviour as criminal or not.

The concept of 'white-collar crime' encompasses a heterogeneous range of actions, with different kinds of offenders, offences, victims, consequences, modus operandi, goals, capacities to avoid detection, and likely outcomes of legal processes. Sutherland also applied it to corporate activity (Cressey, 1989).

An immediate, systematic critique of Sutherland's work was set out by the legal scholar Paul Tappan (1947), who argued that the label 'crime' should be applied only to those acts successfully prosecuted as violations of criminal law (see also Chapter 1). Tappan's critique raised at least three substantial points, which remain of significance:

1   Those offences typically committed by business people are inherently different from criminal offences.

2   Many of the actions that Sutherland's definition would criminalise are in fact 'within the framework of the norms of ordinary business practice' (Tappan, 1947, p. 99).

3   To extend the definition of crime beyond the fact of successful processing through the criminal courts is to enter the sphere of moralising or 'propaganda' (Tappan, 1947).

Sutherland retained a definition of 'crime' that made reference to law – in so far as he defined offences in terms of what was punishable, rather than those that had actually been punished, by law; but he also extended the term 'crime' to cover offences beyond those prescribed by criminal law. That is, he recognised that a large number of offences that could be punished in law were not in fact punished – they went undetected, or, if detected, were not acted upon, or, if acted upon, were then subject to forms of enforcement action different from normal criminal processing. Whereas for Tappan, Sutherland obscured the very real differences between 'criminal' and 'harmful' behaviour, for Sutherland these differences were in many respects contingent – and, more specifically, an effect of relations of power. Sutherland was quite clear that the differential interpretation and enforcement of law against 'white-collar crime' is based partly on the fact that legislators, judges and administrators within the criminal justice system are either subject to the material and ideological influence of business people, or share their ideological and/or cultural worldviews (Sutherland, 1945). These aspects of corporate power are considered in greater detail below.

Activity 5.2

Now return to the case you identified in Activity 5.1. Re-examine that case in relation to the following questions:

■ What terms were employed to talk about your case? Was it framed as an 'accident', as 'malpractice', as 'harm' or as a 'crime'?

■ Did the case involve clear breaches of the criminal law? (Had it been successfully prosecuted by the criminal courts?)

■ Or, were other types of law (or regulation) being used to control or respond to this case?

■ If the criminal law was not evoked, what authorities were given responsibility for dealing with the case?

Comment

Distinguishing crime from harm is not an easy task, certainly in the corporate context. The extent to which crime is defined only in terms of a (successfully prosecuted) violation of criminal law radically affects the amount of crime that can be identified. Yet if much corporate conduct is subject to law other than criminal law, and is dealt with by bodies (not the police, of course, who deal with 'real crime') that prefer to use informal methods of responding to offences (without resorting to formal enforcement), this will have significant effects on the volume of recorded corporate offending (and will, arguably, also affect popular and political assessments of its seriousness).

3.2 The 'hidden figure' of corporate crime

The view one takes as to how to define a corporate crime has real consequences. Thus, the majority of corporate harms, even if they are punishable, remain largely unregulated in practice. The term 'regulated' is used to indicate that those crimes are not policed in the usual sense of the word. As you have already discovered in this chapter, corporate crimes are normally dealt with using different types of enforcement authorities ('regulatory agencies') and often with different types of ('administrative' or 'regulatory') law. As a result, they typically remain outside the ambit of mainstream criminal legal procedure. If they do become subject to law enforcement, they tend to be separated from the criminal law (and processed using administrative or informal disposals rather than prosecution). Even if they are subject to the formal processes of criminal law, corporate crimes are rarely viewed as equivalent to 'real' crimes. These issues are now explored further.

In the case of environmental pollution-related deaths, for example, it is highly unlikely that any will result in prosecution. This is partly because cases of deaths 'brought forward' (the term used by the Department of Health to describe premature death) by pollution are not generally subjected to any process of investigation, and partly because of the complexities of investigating and prosecuting such cases. Thus, in the seven years between 2000 and 2007, the Environment Agency in the UK prosecuted only ninety-nine industrial pollution offences (personal communication between David Whyte and Environment Agency, 4 April 2008). Does this mean only ninety-nine crimes were committed during this period?

Unless the victim lives or works close to a major source of pollution, it may be difficult to identify a link between the source of the pollution and the victim. However, even in cases where identifying a source may be possible, prosecution for causing a death is likely to be difficult to pursue unless there has been a breach of regulations. One issue that takes this beyond the scope of criminal process is that much of the air and water pollution that has deadly effect is often legalised – it is permitted by government licence.

Of the 1200–1500 work-related fatal injuries each year in the UK, noted in Section 2.2, typically only 80–90 lead to successful prosecutions per annum. Further, as research by the Centre for Corporate Accountability (2002) shows, only 1 per cent of occupational illness and disease that is reported to the Health and Safety Executive (HSE) is prosecuted (and only a very small proportion of cases are ever reported).

Many, if not most, food poisoning cases are likely to be a direct result of criminal breaches of food hygiene and food safety legislation. Nonetheless, prosecutions of any food regulation breaches, including those that lead to death, are rare. In 2000/2001, around half of all local authorities failed to lay one single prosecution for breaches of food law (Food Standards Agency, 2001). In 2006/2007, the Food Standards Agency recorded a total of 443 establishments being prosecuted, of which 372 were convicted (Food Standards Agency, 2008). Those prosecutions followed over half a million (582,167) 'on-the-spot inspections' of food establishments (production, packaging, distributions, retail, and so on).

In the majority of cases, we therefore have little idea about whether the deaths, injuries and illnesses caused by corporate activity might have involved criminal breaches of the law. This is partly because they are so rarely investigated. It should also be noted that a further key contributory factor is the fact that corporate victimisation generally appears to us, even as direct victims, in a relatively abstract form (Whyte, 2007; Tombs and Williams, 2008). Major harms – such as illness caused by work, pollution or food poisoning – tend not to be thought of as having been produced by corporate activity; rather, they are typically constructed as 'accidents' rather than as harms that are preventable and avoidable.

The way in which the law constructs those harms further discourages us from considering them as 'crimes' when compared, for example, to interpersonal crimes. Thus, we do not think about our employer or our local supermarket as a 'habitual criminal', despite the fact that they may break the law routinely in ways that are harmful to us. And if we are relatively unaware that we are being victimised by an identifiable criminal committing a criminal offence, we are hardly likely to report it as such. This is reflected in the fact that only 2–3 per cent of people suffering food poisoning reported their case to their local council or an environmental health officer. Of this percentage, just 11 per cent were aware of any action being taken against the outlet in question (TNS, 2004).

Activity 5.3

Think about your own possible victimisation by corporate crime. Have you ever:

- experienced symptoms that you thought were some form of food poisoning after eating in a café, restaurant or fast food outlet, or after eating something you bought from a store?

- bought goods that did not do what you had been led to think they would do, or paid for a service that was clearly not 'as advertised'?

- suffered an injury or illness that you thought was linked to working – or know someone who has?

- experienced sore eyes or a burning throat when walking through a busy town or city?

If you can answer 'yes' to any of these questions, what did you think of your experience? Or do about it? Did you consider yourself a victim of bad luck, or as clumsy or accident prone, or as learning a lesson? Or did you think about yourself as a potential victim of a crime? If the latter, a crime by whom or what? And if a crime, to whom should you have turned to report it?

Comment

Most of us can probably answer 'yes' to most of the questions above. But we are unlikely to think of ourselves as victims of corporate crime in these cases. Even if we think of ourselves as victims of corporate *harm*, we are unlikely to think of this harm as criminal. If we believe a crime has been committed, we are often unable to link our victimisation to one specific company; even if we could, most of us would have little idea of how or where to report this, or how to seek redress. And even if we did know how to go about both of these, we might (perhaps rationally) calculate that it would not be worth the effort.

Of course, the mass media may play an important role here – for the media offers, by definition, a series of sites in which relatively hidden social phenomena, including social problems and crimes, may be brought to wider attention. This is also particularly pertinent given the extensive, and some would say increasing, attention across all forms of media given to crime per se – to the extent that some have argued that crime is a salient feature of modern life (Garland, 2001).

It would certainly be inaccurate to claim that there is no coverage of corporate crime through various forms of mass media. It is, however, clear that the media tends to operate as a further, and mutually reinforcing (when set alongside law, politics, victimisation, and so on), social process that maintains an enduring and obdurate distinction between corporate crime and corporate offenders on the one hand, and 'real' crime and 'real' criminals' on the other. Thus, whether we survey

Figure 5.3
'If Corporate Crime was as Visible as Street Crime'

fictional or documentary-style treatments of crime on television news, in newspapers or crime fiction, in bookshops or cinema, we find that although some attention may be paid to corporate crime, representations of crime converge to produce 'blanket' conceptualisations regarding 'law and order' that reinforce dominant stereotypes of crime and the criminal (Chibnall, 1977). Thus, where corporate crime is covered, as it undoubtedly is, its presence is vastly outweighed by treatments of conventional crime and tends to be treated in lesser profile outlets or formats. *The Wall Street Journal* or *Financial Times*, for example, are useful sources of corporate crime stories, but have small, specialist circulations. Moreover, when corporate crime is treated, it tends to be represented more factually and in the rather sanitising language of frauds, food scares, drugs scandals, chemical or oil spills, accidents at work, rail accidents, tragedies at sea, financial irregularities, and so on, rather than in the 'sensational' language of 'real' crimes (theft, murder, violence, poisoning) (Tombs and Whyte, 2001).

Activity 5.4

Select one broadsheet and one tabloid newspaper from the same day. Then:

■ find all stories in each newspaper that are related to (a) conventional crime and (b) corporate crime, and cut these out or copy them

■ do a basic count of the stories devoted to conventional crime, on the one hand, and those devoted to corporate crime, on the other

■ record the pages on (and/or sections in) which they are found

■ make a brief summary of the tone/nature of the corporate crime stories when compared with the conventional crime stories.

Comment

One of the points often made about corporate crime is that coverage of this type of crime is absent from the media. But this is rather simplistic and somewhat inaccurate. What you may have found in your survey of crime reports through two newspapers is that, in relative terms: corporate crime is much less visible; corporate crime is reported in a tone and language that is more plainly descriptive and less sensationalised, with an absence of the labels 'crime' or 'criminal'; corporate crime stories are more likely to be tucked away in specialist financial, business or money pages; and corporate crime stories tend to be less visible in the high sales tabloids – they are more likely to be found in broadsheets and in the specialist financial press.

In short, through a series of processes operating at various different levels and stages, the prospect of corporate crimes being treated as 'crime' is systematically screened out. One net effect of these screening processes is that formal records of corporate crimes vastly understate the actual scale of such offending. The hidden figure of corporate crime is likely to be far greater than that for almost all forms of conventional crimes. To return to Sutherland's argument: while it might be important to retain a reference to law in defining corporate crime, if the definition is limited to successfully prosecuted violations through the criminal law, then it cannot hope to get close to the hidden figure of such crimes.

4   Power, crime and regulation

How crime is defined matters a great deal. The role of relations of power – both in obscuring the extent of corporate crime and in being able to successfully apply the criminal law to damaging and harmful activities – needs to be recognised. Further, we might add that a key characteristic of power is to operate with the least possibility of being called to account – and this is certainly the case if much corporate crime is not recognised, or, if recognised, is not treated through the law, or, if treated through the law, is not treated through criminal law, or, if treated through criminal law, is still represented as somewhat distinct from 'real' crime.

This section explores how power operates on a series of levels (covert and overt; informal and formal) and in a vast array of arenas, in both the formal defining of certain activities as harms or crimes and in the processes of effective criminalisation.

4.1 Corporate power 'in action'

One level on which power operates is through observable conflicts of interest and their resolution in formal decision-making processes. Thus, for example, corporations engage in a lot of work to pre-empt or frame nationally and internationally based regulatory regimes. They do so both to avoid legal restriction on their activity and to insulate themselves from critical legal scrutiny.

One obvious manifestation of corporate power is to be found in corporations' direct lobbying of governments and other policy makers, both nationally and internationally (Barker and Mander, 1999). All things being equal, companies prefer less rather than more regulation (viewed as limiting their activity), and seek to remove existing law or to render such law innocuous through challenging interpretations of it or by undermining the possibility of it being enforced. Direct lobbying is a key corporate activity, one to which the corporate sector as a whole devotes a great deal of time, money and effort. This activity is vastly facilitated by the series of institutional and interpersonal links between corporations, their trade associations and governments. Such lobbying was one of the techniques used over many years by the asbestos industry in the UK.

Consider the case given in Box 5.2.

Box 5.2   Lobbying by the asbestos industry

Asbestos was known as a magic mineral 'inextricably linked' to industrialisation in Europe and America (Tweedale, 2000). The first recorded death from 'asbestosis' was made known to a UK government inquiry into the substance in 1907. Any semblance of 'effective' regulation in the UK was to wait until 1969 (Tweedale, 2000). Yet the asbestos industry used a variety of techniques to deny the problem, including:

■ co-opting the medical community (Tweedale, 2000, pp. 53N68, 282N6, and passim)

■ suppressing problematic scientific knowledge, funding 'independent' science producing results favourable to the industry's own position, and forming apparently 'independent' lobbying groups (Tweedale, 2000, p. 191)

■ quite simple, routine cover-ups; manipulation of data; and lying to workers and regulators

■ using the generalised power of scientific discourses, within which there is a presumption in favour of official, scientific–technical knowledge over (often superior) 'local ·knowledges'.

The result of this successful lobbying has been devastating. Currently about 125 million people in the world are exposed to asbestos at the workplace (WHO, 2006). The ILO estimates that 100,000 people die each year from work-related asbestos exposure (Takala, 2006). In the UK, asbestos-related deaths continue to rise: on a conservative (HSE) estimate, standing at 4000 per annum and rising to peak somewhere between the years 2011 and 2015 (Tweedale, 2000). French scientists attributed 35,000 deaths to asbestos between 1965 and 1995 and expect 'another 60,000 to 100,000 deaths' up to 2030 (Takala, 2006). The ILO estimates that over 21,000 deaths per annum in the USA, more than 10,000 per annum in the Russian Federation and over 110,000 per annum in China are attributable to exposure to asbestos (Takala, 2006).

Figure 5.4
Deadly exposure to
asbestos in the
Bangladeshi ship-
breaking industry

Corporate representatives also work actively within government. In the sphere of regulation this is nowhere better exemplified than in the vast array of parliamentary, governmental or quasi-governmental structures that determine much regulatory policy and set standards – in terms of, for example, emissions of noxious substances, acceptable exposures to workplace chemicals, adequate food labelling, and so on. Even where these bodies represent a range of interest groups, there is a likelihood that they are both structured and function in ways that allow business interests to predominate (Dalton, 2000; and see Tweedale, 2000, on the Advisory Committee on Asbestos).

These activities are formal and, in principle at least, overt. But corporations also express power in a different way: through covert actions, non-decision making and the mobilisation of bias, whereby power works to move certain issues off political agendas (Lukes, 1974). One effect of power may be to pre-empt conflicts of interest even emerging (and thereby requiring resolution) by excluding particular issues from the political process and thereby mobilising bias (Lukes, 1974).

'Covert power' is also of particular importance in understanding the regulatory process. This form of power works through the more general shaping of peoples' perceptions and preferences so that certain processes and outcomes seem natural – as opposed to socially constructed effects of power. Thus, power works most effectively where it does not seem to be present at all! There are three aspects of this view of power (as it applies to corporate regulation) that are worth examining briefly.

At the level of enforcement, the front-line policing of corporate crime is framed by the general economic, political and social contexts within which it takes place (Tombs, 2004). These contexts create a 'common sense' regarding regulation – and through this idea of common sense, a crucial link between the micro-level activities of regulators and the macro-level political climate can be found. For example, when encountering violations of law in a corporate setting, regulators are often faced with the decision about how to proceed. Decisions not to take formal enforcement action, or to institute prosecutions, are influenced, if not determined, by power in a way that seeks consensus rather than conflict. Avoidance of conflict and seeking compliance are typically prioritised (Slapper and Tombs, 1999; Tombs, 2004).

Such 'consensus' approaches are based on a series of assumptions – whether explicit or implicit – about the nature of corporate offending and the levers that are most likely to ensure legal compliance. So, it is assumed that:

- in general, corporations are inclined towards being law-abiding citizens – in other words, the corporate personality is one that can be appealed to on moral grounds

- corporations will respond to a business case for offending since without compliance they are likely to incur losses in insurance premiums, losses in production, loss of market share, and so on

- corporations are more likely to be encouraged into compliance by indirect commercial pressure from stakeholder groups, consumers, the public, NGOs and even their industrial client and peer groups.

Even where violations are formally, and successfully, processed through the criminal courts, both the nature of any sentence itself and the social reaction to this, are further framed by the fact that those in the dock do not fit our stereotypical images of 'criminals'. Corporate criminals do not appear to threaten our interests in the same way that individual thieves and murderers do. The existing order of regulatory politics helps perpetuate the idea that corporations and their officers are not 'real' criminals and that, in any case, their crimes are not 'real' crimes.

4.2 Regulation as conflict 'management'

A primary view of regulation is that it is a process that responds to, manages and seeks to dissipate social conflicts. This is important, not simply because it helps us to understand where regulation comes from, and why – but it also provides a clue as to the limits of what regulation might achieve. From this view, regulatory agencies tend to emerge after times of crisis and after sustained periods during which conflicts over corporate activity are highly visible (as in the governmental demand for greater regulation following the collapse of major financial institutions in 2008). They are formed by governments in order to absorb and dissipate struggles between conflicting social groups. They seek to achieve those aims by claiming to represent the interests of pro-regulatory groups at the same time as protecting the general interests of society. This does not mean that regulatory agencies are neutral or balanced in the way that they deal with corporate crime; rather, they are 'unequal structures of representation' (Mahon, 1979, p. 154). Regulatory bodies tend to subordinate the interests of the least powerful to the interests of business, but since their purpose is a stabilising one for capitalist social orders, they may subordinate the immediate interests of particular businesses to the long-term interests of capital as a whole. In turn, the likelihood that governments may regulate in order to placate or dissipate movements of opposition makes regulatory agencies vulnerable to pressure (Shapiro, 1984; Snider, 1991). From this perspective, the shape of regulatory regimes and strategies of enforcement are dependent on a range of external factors that shape the confidence and the capacity of subdominant groups to fight back (Tombs, 1996).

If regulation is a way of managing conflict within an existing social order, the precise form it takes is an effect of the power of the groups involved in the struggle for and against that regulation. And this view also helps us to understand why certain forms of harms and crimes are subject to different levels of regulation – and how this changes over time. Regulation may seem to emerge and then decline in 'waves' – while impacting differentially on different spheres of corporate activity. Barry Goetz (1997), for example, notes a key distinction between 'economic' regulation and 'social' regulation:

> ... stock fraud and bank fraud may be given a good deal of attention by the legal system because these crimes victimize other capitalists and, perhaps more important, threaten the integrity of financial markets if they are not controlled. In contrast, a crackdown on housing codes or other kinds of health and safety violations are less likely to be pursued vigorously by the legal system, least over the long term, not only because such interventions are perceived as contradictory to economic growth but also because social regulations are perceived as having little use in stabilizing and assuring the workings of commerce.
>
> (Goetz, 1997, p. 560)

On this basis, regulation produces conditions within which capitalist production can proceed while managing or pre-empting the public articulation of values, claims and policy positions that are directly antagonistic to such production and its growth. Such a view can only be reached by looking beyond the relationship that exists between regulators and the regulated, and looking at what the regulatory relationship means for social relations of power more generally.

Corporate power operates at different levels and in different ways. This section has explored how corporations can influence definitions of crime, processes of criminalisation and the nature of regulation through:

■ their direct and often highly organised interventions in the policy-making process

■ various forms of more covert forms of intervention

■ their ability to shape agendas

■ their influence in terms of 'non-decision making'

■ their ability to help to create and maintain understandings about what is both desirable and feasible in terms of their regulation.

In short, the level of regulation in any given society at any one time in relation to any specific issue can be understood in terms of an effect of the distribution of power.

5 The space between and within the laws

In this section the emergence and social significance of corporate crime and its regulation are considered further in the context of the following propositions about the global economy:

■ The majority of the biggest transnational corporations have production facilities in the 'global South', a feature of the international economy that places downward pressure on safety and environmental standards.

■ The growth of exports of consumer goods to the global South has at the same time generated consumer safety problems.

■ Inequalities of power in labour and consumer markets provide distinct problems for the development of regulation in the global South.

■ In the global South, laws in relation to workplace, environmental and consumer harms are less developed than those found in developed countries.

■ International law has so far failed to develop universal legal standards for corporations.

5.1 The space between the laws

Raymond Michalowski and Ronald Kramer (1987) have noted that the vast expansion of transnational corporations in relatively poor countries has exposed the citizens of those countries to a growing number of corporate harms. For example, when the Malaysian Government indicated that it might allow electronics workers to set up a trade union, and several US electronics firms threatened to relocate, the government was forced to reverse its position. It is through orchestrating a 'space between the laws' that the export of harms is encouraged. For Michalowski and Kramer, corporations can exert both direct and indirect influences. Direct influences refer to the straightforward use by corporations of their economic power to influence government decisions. Indirect influences refer more to the ways in which what is considered to be politically feasible can be structured. Making an economy 'attractive' to global investment often means 'playing easy to get' and ensuring that social and environmental regulations are lax and corporate taxes are low, and so on.

One attempt to close such 'space between the laws' has been the establishment of the *Norms on the Responsibilities of Transnational Corporations and Other Business Enterprises with Regard to Human Rights*, published by the UN Commission on Human Rights. The Norms, based on the Universal Declaration of Human Rights, were adopted by the UN in 2003 and call for human rights obligations to apply to corporations. The Norms include:

- *The right to equal opportunity and non-discriminatory treatment* (the onus here is on corporations to ensure equality rights are derived from relevant international instruments and national legislation).

- *The right to security of persons* (corporations should not benefit from war crimes, crimes against humanity, genocide and torture, and security provision must observe international human rights norms).

- *Basic rights of workers* (corporations shall not use forced or compulsory labour, shall abide by international law on child labour and shall provide a safe and healthy working environment).

- *The right to an adequate standard of living* (wages must be high enough to ensure adequate living conditions for workers and their families).

- *The right to freedom of association* (corporations must ensure that workers are free to join and form their own trade unions and have the right to collective bargaining).

■ *The right to consumer protection* (corporations shall not produce, distribute, market, or advertise harmful or potentially harmful products for use by consumers).

■ *Obligations with regard to environmental protection* (corporations should not only observe national laws and regulations relating to the preservation of the environment, but also pursue practices and policies in accordance with relevant international agreements, principles, objectives, responsibilities and standards).

(Adapted from UNCHR, 2003)

As an initial step towards implementation, the UN calls on corporations to comply voluntarily with the principles outlined in the Norms. As a further step, the UN expects the Norms to be given legal force by common-law decisions made in national courts and by the development of international legal instruments. Although no formal enforcement or prosecution mechanism exists for this purpose, the UN appeals to nation states to establish the necessary legal and administrative networks. Moreover, the UN Commission on Human Rights notes that corporations 'shall be subject to periodic monitoring and verification by United Nations, other international and national mechanisms already in existence or yet to be created, regarding application of the Norms' (UNCHR, 2003, para. 16).

Although we are a long way from an international jurisprudence that allows corporations to be put on trial for human rights violations, the UN Norms do raise key questions about the prospect for developing the Inter-American Court of Human Rights or the European Court of Human Rights in this direction.

5.2 Export processing zones

Export processing zones (EPZs) are the paradigm of the space between the laws, since they are created by governments as lawless or liminal zones with the deliberate intent of attracting corporations. The International Labour Organization defines EPZs as 'industrial zones with special incentives set up to attract foreign investors, in which imported materials undergo some degree of processing before being re-exported' (International Labour Office, 2003, p. 1). Those special incentives may include suspension of normal rates of export and import duties, tax exemption and exemption from labour rights and health and safety regulations.

EPZs are therefore set up with the express aim of creating a haven from law. The first was established around Shannon airport in Ireland in 1954. During the 1960s and 1970s a series of *maquilas*, or factories/assembly plants run by foreign companies for tax exemption purposes, were established along the Mexican–US border to produce cheap clothes and toys for export to the American market. By 1987, there were around 260 EPZs in 67 countries, and it is now estimated that there are 5000 such zones employing a total of 43 million workers; most of those zones are located in China (Nielsen, 2007).

The USA operates a huge EPZ in Saipan, a US Island in the South Pacific where immigration controls and controls on labour rights and the minimum wage are structured differently from the way in which they are structured in the USA. In this sense, Saipan can be understood as the 'Guantánamo' of the sweatshop world: a US territory where US laws do not apply. Saipan exists in a 'space between the laws'. For the purpose of regulation it is outside the USA, but for marketing purposes it is inside the USA. So, for example, US clothing firms use their location in Saipan to label their clothes 'Made in the USA'. Many sweatshop workers, most of them women, pay thousands of dollars in recruitment fees for jobs in Saipan and then have to work until they have paid off the debt. For some this takes years (Bas et al., 2004).

In 1999, a group of NGOs acting on behalf of Saipan garment workers brought a civil lawsuit (Bas et al., 2004), in relation to violations of US labour laws and international human rights standards, against twenty-seven US retailers and twenty-three Saipan garment factories. It alleged that workers lived and worked in intolerable conditions, including working shifts of up to twelve hours a day, seven days a week. Further allegations included under-payment of workers, failure to pay for overtime, and living conditions that were claimed to be cramped and unsanitary, with inadequate food and contaminated water supplies. The companies cited in the case included many household names: Levi Strauss, Abercrombie & Fitch, Calvin Klein, Donna Karan, Gap, Banana Republic, Gymboree, Liz Claiborne, Phillips-Van Heusen, Polo Ralph Lauren, Tommy Hilfiger. All of the companies settled out of court, with the exception of Levi Strauss, which won its case in 2007.

EPZs reflect a wider phenomenon in global production, known sometimes as the 'race to the bottom', whereby regulatory standards are lowered precisely because developing countries are under pressure (sometimes as a proviso in International Monetary Fund or World Bank loan agreements) to provide favourable conditions for business. The 'space between the laws' therefore does not emerge because of 'under-development' or 'backwardness' on the part of poor countries. Nor does it emerge as an inevitable consequence of globalisation

(Tombs and Whyte, 2003). A key assumption in dominant ideas around globalisation is that governments have less political control over economies. Economic management is increasingly relegated to the task of overseeing the operation of 'free' markets and the promotion of corporate activity – most significantly, multi- or transnational corporate activity – within those markets. It is a process that, it is claimed, makes the state weak in the context of the global marketplace (e.g. Hertz, 2001). Alongside this 'pragmatic' recognition of the declining power of the state comes a sustained attack on state, public and, in particular, regulatory activity. This understanding of the process of globalisation provides support for the idea that in a globally competitive market, social and environmental regulation will harm the 'competitiveness' of a nation's economy. Notions of 'globalisation' are commonly invoked by governments as they seek to attract or retain private capital through various forms of de- and reregulation or by imposing cutbacks in social expenditure. This view of globalisation as all pervasive is said to reproduce a 'political construction of helplessness' (Weiss, 1997, p. 15). As a result, state interventions to protect consumers and workers are typically constructed as counterproductive to prosperity in that they repel prospective investors or force existing businesses to relocate elsewhere (Tombs and Whyte, 1998). Such phraseology as 'burdens on business' and 'red tape', then, takes on a heightened meaning and significance in debates on globalisation.

Figure 5.5
Workers resist the establishment of an EPZ in Bengal

Activity 5.5

List the benefits to workers, consumers, other businesses and local and national political rulers of corporate activity in a particular region or country (e.g. setting up a sports shoe or car production facility, a call centre or research facility, or a company that provides water or telecommunications).

Then list the problems that this corporate activity might cause for local communities, workers and consumers. Might those problems need regulation? What types of response from the company and the government are arguments for regulation likely to provoke? How might those responses differ under different political or economic conditions? (For example, are such arguments likely to depend on the stability of the political or economic environment?)

Comment

Listing the benefits of corporate activity is fairly straightforward – especially in a world in which the state itself (through the public sector) provides fewer and fewer goods and services. Any argument for regulation always involves arguing against maximising what seem to be well-known goods – often in the name of some rather intangible aims such as 'safety' or 'the environment'. This illustrates one of the basic ways in which spaces between and within laws are created, maintained and justified.

There is convincing evidence, however, to show that the effects of 'globalisation' have been grossly overstated, along with a growing recognition that nation states have not only been the 'principal agents of globalization', but remain 'the guarantors of the political and material conditions necessary for global capital accumulation' (Barrow, 2005, p. 125). Thus, neither is the state particularly constrained by 'globalisation' (Somerville, 2004; Weiss, 2005), nor is the logic of deregulation a necessity (Mosley, 2005). In this sense, government decisions to regulate in a particular way cannot be explained simply by uncontrollable market forces or by an abstract notion of 'globalisation'. As was witnessed in the global financial crisis of 2008, governments can insist on stronger regulation of some aspects of corporate power (such as the banking system) in return for their (i.e. taxpayer) monetary support. In other words, it is governments that still decide when, how and to what extent corporations should be regulated (Tombs and Whyte, 2003).

A focus on globalisation should also not obscure what is being regulated at the level of the nation state. Extending the argument made by Michalowski and Kramer (1987), it is also possible to identify an endemic space within the laws in relation to the political economies of developed states. For all of the reasons outlined in our discussion of power and criminalisation above, even when cases are discovered and investigated, regulatory agencies tend to prosecute only as a last resort (Hawkins, 2002), not least because the dominant regulatory approach is to seek compliance rather than strict enforcement of the criminal law (Davis, 2004).

5.3 Corporate social responsibility: plugging the space between the laws?

In the face of states' apparent inability or unwillingness to regulate corporate activity, the idea of corporate social responsibility (CSR) has emerged. This is based essentially on the claim that corporations will recognise either their own self-interest in meeting and, indeed, going beyond legal minima in their operations, or that, as dominant social actors, they have social obligations that they should meet in the absence of external law and enforcement.

The idea of CSR dates back to the 1970s, but re-emerged in the twenty-first century as crucial, not so much for upholding social responsibility, but for providing arguments for the continuance of market-based forms of self-regulation. This much is made clear in two relatively recent studies of the discourse and practice of CSR. *Behind the Mask* (2004), produced by UK charity, Christian Aid, and *What's Wrong With Corporate Responsibility?*, produced by independent research organisation, Corporate Watch (Fauset, 2006), both argue that CSR strategies are not only aimed at offsetting criticism for environmental damage and working conditions, but are used as a means of challenging arguments for legal regulation. Indeed, CSR is used strategically to support 'self-regulation' and to claim that corporations can comply with the law with little or no external oversight. Corporations typically argue that legal regulation is counterproductive because it is likely to encourage companies merely to abide by minimum standards, and that it stifles innovative good practice. This rather odd logic is always presented without any empirical evidence (in fact, it flies in the face of evidence regarding the effects of unregulated corporate activity).

Both of these reports concluded that corporate accountability is the necessary counterpoint to CSR. *Behind the Mask* argues that 'corporate ethical commitments have to be given "teeth" by underpinning them with binding regulation. We are advocating a move beyond corporate social responsibility to corporate social accountability – meaning that companies in future will have a legal obligation to uphold international standards' (Christian Aid, 2004, p. 3). The two reports envisage different forms of accountability, but converge on the point that changes in the law and new enforcement mechanisms are necessary because corporations, as they are currently constructed, cannot be expected to self-regulate or to behave responsibly in any autonomous fashion.

If the search for means to fill spaces – both 'between' and 'within' the laws – has led to the re-emergence of claims for corporate social responsibility, then whether corporations could or would exercise such social responsibility without external pressure remains, to say the least, a contested issue. Thus, what Laureen Snider (1991) has termed 'pro-regulatory forces' are crucial in the struggle for more effective regulation – whether this is couched in the language of greater corporate social responsibility or accountability or simple compliance with existing law. However, by definition, pro-regulatory forces – whether they be trade unions, environmental organisations, victims' movements or, at the most general level, social justice, anti-globalisation or anti-capitalist campaigns – are far more likely to reside on the periphery or well beyond formal economic and political processes.

6   Conclusion

Corporations, as powerful economic, political and social actors, have enormous potential for producing harms. This chapter began by introducing a range of such harms, and demonstrated that their scale and impact dwarfs those usually designated as 'crime' and which are the focus of criminal justice systems.

But a somewhat separate question remained: to what extent can these harms be considered as 'crime' – and why, if at all, does this distinction matter? Distinguishing corporate crime from corporate harm is a complex task. In addition, the prospect of corporate harms being treated as crimes is systematically minimised through mutually reinforcing legal, political and social filters (or screening processes). One net effect of these filters is that formal records of corporate crimes vastly understate the actual scale of such offending. The problem of corporate crime typically appears, albeit as a tautology, as a relatively insignificant crime problem.

It was then argued that what lies at the core of these processes of obscuring corporate crime is the nature and exercise of power. Indeed, a key defining characteristic of power is the ability to operate with the least possibility of being called to account. The case was made that most corporate harm is not even recognised as harm. If it is recognised it is generally not treated through the law; if treated through the law, it is not treated through criminal law; and if treated through criminal law it remains represented as somewhat distinct from 'real' crime. Herein lies the argument that if 'crime' can never be a category that entirely captures corporate harm, or indeed even the most harmful subset of corporate activities, the criminalisation of harm remains one crucial means of developing accountability and concrete forms of responsibility within corporations.

Thus, we sought to identify some of the levels and processes through which corporate power operates. Corporations can influence definitions of crime, processes of criminalisation and the nature of regulation through: direct interventions in the policy-making process; more covert forms of intervention; their ability to shape agendas; and, crucially, their more general ability to help to create and maintain understandings about what is both desirable and feasible in terms of their regulation. Further, we indicated that the level of regulation in any given society at any time in relation to any specific issue can be understood in terms of an effect of the distribution of power.

The issue of regulation also needs increasingly to be understood in the context of an international economy, since placing national regulatory systems within this international context helps to make sense of the existence, maintenance and durability of what we referred to as 'spaces between and within the laws' – spaces that corporations, as profit-maximising entities, necessarily exploit.

More generally, this chapter has sought to provide a critique of taken-for-granted assumptions about crime, criminalisation and criminal justice through a focus on various dimensions of corporate 'crime'. Such assumptions can only be understood through the lens of power. A key effect of corporate power is to insulate corporate activities and their effects from public, political and academic scrutiny. This in turn implies that challenges to corporate power – efforts to render corporations more accountable – must in part entail exposing the effect of power in the form of corporate fraud, theft and violence.

References

Barker, D. and Mander, J. (1999) *Invisible Government*, San Francisco, CA, International Forum on Globalization.

Barrow, C. (2005) 'The return of the state: globalization, state theory, and the new imperialism', *New Political Science*, vol. 27, no. 2, pp. 113–45.

Bas, N., Benjamin, M. and Chang, J. (2004) *Saipan Sweatshop Lawsuit Ends with Important Gains for Workers and Lessons for Activists*, London, Clean Clothes Campaign [online], www.cleanclothes.org/legal/04-01-08.htm (Accessed 30 July 2008).

BBC (2007) *Cadbury Fined £1m over Salmonella*, BBC News, 16 July [online], http://news.bbc.co.uk/1/hi/england/6900467.stm (Accessed 30 July 2008).

Cadbury Schweppes (2006) *Corporate and Social Responsibility Report 2006*, London, Cadbury Schweppes; also available online at http://csr2006.cadburyschweppes.com/cspdf/Cadbury_CSR_Report.pdf (Accessed 5 February 2009).

Cadbury Schweppes (2008) *Annual Report and Accounts 2007*, London, Cadbury Schweppes; also available online at www.cadburyschweppes.com/NR/rdonlyres/0E5F368D-6274-42A4-966A-BACA11EA2C8A/0/2007AnnualReport.pdf (Accessed 30 July 2008).

Centre for Corporate Accountability (2002) *Safety Last: The Under-enforcement of Health and Safety Law*, London, Centre for Corporate Accountability and Unison.

Chibnall, S. (1977) *Law-and-Order News: An Analysis of Crime Reporting in the British Press*, London, Tavistock.

Christian Aid (2004) *Behind the Mask: The Real Face of Corporate Social Responsibility*, London, Christian Aid.

Cohen, A., Ross, A., Ostro, B., Pandey, K., Krzyzanowski, M., Künzli, N., Gutschmidt, K., Pope, A., Romieu, I., Samet, J. and Smith, K. (2005) 'The global burden of disease due to outdoor air pollution', *Journal of Toxicology and Environmental Health*, vol. 68, nos 13–14, pp. 9–23.

Consumers' Association (undated) *Which? Consumer Factsheet: Endowment Action*, London, Consumers' Association.

Cressey, D. (1989) 'The poverty of theory in corporate crime research' in Adler, F. and Laufer, W.S. (eds) *Advances in Criminological Theory*, New Brunswick, NJ, Translation.

Croall, H. (2001) *Understanding White Collar Crime*, Buckingham, Open University Press.

Dalton, A. (2000) *Consensus Kills. Health and Safety Tripartism: Hazard to Workers' Health*, London, AJP Dalton.

Davis, C. (2004) *Making Companies Safe: What Works?*, London, Centre for Corporate Accountability.

Department of Health Committee on the Medical Effects of Air Pollutants (2001) *Statement and Report on Long-term Effects of Particles on Mortality*, London, The Stationery Office; also available online at www.advisorybodies.doh.gov.uk/comeap/statementsreports/longtermeffects.pdf (Accessed 30 July 2008).

Elliott, V. (2007) 'Cadbury fined £1m for selling contaminated chocolate bars', *The Times*, 17 July [online], www.timesonline.co.uk/tol/money/consumer_affairs/article2087475.ece (Accessed 16 January 2009).

European Competition Commission (2008) 'Antitrust: Commission fines car glass producers over €1.3 billion for market sharing cartel', *IP/08/1685* Brussels, 12 November 2008, [online] http://europa.eu/rapid/pressReleasesAction.do?reference=IP/08/1685&format= HTML&aged=0&language=EN&guiLanguage=en, (Accessed 1 March 2009).

Fauset, C. (2006) *What's Wrong with Corporate Responsibility?*, Oxford, Corporate Watch.

Financial Services Authority (1999) *FSA Launches Publicity Campaign to Ask Consumers, 'Were You Mis-sold?'*, Press Release, 5 January, London, Financial Services Authority.

Food Standards Agency (2001) *Draft Report on Local Authority Food Enforcement in the UK*, London, Food Standards Agency.

Food Standards Agency (2006) *Cadbury Schweppes plc Recalls a Range of its Own Brand Chocolate Products due to Possible Contamination with Salmonella*, 23 June, Food Alert: for Action, Ref: 36/2006 (38/2006 Scotland) [online], www.food.gov.uk/enforcement/alerts/2006/jun/cadburychoc (Accessed 30 July 2008).

Food Standards Agency (2008) *INFO 08/03/02 – Local Authority Monitoring Data on Food Law Enforcement: April 2006 to March 2007*, Paper for the FSA Board [online], www.food.gov.uk/multimedia/pdfs/board/info080302.pdf (Accessed 30 July 2008).

Fooks, G. (2003) 'In the Valley of the Blind the One Eyed Man is King: corporate crime and the myopia of financial regulation' in Tombs, S. and Whyte, D. (eds) *Unmasking the Crimes of the Powerful: Scrutinising States and Corporations*, New York, Peter Lang.

Garland, D. (2001) *The Culture of Control. Crime and social order in contemporary society*, Oxford: Oxford University Press.

Glasbeek, H. (2002) *Wealth By Stealth: Corporate Crime, Corporate Law and the Perversion of Democracy*, Toronto, Between the Lines.

Global Atmospheric Pollution Forum (undated) *Why Be Concerned?* [online], www.gapforum.org (Accessed 30 July 2008).

Goetz, B. (1997) 'Organization as class bias in local law enforcement: arson-for-profit as a "nonissue"', *Law and Society Review*, vol. 31, no. 3, pp. 557–85.

Hawkins, K. (2002) *Law as a Last Resort: Prosecution Decision Making in a Regulatory Authority*, Oxford, Oxford University Press.

Helms, M., Vastrup, P., Gerner-Smidt, P. and Molbak, K. (2003) 'Short and long term mortality associated with foodborne bacterial gastrointestinal infections: registry based study', *British Medical Journal*, no. 326, pp. 357–60.

Hertz, N. (2001) *The Silent Takeover: Global Capitalism and the Death of Democracy*, London, Arrow Books.

International Labour Office (2003) Governing Body Committee on Employment and Social Policy, Geneva, March, GB.286/ESP/3 286th Session, Geneva, International Labour Office.

International Labour Organization (2005) *World Day for Safety and Health at Work 2005: A Background Paper*, Geneva, International Labour Organization.

Lukes, S. (1974) *Power: A Radical View*, London, Macmillan.

Mahon, R. (1979) 'Regulatory agencies: captive agents or hegemonic apparatuses?', *Studies in Political Economy*, vol. 1, no. 1, pp. 154–68.

Michalowski, R. and Kramer, R. (1987) 'The space between laws: the problem of corporate crime in a transnational context', *Social Problems*, vol. 34, no. 1, pp. 34–53.

Mosley, L. (2005) 'Globalisation and the state: still room to move?', *New Political Economy*, vol. 10, no. 3, pp. 356–62.

Nielsen, J. (2007) *Export Processing Zones or Free Zones – The Experience Seen from a Trade Union Point of View* [online], www.labour-inspection.org/EPZ.experiences.tradeunionpoint.htm (Accessed 16 January 2009).

Office of Fair Trading (2007) 'OFT welcomes early resolution agreements and agrees over £116m penalties'. 170/07, 7 December 2007, [online], www.oft.gov.uk/news/press/2007/170-07, (Accessed 1 March 2009).

O'Neill, R., Pickvance, S. and Watterson, A. (2007) 'Burying the evidence: how Great Britain is prolonging the occupational cancer epidemic', *International Journal of Occupational and Environmental Health*, vol. 13, no. 4, pp. 428–36.

Passas, N. and Goodwin, N. (eds) (2007) *It's Legal But It Ain't Right: Harmful Social Consequences of Legal Industries*, Ann Arbor, MI, University of Michigan Press.

Pearce, F. (2001) 'Crime and capitalist business organisations' in Shover, N. and Wright, J. (eds) *Crimes of Privilege*, Oxford, Oxford University Press.

Rebovich, D. and Kane, J. (2002) 'An eye for an eye in the electronic age: gauging public attitude toward white collar crime and punishment', *Journal of Economic Crime Management*, vol. 1, no. 2. [online], www.utica.edu/academic/institutes/ecii/publications/articles/BA296422-B592-E761-E0A21050AFFB2EAB.pdf, (Accessed 1 March 2009).

Shapiro, S. (1984) *Wayward Capitalists*, New Haven, CT, Yale University Press.

Slapper, G. and Tombs, S. (1999) *Corporate Crime*, Harlow, Longman.

Smithers, R. (2007) 'Cadbury facing prosecution under health laws following contamination of chocolate', *The Guardian*, 13 February [online], www.guardian.co.uk/society/2007/feb/13/health.food (Accessed 2 February 2009).

Snider, L. (1991) 'The regulatory dance: understanding reform processes in corporate crime', *International Journal of the Sociology of Law*, vol. 19, pp. 209–36.

Somerville, P. (2004) 'State rescaling and democratic transformation', *Space and Polity*, vol. 8, no. 2, pp. 137–56.

Sutherland, E. (1945) 'Is "White-Collar Crime" Crime?', *American Sociological Review*, no. 10, pp. 132–39.

Sutherland, E. (1983) *White Collar Crime: The Uncut Version*, New Haven, CT, Yale University Press.

Takala, J. (2006) *Asbestos: The Iron Grip of Latency*, Geneva, International Labour Organization; also available online at www.ilo.org/global/About_the_ILO/Media_and_public_information/Press_releases/lang–en/WCMS_076282/index.htm (Accessed 30 July 2008).

Tappan, P.R. (1947) 'Who is the criminal?', *American Sociological Review*, vol. 12, no. 1, pp. 96–102.

TNS (2004) *Consumer Attitudes to Food Standards Wave 4*, UK Report, prepared for Food Standards Agency and COI Communications, London, TNS; also available online at www.foodstandards.gov.uk/multimedia/pdfs/cas2003.pdf (Accessed 30 July 2008).

Tombs, S. (1996) 'Injury, death and the deregulation fetish: the politics of occupational safety regulation in UK manufacturing industries', *International Journal of Health Services*, vol. 26, no. 2, pp. 309–26.

Tombs, S. (2004) 'Review: Keith Hawkins, law as last resort', *The Modern Law Review*, vol. 67, no. 4, pp. 704–9.

Tombs, S. and Whyte, D. (1998) 'Capital fights back: from Cullen to crime in the offshore oil industry', *Studies in Political Economy*, no. 57 (September), pp. 73–101.

Tombs, S. and Whyte, D. (2001) 'Media reporting of crime: defining corporate crime out of existence?', *Criminal Justice Matters*, no. 43 (Spring), pp. 22–3.

Tombs, S. and Whyte, D. (2003) 'Corporations beyond the law? Regulation, risk and corporate crime in a globalised era', *Risk Management*, vol. 5, no. 2, pp. 9–16.

Tombs, S. and Whyte, D. (2007) *Safety Crimes*, Cullompton, Willan.

Tombs, S. and Whyte, D. (2008) *A Crisis of Enforcement: The Decriminalisation of Death and Injury at Work*, London, Harm and Society Foundation.

Tombs, S. and Whyte, D. (2009) 'The State and corporate crime' in Coleman, R., Sim, J., Tombs, S. and Whyte. D. (eds) *State, Power, Crime*, London, Sage.

Tombs, S. and Williams, B. (2008) 'Corporate crime and its victims' in Stout, B., Yates, J. and Williams, B. (eds) *Applied Criminology*, London, Sage.

Tweedale, G. (2000) *Magic Mineral to Killer Dust: Turner and Newall and the Asbestos Hazard*, Oxford, Oxford University Press.

UK Parliament (2003) *Postnote: Food Poisoning*, London, Parliamentary Office of Science and Technology.

UN Commission on Human Rights (UNCHR) (2003) *Norms on the Responsibilities of Transnational Corporations and Other Business Enterprises with Regard to Human Rights*, Geneva, UN Commission on Human Rights.

Vidal, J. (2005) 'Climate change and pollution are killing millions, says study', *The Guardian*, 6 October [online], www.guardian.co.uk/environment/2005/oct/06/health.climatechange (Accessed 6 March 2009).

Walsh, F. (2007) 'OFT hands out £116m in fines for milk price fixing', *The Guardian*, 7 December, [online], www.guardian.co.uk/business/2007/dec/07/supermarkets (Accessed 1 March 2009).

Weiss, L. (1997) 'Globalization and the myth of the powerless state', *New Left Review*, no. 225 (September/October), pp. 3–27.

Weiss, L. (2005) 'The state-augmenting effects of globalisation', *New Political Economy*, vol. 10, no. 3, pp. 345–53.

Whyte, D. (2004a) 'Regulation and corporate crime' in Muncie, J. and Wilson, D. (eds) *Student Handbook of Criminal Justice and Criminology*, London, Cavendish.

Whyte, D. (2004b) 'All that glitters isn't gold: environmental crimes and the production of local criminological knowledge', *Crime Prevention and Community Safety*, vol. 6, no. 1, pp. 53–64.

Whyte, D. (2007) 'Victims of corporate crime' in Walklate, S. (ed.) *A Handbook of Victimology*, Cullompton, Willan.

Woolfson, C. (2005) 'Un-social Europe', *Transitions Online*, 10 June [online], www.tol.cz/look/TOL/article.tpl?IdLanguage=1&IdPublication=4&NrIssue=119&NrSection=4&NrArticle=14149&tpid=6 (Accessed 30 July 2008).

World Health Organization (WHO) (2006) *Elimination of Asbestos-Related Diseases*, Geneva, World Health Organization; also available online at www.who.int/occupational_health/publications/asbestosrelateddiseases.pdf (Accessed 30 July 2008).

Chapter 6
Eco crime

Reece Walters

Contents

1 Introduction

This book has been examining the ways in which crime interacts with notions of harm, violence and power at both the local and the global level. Previous chapters have explored how crime is constructed, manifested and regulated through and within areas such as cyberspace, the city, the human body and the corporation. This chapter focuses attention on the environment.

Why is this topic important? Issues pertaining to the protection of the planet continue to capture centre stage of international policy. There is mounting evidence regarding the perils facing Earth's sustainable development and the causes and consequences of environment-threatening events. As such, the United Nations Intergovernmental Panel on Climate Change (IPCC) has referred to global warming as a 'weapon of mass destruction' (IPCC, 2007). The need to protect natural resources and curtail environmental destruction has been reflected in an expanding amount of environmental law. Collectively, there are more treaties, protocols, directives and statutes that address environmental issues than any other area of law, including trade, health, security, employment and education (Bodansky et al., 2007).

Yet, it is important to note that international agreements that seek to protect the natural environment and all of its resources require nation states to sign up and legally bind themselves to the terms and conditions of those agreements, through, for example, reforming domestic policy to meet agreed-upon objectives. But not all nation states sign agreements, and those that do often fail to implement change. Many states and corporations profit from wilful actions of environmental degradation. Therefore, we must ask, what is the best way of dealing with such lawbreakers? Can law be expected to prevent illegal acts resulting in environmental damage? Should acts of environmental harm be criminalised?

For many, the destruction of natural habitats and the pollution of oceans, waterways and the atmosphere is a global catastrophe; for others (including some states and corporations), it is a necessary by-product of commercial profit and capital accumulation (see Chapter 5). The challenge for environmental protection and regulation is that it often competes with or is superseded by trade law – whereby economic prosperity and quality of human life are viewed as paramount political and social objectives.

This chapter aims to:

- explore concepts of eco crime and its relationship to transnational harm

- examine the emerging discourse of green criminology

- critique the ways in which states and corporations exploit and damage the environment

- analyse the role of law and social movements in preventing eco crimes and protecting the environment

- investigate notions of environmental, ecological and species justice.

In particular, Section 2 exposes the various dimensions of eco crime and Section 3 explores how criminology has, in recent years, begun to respond to the global challenges presented by illegal and harmful acts that damage the environment. Sections 4 and 5 examine the strengths and limitations of existing legal and social mechanisms that have attempted to prevent and regulate eco crime. The chapter concludes by charting possible orientations for the future of environmental justice and green criminology.

Activity 6.1

Examine the photographs in Figure 6.1. The actions the pictures illustrate have been referred to as eco crimes by various commentators. Rank the actions in order from 1 to 7 according to what you consider to be their seriousness as examples of eco crime (with 1 being the most serious, 7 the least) and note down why you have ranked them in this way. To assist your ranking, the photographs convey a range of activities, from air pollution, illegal logging, chemical waste and acts of vandalism, to illegal killing of endangered wildlife and having too many children (which has been identified as a threat to the planet: that is, 'population explosion'). The final picture (labelled (g)) provides an image of Greenpeace campaigners protesting against the development of a third runway at Heathrow Airport, UK, in 2008. Governments and policing agencies, such as the Federal Bureau of Investigation (FBI) in the USA, refer to activities that destroy, deface and damage property while disrupting services and production in the name of protest, as 'eco terrorism'.

Figure 6.1

Examples of eco crime. The images identify various acts that have been defined by different commentators as 'eco crimes'

Comment

There is no right or wrong ranking for the images in Figure 6.1. It is a difficult exercise that requires you to think through various issues involving, for example, harm, cost and injury. It is a ranking that will differ from one person to the next. But it is important for you to reflect on why you consider some acts to be more serious than others. Such reasonings are in turn important for the way we define and respond to eco crime.

Some of the images identify wilful corporate acts of environmental pollution and destruction: sometimes within the law, but often not. There are environmental costs to ensuring that people have the resources and technologies to enhance their lives. For example, transporting oil for use in commercial and personal machinery and vehicles can result in devastating ocean spills; factories that supply products for our furnishing and building needs may produce alarmingly dangerous levels of pollutant air emissions; timber from rainforests and native woodlands for housing and construction results in the destruction of habitats and essential biodiversity; and factories that produce clothing or food often burn off or release toxic chemicals into the atmosphere and our waterways, which not only compromise soil and water quality while destroying numerous species of flora and fauna, but also adversely affect human health. Can human beings maintain high standards of living without compromising the integrity of the environment? Are the two ever compatible? Sometimes state actions purportedly designed to bring about peace and security also result in environmental damage. For example, the US-led invasions of Iraq and Afghanistan have left several Iraqi and Afghani cities exposed to radiation from depleted uranium weaponry at up to 2000 times the normal level (Patton, 2003; Azami, 2008). Thus, adverse environmental consequences can result from trade and progress and from war and peace keeping, as well as from illegal acts of environmental crime. All of these may be termed 'eco crimes'. However, as we shall discover, this term is a slippery one, with differing meanings and interpretations across different cultures and societies.

Eco crime comprises a range of different acts, not all of which are illegal in all jurisdictions. Indeed, one of the major problems facing the prevention of acts that damage the environment is that they can be perfectly legal in some countries and not in others. Most countries do not have 'environmental courts' or environment judges, and most do not even use the language of 'crime' with reference to the environment, preferring other terms such as 'offences' or 'breaches'.

Moreover, when governments do use the language of environmental crime or of eco crime, such terms tend to be used to describe graffiti, littering, fly-tipping and vandalism. While these acts have anti-social aspects, they are of course minuscule when compared to the damage caused by large companies and governments of 'the powerful' who, whether intentionally or negligently, contaminate and destroy the natural environment. As discussed in Chapter 1, Jeffrey Reiman (1979) has succinctly argued in his text *The Rich Get Richer and the Poor Get Prison*, 'the more likely it is for a particular form of crime to be committed by middle- and upper-class people, the less likely it is that it will be treated as a criminal offence' (quoted in Carrabine et al., 2004, p. 77).

Take, for example, the USA's 'war on drugs' under the Reagan Administration in the 1980s. This included a strategy to eliminate drugs 'at supply'. Official US policies of crop eradication (which have continued into the twenty-first century) sprayed toxic chemicals in South America as a crime prevention technique. 'Eliminate the crop and you eliminate the drug crime in the US' was the logic behind what has become an environmental disaster. Rather than annihilate the poppy plant (the crop of origin for opiate drugs, which has spread to new regions across the world and expanded the industry), the US Government has succeeded in contaminating waterways, killing wildlife and causing the premature deaths of thousands of people affected by the toxic sprays in what some have referred to as acts of 'eco-cide' and 'culture-cide' (Del Olmo, 1998).

2   Charting the terrain

This section disentangles terminology and identifies the substantive areas to be covered in the rest of the chapter.

2.1 What is eco crime?

The Oxford Handbook of International Environmental Law (Bodansky et al., 2007) provides a comprehensive collection of articles pertaining to the various areas of law that protect the environment. Not a single paragraph is devoted to 'environmental' or 'eco crime'. Although a language of precaution, liability and responsibility is used in the *Oxford Handbook*, the actions of those who harm the environment are rarely referred to as crimes. From a purely legal perspective this is best explained by the fact that environmental offences are not contained within either international or national criminal law. Rather, they are dealt with as administrative offences and prosecuted in civil courts. Such offences only become issues for the criminal courts when offenders fail to comply with a court sanction (such as not paying a fine). Within domestic law this is typically used only in reaction to anti-social behaviour. For example, in the UK, the Home Office defines 'environmental crime' as:

- fly-tipping – dumping household or commercial rubbish in private or communal areas

- littering – deliberately dropping litter on the streets

- graffiti – spray-painting or otherwise marking private property or communal areas like the sides of bus-shelters and houses

- vandalism – damaging private property or communal facilities like telephone boxes or play-ground equipment

(Home Office, 2007)

The House of Commons Environmental Audit Committee has also published findings on what it refers to as 'Corporate Environmental Crime', which it has defined as 'any environmental crime that has been committed by a corporate body (Environmental Audit Committee, 2005, p. 8). Interestingly, the transnational issues mentioned above are not included, while issues to do with water, sewerage and landfill are. Many countries see environmental crimes as acts of civilian disorder and not as acts of serious environmental degradation caused by international corporations. International law, including European Union (EU) law, does not define 'eco crime'. International crimes expressed within international law include acts such as genocide, aggression, torture and terrorism, but not acts that destroy the environment. As a result, green criminology (discussed further in Section 3) seeks to shift political and legal discourses to include acts of environmental harm within a criminal law rubric.

Existing academic texts often use the term 'eco crime' synonymously with that of 'environmental crime'. But throughout this chapter the term 'eco crime' will be preferred. There are several reasons for this.

- 'Environmental crime' is a legal and government-dominated term that has been constructed and used to define specific disorder-type offences, such as property abuse and anti-social behaviour. Environmental crimes referred to by governments routinely ignore or pay lip service to corporations that pollute and destroy the environment. As a result, the serious harms caused to the environment, committed by states and corporations (air pollution, toxic dumping, destruction of native woodlands and natural habitats, contamination of waterways – just to mention a few), are omitted from the definition and lexicon of 'environmental crime'.

- Existing government usages of the term 'environmental crime' fail to acknowledge the social, cultural and economic consequences experienced by people who are the victims of acts that damage the environment. In contrast, an important dimension of 'eco crime' is recognition that the 'environment' includes impacts on both human and non-human species.

- 'Environmental crime' within criminological discourses is widely thought of as being confined to 'environmental criminology' (Bottoms and Wiles, 2003; Wortley et al., 2008); that is, 'crime mapping' or charting the spatial and geographical occurrence of recorded crime.

- 'Environmental crime' – in the sense of pollution and environmental degradation – while adopting the term 'crime', is typically viewed and dealt with as an administrative offence, if it is dealt with at all.

This chapter argues that the term 'eco crime' is better able to encapsulate existing legal definitions of environmental crime, as well as sociological analyses of those environmental harms not necessarily specified by law. The term also permits analyses that transcend national borders. In doing so, it provides criminology with substantial challenges, such as those posed by Richard Harding in 1983 when discussing nuclearism: notably, 'What can criminology and criminologists do to decrease the chances of the extinction of mankind and the destruction of the planet?' (Harding, 1983, p. 81). This demanding question requires criminology to engage with issues of global concern and allows it to explore a range of acts that often result in widespread social and environmental harm, but which are not necessarily covered in legal statutes. It also allows an assessment of big issues, such as threats to the extinction of human and non-human life. If the natural resources that maintain life are damaged or threatened, surely criminology should be involved in such debates? If an assault causing injury is relevant to criminology, surely the compromising or eradicating of the essentials of life – for example, food, water and air – must also be relevant? Friedo Herbig and Sandra Joubert (2006) refer to this as a 'conservation criminology'. For them, criminology must examine what they call 'natural resources crime': actions that damage or threaten 'nature' and the resources necessary for conservation.

When eco crime is contextualised within notions of harm we can observe a broadening of the gaze beyond legal terrains to include discourses on risk, rights and regulation. As a result, eco crime extends existing definitions of environmental crime to include licensed or lawful acts of ecological degradation committed by states and corporations. For Laura Westra (2004, p. 309), eco crime is unprovoked aggression 'committed in the pursuit of other goals and "necessities" such as economic advantage'. Westra's work broadens the definition of eco crime to include issues of human health, global security and justice. She suggests that harmful environmental actions committed in pursuit of free trade or progress are 'attacks on the human person' that deprive civilians (notably the poor and marginalised) of the social, cultural and economic benefits of their environment (Westra, 2004, p. 309). As a result, such actions are 'violent' and should be viewed as akin to human rights violations.

That Westra's framework extends eco crimes beyond acts that damage the environment to those that have widespread social and cultural consequences is an important point to note. For example, in 1988 a US ship carrying 4000 tons of toxic incinerator ash dumped this ash on a beach outside the Haitian port city of Gonaive. Haitian people suffered skin diseases and vision disorders as result of the toxic chemicals that subsequently littered their lands and waterways (UNEP 1991). Such acts of eco crime create devastating conditions for the lives of local people. The contamination of drinking water, the degradation of soil and the pollution of air and land all expose people (usually those in poor and developing countries) to substantial health risks (see Chapter 1). International environmental law attempts to prevent the dumping of toxic waste and activities that pollute other countries, yet these still occur. As Maria Hauck (2007) has observed, acts of eco crime are linked to the poverty and social dislocation, as well as the mental and physical debilitation, of people who are victims of corporations and states that deliberately violate environmental agreements.

Activity 6.2

In light of the definitions presented above, including the social and cultural impacts of acts that damage the environment, read the following extract and assess whether or not you think BP has committed an eco crime.

Extract 6.1

Greenpeace calls BP's oil sands plan an environmental crime

Terry Macalister

BP will be involved in the 'greatest climate crime' in history by backing tar sands projects to extract oil in Canada and is likely to face direct action, Greenpeace warned last night.

The threat came as state officials in Alaska confirmed they were preparing a civil law suit against BP for the Prudhoe Bay oil spill when 200,000 gallons of crude [oil] were released into the wilderness.

The Greenpeace warning followed BP's announcement on Wednesday that it was buying into the tar sands schemes through a deal with Husky Oil, reversing a decision by former chief executive John Browne to stay away from an expensive and environmentally dirty business ...

'In the tar sands you are looking at the greatest climate crime because not only will these developments produce 100m tonnes of greenhouse gases annually by 2012 but also kill off 147,000 sq km [56,000 sq miles] of forest that is the greatest carbon sink in the world,' said Mike Hudema, a climate campaigner with Greenpeace in Edmonton ...

BP accepted that tar sands operations were energy-intensive and would increase its carbon footprint but said it needed to find new supplies to meet increasing demand for oil products. 'Someone is going to develop these resources and we will bring our standards to bear and will be developing them as best as possible,' a spokesman said.

Source: *The Guardian*, 7 December 2007

Comment

BP has not violated any laws in the UK or Canada, but its actions may damage the environment. Do you consider that BP's actions constitute an eco crime? In reaching your conclusion, consider the importance of oil in contemporary society and whether it is reasonable to expect that certain natural environments should be compromised to yield essential fuel supplies. It could be argued that oil is a necessary natural resource for human existence and that, provided it is extracted legally, any environmental consequences are unavoidable side-effects. If this line of argument informs your reasoning, consider the case of the Achuar people who have lived in the north-east Peruvian rainforest for thousands of years. In 2007, these indigenous peoples filed a lawsuit in California against oil giant Occidental Petroleum (OP). The drilling activities of OP ceased in 2002, but thirty years of extracting oil has resulted in the contamination of water, the extinction of plant and animal life and generations of ill health for the Achuar. The petroleum corporation's spokesperson has responded to this unresolved litigation by stating: 'This oil industry should be of benefit for everybody – maybe today it's not of benefit to indigenous peoples and the government should find the best way to solve that problem' (quoted in Collyns, 2008). Cases such as these also emphasise the ways in which eco crimes occur across borders. Should the livelihoods of indigenous peoples be jeopardised or harmed for oil? Is it acceptable that the environment be damaged to extract oil? What lessons can be learned from the Achuar for future oil explorations in rainforests, where human and non-human life has been flourishing for thousands of years?

2.2 Transnational dimensions to eco crime

Interpol (2007) divides eco crime into 'pollution' and 'wildlife', which respectively denote the illegal disposal of waste that contaminates air, water and land; and the unlawful trade in endangered species. These two broad categories have been further expanded on by the United Nations Interregional Crime and Justice Research Institute (UNICRI), which focuses on 'crimes against the environment' as prohibited by international law. UNICRI categorises eco crime as:

- illegal trade in wildlife in contravention to the 1973 Washington Convention on International Trade in Endangered Species of Fauna and Flora (CITES);

- illegal trade in ozone-depleting substances (ODS) in contravention to the 1987 Montreal Protocol on Substances that Deplete the Ozone Layer;

- dumping and illegal transport of various kinds of hazardous waste in contravention to the 1989 Basel Convention on the Control of Transboundary Movement of Hazardous Wastes and Other Wastes and their Disposal;

- illegal, unregulated and unreported (IUU) fishing in contravention to controls imposed by various regional fisheries management organizations (RFMOs);

- illegal logging and trade in timber when timber is harvested, transported, bought or sold in violation of national laws.

(UNICRI quoted in Brack and Hayman, 2002, p. 5)

Other environmental offences identified by UNICRI share similar characteristics with these five main categories. They include:

- bio-piracy and transport of controlled biological or genetically modified material;

- illegal dumping of oil and other wastes in oceans (that is, offences under the 1973 International Convention on the Prevention of

Pollution from Ships (MARPOL) and the 1972 London Convention on Dumping);

■ violations of potential trade restrictions under the 1998 Rotterdam Convention on the Prior Informed Consent Procedure for Certain Hazardous Chemicals and Pesticides in International Trade;

■ trade in chemicals in contravention to the 2001 Stockholm Convention on Persistent Organic Pollutants;

■ fuel smuggling to avoid taxes or future controls on carbon emissions.
(UNICRI, quoted in Brack and Hayman, 2002, p. 5)

All of the eco crimes listed above are covered by law (discussed further in Section 5). They are prohibited under international agreements that seek to protect the environment against hazardous and dangerous acts that threaten the ongoing development and sustainability of flora and fauna.

Activity 6.3

At an international level, governments have been accused of ignoring some of the eco crimes listed above. Consider the following extract. It identifies how government authorities often evade national and international laws that protect endangered wildlife. It also highlights how trade in protected animals (for skins, trophies and medicinal purposes) are lucrative industries in which governments, businesses and consumers seek benefits from trade at environmental expense. Does any aspect of the content of the extract give rise to serious concern? If so, what kinds of concern?

Extract 6.2

ENVIRONMENT-INDIA: Illegal Trade Decimating Wildlife

Malini Shankar

A great variety of endangered wildlife species end up feeding the illegal market for Traditional Chinese Medicine (TCM) thanks to poor enforcement in stopping the trade, say experts and activists.

'The Chinese market is like a "black hole" sucking in wildlife products from neighbouring countries,' said Peter Pueschel, head of global Wildlife Trade Programme at the International Fund for Animal Welfare (IFAW), in an e-mail interview with IPS ...

According to the wildlife crime database maintained by the Wildlife Protection Society of India (WPSI), 846 tigers, 3,140 leopards and 585 freshwater otter (skins) were poached between 1994 and Aug. 31, 2008 and another 320 elephants were poached between 2000 and 2008 in India.

'Although many species used in TCM are now protected by national and international laws, illegal trade and poaching have increased to crisis levels as TCM's popularity has expanded over the last two decades,' says Samir Sinha of the Indian chapter of the TRAFFIC, the Britain-based wildlife trade monitoring network.

'The problem is widespread, and mostly boils down to lack of political support,' says Belinda Wright of the WPSI.

Elephants, tigers, leopards, mongoose, black bears, rhinos, snakes, butterflies, gorillas, otters, musk deer, antelopes, reptiles and products such as caterpillar fungus and porcupine quills form the bulk of the raw material for the TCM industry that, according to Interpol, is worth 20 billion dollars per year.

'We believe there is organised wildlife trade but it is difficult to identify,' said Xu Hongfa, director of TRAFFIC – China in e-mail responses to queries from IPS.

According to most wildlife experts the illegal trade is helped along by the fact that Chinese authorities do little to curb the TCM industry because it is regarded as a part of East Asian culture. But Beijing can and does vigorously protect certain species such as the Giant Panda which has iconic status ...

'During a five-day period in June 2008, EIA (Environment Investigation Agency) investigators observed five traders who have been documented selling Asian big cat skins in previous years,' said Debbie Banks of the London-based EIA, adding that Chinese authorities failed to act on information passed on to them ...

Pueschel referred to a stock of 110 tonnes of ivory that disappeared from Chinese government custody in July 2008. 'The main point here is that these incidents have not been taken seriously. It remains totally unclear where this ivory has gone. Nevertheless China has been designated an ivory importing country ("trading partner") supported by the Convention on International Trade in Endangered Species of Wild Fauna and Flora (CITES) secretariat.'

In May 2006 a consignment of 3,900 kg of ivory tusks was found concealed in a container of timber logs seized by customs officials in Hong Kong, revealing the ingenious methods used by wildlife racketeers. 'The "standard sizes" of cut ivory pieces make it easier to hide them inside any kind of packaging material,' says Pablo Tachil a wildlife investigator based in Bangalore.

According to Tachil, Burma has emerged as a major staging point for the wildlife trade because of its location close to India ... and the major markets of South-east Asia. 'Burma is also an ideal hideout for poachers and traders, because of weak policing,' he said ...

An IFAW report in 2007 revealed that at least 90 percent of all investigated ivory listings on eBay were legally suspect. While eBay claims that its site allows 'shoppers to see the positive social and environmental impact' of each purchase, including whether it 'supports animal species preservation', activists say nothing is done by way of monitoring.

The animal most at risk of ending up as raw material for TCM is the tiger because it has long been revered in China as a symbol of power and strength and the belief that its products have potent medicinal properties. Only a century ago there were eight kinds of tigers, with over 100,000 wild tigers in the world. Today only five tiger subspecies exist, with fewer than 5,000 wild tigers in the world ...

Source: Inter Press Service (IPS), Bangalore, 13 October 2008

Comment

The article in Extract 6.2 identifies the links between transnational organised crime and the environment: that is, international networks of criminality, involving state officials, exploiting the environment for commercial gain. The environment provides a profitable domain for manipulation, with substantial consequences for indigenous communities and surrounding flora and fauna. Moreover, the money to be made from the illegal trade in endangered species is often used to purchase weapons, fund civil wars and commit acts of ethnic cleansing. For example, the Zakouma National Park in Chad has become the target of the illegal poaching of elephants, and the subsequent selling of ivory tusks is a multimillion pound per annum industry. The Janjaweed, a guerrilla militia in north-east Africa, uses the profits made from the sale of tusks to buy weapons for use in privately sponsored warfare, which has reportedly included the genocidal acts in Darfur (Begley, 2008).

There are also numerous examples (as discussed in Chapter 5) of corporations polluting the environment and forcibly relocating people as a result of commercial activities. Yet more often than not, such corporate actions go unpunished. Indeed, they are often seen as 'part and parcel' of commercial activity. In Activity 6.2 above, for example, it was noted how some corporations view the violation of the environment and other people's rights as an unfortunate by-product of obtaining essential natural resources.

As an academic field of study, criminology has latterly begun to engage with acts that damage and destroy the environment. But what sort of criminology is capable of doing this? The following section explores this question.

3   Greening criminology

Green criminology asserts that eco crimes at both an international and a domestic level should encapsulate all acts of environmental harm to human and non-human species, as well as to the natural environment itself (Lynch and Stretesky, 2003; Beirne and South, 2007; White, 2008).

3.1 Exploring green criminology

Green criminology remains an undeveloped criminological narrative, yet its various perspectives aim to provide an interdisciplinary scholarship committed to the protection and conservation of environmental resources and to the prevention of illegal and harmful acts that unnecessarily threaten or damage the natural environment.

Two key figures in the founding of green criminology, Piers Beirne and Nigel South (2007, p. xiii), argue that, at its 'most abstract level', it includes 'those harms against humanity, against the environment (including space) and against non-human animals committed by both powerful organisations (e.g. governments, transnational corporations, military apparatuses) and also by ordinary people'. This broad definition acknowledges governmental understandings of individual irresponsibility (vandalism, graffiti and fly-tipping), but is also capable of focusing primary attention on acts of the 'powerful' in causing widespread and long-term environmental damage. This focus is consistent with the origins of green criminology. When the term was first coined by Michael Lynch in 1990, it was designed to harness green environmentalism (achieving sustainable development through changes to public policy and individual behaviour) and green political theories to examine 'environmental destruction as an outcome of the structure of modern capitalist production and consumption patterns' (Lynch, 1990, p. 1). In this sense, the theoretical roots of green criminology are embedded within the traditions of radical criminological schools of thought, such as feminism, Marxism and social constructionism (these radical criminologies emerged in the late 1960s and early 1970s in the UK and the USA, arguing, among other things, that crime is to be found in relations of power, oppression and selective processes of criminalisation – see Muncie, 2006).

3.2 Guiding perspectives

Rob White (2008) argues that there is no one green criminological theory, but rather a series of 'perspectives' or narratives that draw on various philosophical, sociological, legal and scientific traditions. He argues that the three 'theoretical tendencies' that inform green criminology are 'environmental justice', 'ecological justice' and 'species justice' (White, 2008, p. 15).

Environmental justice is a human-centred or anthropocentric discourse with two distinct dimensions. First, it assesses the equity of access and use of environmental resources across social and cultural divides. Who has access to the benefits and profits of natural resources, and why? What factors prevent all people from sharing equally in the environment? The European Court of Human Rights has ruled that all EU member states and their subjects have a 'right to a safe environment' (Mularoni, 2003). Actions that prevent, jeopardise or compromise this right are actions that violate environmental justice. Second, it explores how people (notably marginalised, poor and powerless people) are affected by natural disasters, corporate activity and state actions that damage the environment. For example, toxic dumping, chemical spills, industrial pollution, nuclear testing, illegal fishing, wildlife poaching and contamination of drinking water have adverse side-effects but do not victimise all people equally. It is indigenous peoples, minority ethnic communities, the poor and often women who are most affected by such eco crimes.

Ecological justice focuses on the relationship or interaction between humans and the natural environment. When humans develop the environment for material needs (housing, agriculture, business, consumption), this approach insists that such actions be assessed within the context of damage or harm to other living things. This position is often referred to as an 'ecocentric' understanding of the interaction between humans and nature. Some may criticise it because it does not acknowledge that the reality of harm, development, progress, and so on, will always be defined and responded to by humans. Yet ecological justice argues that an environmentally centred perspective, which upholds the importance of living creatures as well as inanimate and non-living objects (such as soil, rock, water, air), provides useful insights for guiding future economic and developmental decisions. It asserts the intrinsic value and equal status of non-humans (discussed in Section 5) and explores the potential for sustainability while utilising environmental resources for fundamental human needs.

For example, with this emphasis, a green criminology may draw on and learn through actor-network theory (ANT) (developed from the work of Michael Callon, 1991, and Bruno Latour, 1992, 2005) and social studies of science and technology. Callon and Latour perceive of a network in which both human and non-human actors assume and create identities through their connectedness and dependence on each other. The often-cited example of human and non-human 'actants' is the driving of a motor vehicle. It is the mechanics of the motor car, combined with road conditions, traffic rules and prior experience, that produce a social and technological network that creates the act of driving. This network approach in green criminology takes the criminological gaze beyond acts of criminal intent to the global dimensions that contribute to environmental harm. In this way, the deforestation of the Amazon Rainforest, for example, is not simply the wilful action of a government permitting timber corporations to log ancient indigenous woodlands. It is much more complex. The act of deforestation in the Amazon Rainforest is a global phenomenon that involves the technologies and consumers of all inputs and outputs of rainforest logging. In other words, the felling of the Amazon trees occurs because a network of participating factors (or actants) – from the lumberjack who controls the saw to the North American family that uses the chipwood to spread across their front garden – contribute, in combination, to the act of deforestation, with widespread ecological consequences.

Species justice is a non-human or biocentric discourse that emphasises the importance of non-human rights. It asserts that human beings are not the only creatures with rights, nor are humans superior beings. In other words, there is no hierarchy of existence with human beings at the pinnacle. All 'living things in existence' share an equal status of importance. Beirne and South (2007) argue that to prohibit or disregard non-human creatures as being not of equal standing within the natural environment denies the value and worth of those species. Conversely, it may be argued that existence or survival, and indeed evolution itself, is dependent on one species consuming another. Linked closely to this is the notion of 'ecological extension' where the importance of human beings is considered no more significant, in the long-term existence of the environment, than that of all other creatures that combine to form the natural environment. As White (2008, p. 17) identifies, an analysis from this perspective aids a critique of how rights are constructed. It allows us to question the bases from which rights are created and protected. If rights are about ensuring health and well-being while minimising pain and suffering, humans are not the only species to experience these. Some animals have been assigned legal rights, such as chimpanzees in Germany. In 2002, Germany became the first EU country to integrate animal rights into its constitution. This requires the state to 'respect and protect the dignity' of animals (Welfare for Animals Global, 2002).

The perspectives discussed above centre critical attention on the key issues of how and why certain things come to be called 'criminal', whereas others do not. In doing so, they open up debate about whether certain harms should be criminalised. Importantly, green criminology is not only a response to official and scientific evidence about environmental damage and species decline; it is also an engagement with emerging social movements and public opinions of resistance (such as the European Social Forum, Statewatch, Greenpeace and the Centre for Corporate Accountability). Chaia Heller (a French anti-genetic engineering campaigner) suggests that green criminology moves away from a sole reliance on risk and measurement, as presented by science and government, and incorporates social and cultural meanings of harm, as defined by ordinary citizens (Beirne and South, 2007). In these ways, green criminology itself can be considered an evolving knowledge base that challenges mainstream disciplinary discourses as well as neo-liberal government and corporate rationalities (Scraton, 2001). It questions the moral and ethical bases on which contemporary laws permit the exploitation of nature and examines the conditions in which coexistence and inter-species cooperation can be achieved. Moreover, its globalising of the criminological lens (viewing crime beyond the local and national level to include international and global actions of criminality) permits the involvement of movements and organisations that are outside the state to contribute to emerging notions of environmental justice.

4 The corporate colonisation of nature

In a rapidly globalising world where free-trade ideology continues to expand in new markets in South East Asia, the green perspectives discussed above emerge as central to debates about environmental protection. South argues that speedy developments in globalised trade place the environment at greater risk of exploitation and damage. Indeed, he argues that within competitive trade economies, the environment becomes a target for commercial profit. This is what he calls 'the corporate colonisation of nature' (South, 2007, p. 230).

As discussed in Chapter 1, it is widely recognised that some of the most polluted areas on Earth are also home to the poorest people. Where environments are degraded for economic prosperity, it is the surrounding populations of impoverished people who fall victim and suffer the greatest harm to their economy, their health and their food and water sources. Emerging notions of environmental justice (discussed further in Section 5) attempt to redress this imbalance by aspiring to equal access to environmental resources across cultures and classes.

4.1 Biopiracy

The environment is often viewed as a commodity that provides valuable resources for goods and services. These diverse resources have considerable value for a multiplicity of global industries. Many of these resources are to be found in rainforests, savannahs and waterways in poor countries, which then become targets for exploitation by large multinational companies. For example, organisms found in the soils and rivers of a sovereign nation come to be patented and subsequently owned by corporations in other countries. This practice is often referred to as 'biopiracy'. Biopiracy is the illegal practice of taking control and ownership of organisms (from plants and animals) and depriving indigenous peoples of access to, and the benefits of, their own ecological sovereignty. As Ikechi Mgbeoji (2006, p. 13) argues; 'bio-piracy may be defined as the unauthorised commercial use of biological resources and/ or traditional knowledge, or the patenting of spurious inventions based on such knowledge, without compensation'. White has also identified that increases in biopiracy are aided by the World Trade Organization (WTO) and international agreements that permit corporations to assert trade-related intellectual property rights. Government officials and business representatives in poorer countries are often required by large transnational corporations to sign agreements that override plant and animal protections. Such contractual arrangements are often made in secret, without government or public oversight (White, 2008, p. 134).

Activity 6.4

Consider the case in Extract 6.3 in light of the discussion of biopiracy above and of the reference to ecological sovereignty in particular.

Extract 6.3

BIODIVERSITY: Indigenous Peoples Fight Theft

Julio Godoy

Amongst the suits in the luxurious hotel hall, Sebastian Haji immediately catches the eye. He is small, dark-skinned, and wears a crown of feathers on his head.

Sebastian is a Machineri Indian from the Amazons region in Brazil, and he is in Bonn for serious business with the suits. He is here to fight biopiracy.

'Multinational companies are stealing the knowledge and resources of Amazonian people, and international institutions and our own government are just looking at the thieves,' Sebastian told IPS. 'And this robbery is taking place despite international conventions and alleged legal protection of our rights anchored even in the Brazilian constitution.'

Like many other representatives of indigenous peoples from around the world, Sebastian is in Bonn for the UN conference on biodiversity May 19–30. The conference is taking place within the framework of the UN Convention on Biological Diversity (CBD), the international treaty adopted at the Earth Summit in Rio in June 1992 to protect biodiversity ...

Biopiracy means, for example, how Amazonian indigenous peoples might lose two of their traditional healing methods to multinational companies.

'We have a plant, the ayahuasca (banisteriopsis caapi), and the sweat of frog, the kambô (phyllomedusa bicolour), which our spiritual leaders (healers) use as medicine,' Sebastian told IPS.

The ayahuasca, which means 'wine of the soul', has been used for centuries by the indigenous peoples of the western Amazon Basin to brew a ceremonial drink which contains a hallucinogenic, dimethyltryptamine.

'Our spiritual leaders use the ayahuasca in religious and healing ceremonies to meet with good spirits, expel bad energy, diagnose and treat illnesses, and divine the future,' Sebastian said.

For more than 20 years, ayahuasca has been at the centre of a legal battle between representatives of indigenous peoples and the U.S. company Cielo Herbals. The U.S. company is now growing the plant in Hawaii and other territories, and commercialising the drink.

The case of the kambô frog, also known as the monkey frog, is similar. Amazonian people have for centuries used sweat secretion from the frog on burns.

Scientific researchers have found that the secretion contains peptides and opiates that have analgesic properties and are capable of combating ischemia, a condition in which the blood flow (and thus oxygen) is restricted to a part of the body.

'Our healers know how to use the frog's secretion,' Sebastian told IPS. 'Now, it is being used in other places incorrectly, and this has led to the death of patients.'

Several U.S. companies, universities and researchers, including the Seattle-based ZymoGenetics Inc., have filed for patents on the frog's sweat.

Sebastian said such biopiracy occurs despite numerous international conventions and Brazil's own constitution of 1988. Brazil has also ratified the International Labour Organization's Indigenous and Tribal Peoples Convention, also known as ILO Convention 169. Another is the UN convention on biodiversity, which is being debated in Bonn ...

'All these international conventions are dead letter,' Sebastian said.

'For us indigenous peoples, the protection of our biodiversity resources is also the protection of ourselves,' Hernández [a Machineri Indian from the Amazons region in Brazil] told IPS. 'But our governments and the international organisations are not really concerned with that.'

'We do not protect just ourselves,' Sebastian said. 'We protect the whole of humanity. Look at the weather: never in human history has nature shown so many symbols of resistance towards human action.'

Source: Inter Press Service (IPS), Bonn,
24 May 2008

Comment

The term 'ecological sovereignty' was used in the discussion above Activity 6.4 to describe a country's right to use and benefit from natural resources that originate within its own territory. But should such sovereignty exist? On the one hand, it could be argued that the example given in Extract 6.3 represents an eco crime (the theft of culture and biological diversity); on the other hand, it provides an example of essential corporate activity seeking solutions to global medical problems. International conservation areas protected by law are land, forest, water and sea regions with untold biological significance. In the Amazon Rainforest, for example, the overwhelming majority of flora and fauna species have not been classified. Such organisms may hold the keys to solving terminal illness and to seeking answers to global energy and food needs. Should only one country have the right to access unique resources within its borders? Or should those resources be available, perhaps at a cost, to all countries and corporations for global benefit?

4.2 Corporate engineering of nature

Alongside the Amazon Rainforest, Africa is regarded as the most biodiversity-rich region on Earth. As a relatively undeveloped continent, the potential for such diversity remains hidden and unexplored. Some African nations wish to preserve their genetic and biological wealth amid devastating circumstances such as human hunger. Corporations threaten biodiversity not only through theft, but also as a result of contamination or corporate engineering. Take, for example, the issue of genetically modified organisms (GMOs). With the world reportedly experiencing a 'food crisis', many have hailed genetically modified (GM) foods as the answer to world hunger. Concerns over GM food safety received international headlines when the Zambian president referred to it as poison. The introduction of genetic technology into the food chain has posed a perceived danger to the staple food of Zambians, which has generated a discourse of fear and moral panic among many in the population (Walters, 2006). It has been proven that GM plants (the seeds of which are owned by large corporations) can irreversibly contaminate other plants (Walters, 2009).

Zambia is one of six southern African nations that has faced food shortages for most of the time since its independence in 1964. Despite this, however, the Zambian Government has continued to reject GM food out of fear of potential harm to its population and biodiversity. For some US geneticists, the stance adopted by the Zambian president is 'incomprehensible' (see Fedoroff and Brown, 2004, p. 31). Moreover, senior US authorities have placed intolerable pressure on African nations to accept what is now a surplus of GM food from US farmers. For example, the US ambassador to the UN, Tony Hall, suggested that Zambia's political leaders be convicted as criminals by stating, 'people that deny food to their people, that are in fact starving people to death, should be held responsible ... for the highest crimes against humanity in the highest courts in the world' (quoted in Walters, 2006, p. 30).

Yet Zambian officials have continually argued that external political pressure from countries such as the USA, wanting to 'dump' surplus and unwanted GM food, is illegal and threatens the rich, natural genetic resources that the Zambian Government wishes to protect. The Minister of Agriculture stated that:

> Food is a weapon of mass destruction. It is used by some countries to control and pressure the poorer African nations. Western leaders have accused my President of untruths. We are adopting the precautionary principle on GM food and until we have more accurate scientific facts that clearly show that it is safe, we will not introduce it to our environment ... I am wanting to explore the potential of our

biodiversity before we destroy what we already freely have, what God has given us for free. How can we accept GMOs when I know that such technology could destroy our biodiversity, the possibilities of which are still unknown?

(quoted in Walters, 2006, p. 30).

The Zambian Government is also conscious that, should their environment be polluted by the genes of GM crops, the consequences will not only be irreversible, but according to international patent law, there is a risk that a vast amount of Zambian plant life will be claimed by offshore corporations (Walters, 2009).

With the production of GM products being controlled by a diminishing number of GM biotechnology giants, we are witnessing a growing form of 'monopoly capitalism' (Walters, 2006, p. 35). The aggressive corporate policies of control are openly acknowledged by the directors of the biotech industries. Rob Fraley, from the chemical corporation Du Pont, has stated that 'what we are seeing is not just a consolidation of seed companies, it's really a consolidation of the entire food chain' (quoted in Assouline et al., 2001, p. 30). Such monopoly capitalism infringes human rights and international trade law (see Cottier et al., 2005) and is in direct opposition to the competitive and free-trade policies of the WTO. Yet, it is from the WTO that the US Government has sought a ruling for the ongoing biotech hegemony in world food trade (Walters, 2009). The overwhelming percentage of GM food and its accompanying fertilisers, seeds and herbicides is produced by four chemical corporations, namely: Monsanto, Syngenta, Du Pont and Bayer (see Nottingham, 2003). That the global trade in GM food is lucrative for governments and the four GM giants is essential for understanding pressures and the unethical and illegal actions discussed in relation to Zambia. Yet free-trade ideologies espoused by the WTO, in order to enhance notions of competitive capitalism, are compromised by a status quo of monopoly capitalism.

As Mark Winston (2002, p. 174) argues, 'genetically modified organisms would be only an interesting academic sideline if there was no money to be made. The heavy investments in research that have driven corporate biotechnology would not have been forthcoming without the product protection provided by patents'. The monopolisation of four biotech companies in what some refer to as 'bio-imperialism' (see Engdahl, 2004) continues to mount concerns and fears within agricultural and consumer groups. Farmers, for example, remain sceptical of the motivations and tactics of corporations that attempt to control and profit from food production through the laws of patent and intellectual property.

In addition, the aggressive and monopolised business practices of the GM giants have heightened widespread anxiety about the technology. The biotech corporate lobbying of government officials, the bribing and threatening of scientists, the theft, manipulation and subversion of scientific data, the strategic placement of GM corporate employees on regulatory, funding and government decision-making bodies, have all been documented and continue to raise serious concerns about the actions and motives of the GM giants (Smith, 2003; Rees, 2006; Walters, 2009).

5 Preventing eco crime and promoting environmental justice

This section explores the ways in which eco crimes may be prevented. It charts existing legal approaches and explores non-legal initiatives through examples of consumer action and social movements.

5.1 Existing legal regimes

International law has not specifically defined what the 'environment' is, or what it is not. Instead, it has allowed different UN-affiliated bodies to provide various meanings, which together form customs and principles that are recognised by law. As a result, the environment tends to be referred to either in broad terms, such as 'where we all live' (UNEP, 1972), or in more specific ways, such as 'the combination of elements whose complex inter-relationship make up the setting, the surroundings and the conditions of life of the individual and of society as they are and as they are felt' (EEC Regulation 1872/84). It is apparent that the UN, and its International Court of Justice (based in The Hague), have quite deliberately avoided defining 'environment'. The preferred position of the international community appears to be that of accepting that the environment is 'a term that everyone understands and no one is able to define' (Caldwell, quoted in Birnie and Boyle, 2002, p. 4).

As mentioned above, the protection of the environment is often viewed as being in conflict with progress and development. As a result, emerging environmental regulations and regimes are often influenced, or indeed shaped, by lobby groups and industries that seek to maintain economic prosperity as the cornerstone of contemporary social life.

Guiding legal principles of international environmental regulation

Numerous general principles have been formulated by the UN not only to guide, but also to form an important component of the development of all international environmental law directed at the prevention of eco crime. These have been repeatedly emphasised at official international environment summits, enshrined into the wording of multilateral environmental agreements and articulated in the rulings of international judicial decisions (Beyerlin, 2007). In the main, they derive from the Rio Declaration on Environment and Development of 1992 (UNEP, 1992) and include the following:

- *The principle 'not to cause transboundary environmental damage'.* This principle, often referred to as the 'preventative action or no harm principle', bestows a duty on countries to prevent any actions within their borders that may damage the environment of other nations. A nation must not knowingly cause or allow activities within its sovereign territory to adversely affect the environment of another sovereign nation.

- *The principle of environmental impact assessment.* This emerges from Principle 17 of the Rio Declaration and requires nations to conduct recognised assessments to determine the risks and harms associated with activities likely to damage the environment. This is not a mere suggestion but a mandatory duty and legal requirement.

- *The precautionary principle.* Principle 15 of the Rio Declaration identifies that 'where there are threats of serious or irreversible damage, lack of full scientific certainty shall not be used as a reason for postponing cost-effective measures to prevent environmental degradation'. If a country is aware that its actions may result in serious damage to the environment, it is bound to take action to avert the potential harm.

- *The polluter pays principle.* Principle 16 of the Rio Declaration states that 'national authorities should endeavour to promote internationalisation of environmental costs and the use of economic instruments, taking into account that the polluter should, in principle, bear the costs of pollution'.

- *The principle of sustainable development.* Sustainable development has been a core tenet of international law. Following the publication of the Brundtland Report in 1983 (World Commission on Environment and Development, 1987), which defined sustainable development as 'development that meets the needs of the present without compromising the ability of future generations to meet their own needs', this principle has ensured that the protection of the environment is not treated in isolation from issues of trade and progress or what is often referred to as the 'norm of integration'.

- *The principle of common but differentiated responsibilities.* This is a legal rule which stipulates that states 'shall co-operate in a spirit of global partnership to conserve, protect and restore the health and integrity of the Earth's ecosystems'. It asserts that while all nations have a common purpose to protect the environment and avoid environmental damage, those nations that cause the greatest environmental degradation should pay a greater share of the cost of restoring and alleviating environmental damage.

■ *The principle of intergenerational equity.* This requires all nations to forecast the long-term consequences of their actions. In doing so, all nations must not assume that future generations will have the technology and means to make good all of today's environmental problems. The principle is premised on the assumption that 'we hold the Earth in trust for future generations'.

As David Hunter et al. (1998, p. 348) have succinctly identified, there are ongoing deficiencies of obligation and compliance under international regulations that reflect the above principles. What remedies should be available to states who suffer damage? If powerful countries such as the USA and China fail to sign up to and acknowledge certain international treaties, and fail to acknowledge the authority of the International Court of Justice and its decisions, how valid is international law? Is it real law or is it merely symbolic? Can law really protect the environment and prevent eco crime when its power and purpose is not unilaterally agreed or respected? The answers to these questions are complex and continue to provide challenges for parties to environment treaties.

Enforcing environmental regulations

An important litmus test for compliance with international environmental law is whether or not a country is incorporating international agreements into its own national law. In other words, can the law be effective for preventing eco crimes if countries do not comply? The United Nations Environment Programme (UNEP) defines compliance as 'all relevant laws, regulations, policies, and other measures and initiatives, that contracting parties adopt and/or take to meet obligations under a multilateral environmental agreement' (UNEP, 2006). UNEP provides countries with guidelines on and assistance with compliance, yet there is recognition that some countries have difficulties with implementation. There is often an 'implementation deficit', which is explained by, for example, a country's lack of financial and technical resources, limited expertise in international environmental law, inability to keep pace with the rapid expansion in treaties, overstretched and under-resourced ministries and state institutions, and cultural and religious factors (UNEP, 2006).

One key area of international eco crime is the illegal logging and trade in timber. The UK, for example, is a signatory to various agreements that serve to preserve natural habitats. The UK has also been identified as one of the best examples of compliance and implementation, with a growing and expansive body of law and policy in place to protect the environment (Thornton and Beckwith, 2004). Be that as it may, the UK is also the world's third largest importer of illegally logged timber. Up to 3.2 million cubic metres of timber, extracted from the Amazon Rainforest and other protected habitats and sold in the UK for household furniture or garden woodchip, comprises a £700 million per year British industry (EIA, 2007). Thus, those nations that appear to exemplify compliance with regulations face ongoing challenges to curb illegal markets that exploit and damage the environment.

Activity 6.5

Consider the following examples of eco crimes involving powerful states and corporations. What questions do they raise about the effectiveness of law to prevent international eco crimes? Why do you think the enforcement of environmental treaties is weak?

- In Russia, the dumping of radioactive waste at sea has been widely recognised and proven as common practice. Thomas Cochran et al. (1995) document that dozens of damaged submarine nuclear reactors and thousands of radioactive waste containers have been dumped by Russian authorities in the Berents and Kara Seas. Commercial Russian sailing vessels have also been reported to the International Atomic Energy Agency for transporting radioactive waste in substandard containers – which is both illegal and highly dangerous (Greenpeace, 2005).

- The borders of Afghanistan and Pakistan are used for the smuggling of chlorofluorocarbons (CFCs). CFCs are chemicals used in aerosols and refrigeration and are responsible for the depletion of the ozone layer. This illegal trade is being used to enable developing nations to 'benefit' from the technologies long since available in the West (BBC News, 2004).

- The British nuclear industry (regulated, and in some instances operated, by government) has illegally disposed of thousands of barrels of radioactive waste in the Channel Islands, and reportedly 'lost' 30 kg of plutonium from Sellafield nuclear power station – an issue that awaits hearing (Walters, 2007).

- Italy continues to uphold the worst environmental infringement record in the EU. In early 2002, a total of 125 breaches of EU environmental directives were lodged against the Italian authorities, with some cases referred to the European Court of Justice (Ferrigno, 2003). In December 2006, the European Parliament identified sixty environmental infringement notices that remained outstanding against the Italian Government (the highest in Europe), mainly for breaches of waste management. Italy has yet to implement seven different EU environmental directives relating to water, air, soil, waste and nature protection and its legal regimes are often severely criticised for not harmonising with EU law. Throughout the 1990s, international headlines reported 11 million tonnes of industrial waste unaccounted for and large amounts of toxic waste dumped in Italy in what came to be known as acts of the 'eco-mafia' (Edmondson, 2003). Mafia-related enterprises were reported to be monopolising waste disposal contracts from industries producing toxic residues and illegally dumping the pollutants in various areas of the Italian countryside. Furthermore, the Mafia were bidding for, and successfully obtaining, provincial contracts to clean up the very environmental mess they themselves had created (Edmondson, 2003).

Comment

Harmonising environmental legislation across culturally and economically diverse nations within a historical context that prioritises trade and economic stability remains a demanding and challenging enterprise. There are ongoing tensions between trade and economic prosperity on the one hand, and environmental protection on the other. For example, the rapid industrialisation of China has witnessed the opening of hundreds of fossil fuel-burning power stations. It is predicted that China's coal use will more than likely exceed that for all industrialised countries over the next twenty-five years. In doing so, it will breach international law and exceed the expected reductions of Kyoto Protocol emissions five-fold. However, China's ongoing development is considered crucial for world trade (Bradsher, 2007).

The imperatives of trade often supersede the need to protect environmental resources and surrounding communities. While parties to environmental agreements may seek trade restrictions where the trade is deemed to harm human, animal or plant health or threatens the existence of a natural resource, 'there are no internationally agreed set of principles to deal with the potential difficulties caused by the overlap between the GATT [General Agreement on Tariffs and Trade] rules and the trade provisions of environmental provisions' (Thornton and Beckwith, 2004, p. 40).

Law as a mechanism for protecting the environment faces challenges when free trade is prioritised by individual countries. In its place, notions of regulation and mutual agreement often emerge between trading nations. Trade and economic buoyancy are sometimes viewed by nations around the world as the cornerstones of stable and productive societies. Such trade, however, often comes with environmental consequences.

5.2 Innovations in the legal regulation of eco crime

If the laws described above are to have 'teeth', they must be mobilised and administered through a system of justice. But how can environmental justice operate on a global level? A growing number of nations are signing up to an increasing number of international environmental agreements. A global network of collective concern about justice and the environment is emerging. One mechanism for upholding environmental justice has been mooted via a proposed International Environment Court.

The International Court of the Environment Foundation, established in Italy in 1988, continues to promote, research and collaborate with governments, non-governmental organisations (NGOs) and legal practitioners to develop and implement an International Environment Court (see Pirro, 2002). In 2002, at the World Summit on Sustainable Development, 130 senior judges from around the world identified that there were sufficient domestic and international laws to protect the environment, but also a growing number of 'miscreant corporations and backsliding governments' that were unwilling to self-regulate or enforce laws. The judges called for a unified international court of the environment to strengthen the existing legal framework of environmental governance and, in doing so, to protect the world's poor who are 'often the hardest-hit victims of environmental crimes' (quoted in James, 2002).

Further insistence of the need for an international court was recommended at the Conference of the Americas for the Environment and Sustainable Development at Rio de Janeiro in September 2004. In a country regularly exploited for its genetic diversity and richness, the Brazilian Government continues to support an international legal forum which can prosecute and sanction criminal activities that have origins and backing beyond Brazil's jurisdiction. The UN, through its environment programme and, notably, the World Environment Organization, sees the role of a new system of environmental governance as necessitating a mixture of precaution, education, responsibility and control. In other words, an international court cannot solely be about punishment and sanction but must also be premised on notions of dispute resolution and restorative justice. As Judge Postiglione (Director of the International Court of the Environment Foundation) argues, such a court should meet the cultural, ethical, social, economic and religious needs of peoples and their environments as well as the legal needs of global governance (Postiglione, 2004).

5.3 Social movements and citizen participation

Perhaps law is not the best or the only way to achieve environmental justice. Discourses of environmental justice are also emerging from social movements, campaign organisations and citizen action groups. Citizen participation in environmental justice recognises that the world has to be understood as a system or as the interconnection of overlapping networks. It is the coming together of human and non-human actors in such networks that gives them their meaning. So, to redress the injustices of deforestation, wildlife crime and corporate pollution, for example, it could be argued that citizens as consumers are best placed to influence state and corporate practices by 'product boycotts', protests, political lobbying and fair trade purchases (see Cochrane and Walters, 2008). Others might voice their opposition through political campaigns and/or use direct action to disrupt the activities that result in environmental damage. However, such resistance is typically condemned as 'eco terrorism'.

Activity 6.6

Consider the following.

A Dutch journalist has insisted that a court in Amsterdam jail him for eating chocolate. As a protest and a campaign in consumer awareness, Tuen van de Keuken asserts that his crime is to eat chocolate derived from cocoa plants from the Ivory Coast, a war-torn country where child labour provides large corporations with the ingredients they need to produce the confectionary at substantial ecological costs to the local African environment (see Comiteau, 2007). Is this an act of extremism? Or a perfectly valid response to the ways in which networks of exploitation, environmental degradation and capitalism conspire to produce a worldwide consumer product? Are such actions that boycott particular consumer products for environmental reasons a possible way to ensure that large corporations operate their industries ethically? Can eco crimes be prevented by consumer choice?

Comment

In his influential book *The Green Economy* (1991), Michael Jacobs promotes the notion of 'consumer sovereignty' to create environmental justice and hold unethical and illegal corporations to account. In principle, this concept combines the power of consumers through the ethical sourcing of goods and services to influence the market decisions of large corporations. Of course, such sourcing relies on accurate information, which is often not forthcoming. Newspaper stories continue to reveal how corporations 'greenwash' their images while actively lobbying governments to water down regulations requiring the sourcing of product contents and labour (Pearce, 2008).

Public opposition to GM foods (which was discussed earlier) has seen boycotts across Europe severely affect the profits of biotech companies while steering governments towards preventing the commercial planting of GM crops (Walters, 2009). Michael Mehta (2005) has chronicled the ways in which public resistance was successfully mobilised against nuclear power in Canada where 'risk' was defined by the wishes of the community. Christopher Foreman (1998) provides numerous examples of local resistance in the USA, where groups of residents and community activism have influenced pollution controls while being instrumental in bringing the illegal actions of corporations to justice. Other examples of citizens working in conjunction with organisations such as Greenpeace, Friends of the Earth and the Campaign for Nuclear Disarmament, for instance, have demonstrated how issues such as waste management, toxic dumping, deforestation and the illegal trade in wildlife can be exposed, recognised and successfully prosecuted as eco crimes (Cochrane and Walters, 2008). Some scholars have argued that public participation in the regulation of crimes of the powerful is a means of enhancing democracy (Cochrane and Walters, 2008). Ordinary people are not mere passive individuals under government control, but active citizens with a right and role to question how decisions about governance are made. Whether through direct action, public protest, letter of complaint or assisting a campaign organisation, 'people power' is often the initial means of detecting the occurrence of eco crimes.

In addition to law and citizen participation, another possible way forward includes 'working with' transnational corporations. Notions of corporate and social responsibility provide scope for greater transparency, public scrutiny and involvement. The opening up of the corporate world has revealed, to some extent, information, skills, policies and practices that have the potential to be utilised for conservation purposes. In turn, such knowledges can be redirected towards corporations to assist in the development of environmentally responsible practices. However as White (2008, p. 268) warns, the capacity to be critical while in a collaborative relationship and to 'take action may be compromised by what inevitably becomes a corporate dominated partnership and not a conservation one'.

6   Conclusion

Earlier chapters in this book have examined the ways in which crime can be better understood through the utilisation of such concepts as power, violence and harm. Through this lens, this chapter has argued that eco crime necessitates a general rethinking of the parameters and horizons of the criminological landscape. Such a rethinking requires a reflection on how humans relate to the environment and what constitutes acceptable and unacceptable exploitations of flora, fauna and natural resources.

While legal interventions seek to protect the environment, the imperatives of market economies and free trade – perpetuated by powerful institutions and governments – provide the impetus for the continuance of eco crime. Moreover, crimes such as deforestation or air pollution may have environmental and social impacts that extend far beyond the offending country. These are jurisdictional matters that provide serious challenges for legal recourse. The apparent lack of existing political will to address such actions also remains a cause for serious concern. As such, green issues and eco crime will continue to require ongoing criminological imagination and scholarship.

References

Assouline, G., Joly, P. and Lemarie, S. (2001) *PIA Project: Policy Influences on Technology for Agriculture, Chemicals, Biotechnology and Seeds. Interaction Between Public Policies and Company Innovation Strategy: Overview of the Company Monographs*, Strasbourg, European Commission.

Azami, D. (2008) 'Afghan "health link" to uranium', BBC News, 30 April [online], http://news.bbc.co.uk/1/hi/sci/tech/7373946.stm (Accessed 12 February 2009).

BBC News (2004) 'Whistle blown on illegal CFC trade', BBC News, 31 January [online], http://news.bbc.co.uk/1/hi/sci/tech/3442985.stm (Accessed 13 February 2009).

Begley, S. (2008) 'Extinction trade – endangered animals are the new blood diamonds as militias and warlords use poaching to fund death', *Newsweek*, 1 March [online], www.newsweek.com/id/117875/output/print (Accessed 13 February 2009).

Beirne, P. and South, N. (eds) (2007) *Issues in Green Criminology: Confronting Harms Against Environments, Humanity and Other Animals*, Cullompton, Willan.

Beyerlin, U. (2007) 'Different types of norms in international environmental law, policies, principles and rules' in Bodansky et al. (eds) (2007).

Birnie, P.W. and Boyle, A.E. (2002) *International Law and the Environment* (2nd edn), Oxford, Oxford University Press.

Bodansky, D., Brunnee, J. and Hey, E. (eds) (2007) *The Oxford Handbook of International Environmental Law*, Oxford, Oxford University Press.

Bottoms, A. and Wiles, P. (2003) 'Environmental criminology' in Maguire, M., Morgan, R. and Reiner, R. (eds) *The Oxford Handbook of Criminology* (3rd edn), Oxford, Oxford University Press.

Brack, D. and Hayman, G. (2002) *International Environmental Crime: The Nature and Control of Environmental Black Markets*, London, Royal Institute of International Affairs.

Bradsher, K. (2007) 'Push to fix ozone layer and slow global warming', *New York Times*, 15 March.

Callon, M. (1991) 'Techno-economic networks and irreversibility' in Law, J. (ed.) *A Sociology of Monsters: Essays on Power, Technology and Domination*, London, Routledge.

Carrabine, E., Iganski, P., Lee, M., Plumer, K. and South, N. (2004) *Criminology: A Sociological Introduction*, London, Routledge.

Cochran, T.B., Norris, R.S. and Bukharin, O.A. (1995) *Making the Russian Bomb: From Stalin to Yeltsin*, Boulder, CO, Westview.

Cochrane, A. and Walters, R. (2008) 'The globalisation of social justice' in Newman, J. and Yeates, N. (eds) *Social Justice: Welfare, Crime, and Society*, Maidenhead, Open University Press/Milton Keynes, The Open University.

Collyns, D. (2008) 'Peru tribe battles oil giant over pollution', BBC News, 24 March [online]; http://news.bbc.co.uk/1/hi/world/americas/7306639.stm (Accessed 13 February 2009).

Comiteau, L. (2007) 'Slaves to chocolate', *Time*, 25 May.

Cottier, T., Pauwelyn, J. and Burgi, E. (eds) (2005) *Human Rights and International Trade Law*, Oxford, Oxford University Press.

Del Olmo, R. (1998) 'The ecological impact of illicit drug cultivation and crop eradication programs in Latin America', *Theoretical Criminology*, vol. 2, no. 2, pp. 269–78.

Edmondson, M. (2003) 'Italy and the eco-mafia: how billions are made through dumping toxic waste – with little public outcry', *Business Week*, 27 January.

Engdahl, F.W. (2004) *Bio-Imperialism – Why the Biotech Bullies Must be Stopped*, Little Marais, MN, Organic Consumers Association.

Environmental Audit Committee (2005) *Environmental Audit – Fifth Report* [online], www.parliament.the-stationery-office.co.uk/pa/cm200102/cmselect/cmenvaud/582/58202.htm (Accessed 18 March 2009).

Environmental Investigation Agency (EIA) (2007) *British MPs Urged To Legislate Against Trade in Illegal Timber*, 20 July [online],

www.eia-international.org/cgi/news/news.cgi?t=template&a=406&source=
(Accessed 6 March 2009).

Fedoroff, N. and Brown, N. (2004) *Mendel in the Kitchen: A Scientist's View of Genetically Modified Foods*, Washington, DC, Joseph Henry Press.

Ferrigno, R. (2003) *A Case Study on the Implementation of EU Environmental Legislation: Italy* [online], www.eeb.org/activities/waste/ITALY-waste-report-March2003.pdf (Accessed 6 March 2009).

Foreman, C. (1998) *The Promise and Peril of Environmental Justice*, Washington, DC, Brookings Institution Press.

Greenpeace (2005) *Illegal Nuclear Waste Shipment Blocked*, 1 December [online], www.greenpeace.org/international/news/illegal-nuclear-waste-shipment (Accessed 6 March 2009).

Harding, R. (1983) 'Nuclear energy and the destiny of mankind – some criminological perspectives', *The Australian and New Zealand Journal of Criminology*, vol. 16, no. 2, pp. 81–92.

Hauck, M. (2007) 'Non-compliance in small-scale fisheries: a threat to security?' in Beirne, P. and South, N. (eds) (2007).

Herbig, F.J.W. and Joubert, S.J. (2006) 'Criminological semantics: conservation criminology – vision or vagary?', *Acta Criminologica*, vol. 19, no. 3, pp. 88–103.

Home Office (2007) *Anti-Social Behaviour: Environmental Crime* [online], www.homeoffice.gov.uk/anti-social-behaviour/types-of-asb/environmental-crime/ (Accessed 3 February 2009).

Hunter, D., Salzman, J. and Zaelke, D. (1998) *International Environmental Law and Policy*, New York, Foundation Press.

Intergovernmental Panel on Climate Change (IPCC) (2007) *Climate Change: Synthesis Report* [online], www.ipcc.ch/pdf/assessment-report/ar4/syr/ar4_syr.pdf (Accessed 12 November 2008).

Interpol (2007) *Environmental Crime* [online], www.interpol.int/Public/EnvironmentalCrime/Default.asp (Accessed 16 January 2008).

Jacobs, M. (1991) *The Green Economy: Environment, Sustainable Development and the Politics of the Future*, Concord, MA, Pluto Press.

James, B. (2002) 'Enforce the measures in place, panel urges: Judges call for tougher action on environment!', *International Herald Tribune*, 28 August 2002 [online] www.iht.com/articles/2002/08/28/joberg_ed3_3.php (Accessed 18 March 2009).

Latour, B. (1992) 'Where are the missing masses? The sociology of a few mundane artifacts' in Bijker, W. and Law, J. (eds) *Shaping Technology/Building Society: Studies in Sociotechnical Change*, Cambridge, MA, MIT Press.

Latour, B. (2005) *Reassembling the Social: An Introduction to Actor-Network-Theory*, Oxford, Oxford University Press.

Lynch, M. (1990) 'The greening of criminology: a perspective on the 1990s', *The Critical Criminologist*, vol. 2, no. 3, pp. 1–12.

Lynch, M. and Stretesky, P. (2003) 'The meaning of green: contrasting criminological perspectives', *Theoretical Criminology*, vol. 7, no. 2, pp. 217–38.

McLaughlin, E. and Muncie, J. (eds) (2006) *The Sage Dictionary of Criminology* (2nd edn), London, Sage.

Mehta, M. (2005) *Risky Business: Nuclear Power and Public Protest in Canada*, Lanham, MD, Lexington Books.

Mgbeoji, I. (2006) *Global Piracy: Patents, Plants and Indigenous Knowledge*, Vancouver, UBC Press.

Mularoni, A. (2003) 'The right to a safe environment in the case-law of the European Court of Human Rights' in Postiglione, A. (ed.) *The Role of the Judiciary in the Implementation and Enforcement of Environmental Law*, Rome, International Court of the Environment Foundation.

Muncie, J. (2006) 'Radical criminologies' in McLaughlin, E. and Muncie, J. (eds) (2006).

Nottingham, S. (2003) *Eat Your Genes: How Genetically Modified Food is Entering Our Diet*, London, Zed Books.

Patton, J. (2003) 'United States: expert "depleted uranium use is a war crime"', *Green Left Online*, 23 July [online], www.greenleft.org.au/2003/546/29939 (Accessed 12 February 2009).

Pearce, F. (2008) 'The great green swindle', *The Guardian*, *g2*, 23 October, p. 5.

Pirro, D. (2002) *Project for an International Court of the Environment – Origins and Development* [online], www.biopolitics.gr/HTML/PUBS/VOL8/html/Pirro.htm (Accessed 6 March 2009).

Postiglione, A. (2004) *Need for an International Court of the Environment*, Rome, International Court of the Environment Foundation.

Rees, A. (2006) *Genetically Modified Food: A Short Guide for the Confused*, London, Pluto Press.

Reiman, J. (1979) *The Rich Get Richer and The Poor Get Prison: Ideology, Class and Criminal Justice*, New York, Wiley.

Scraton, P. (2001) 'A response to Lynch and Schwendingers', *The Critical Criminologist. Newsletter of the ASC's Division on Critical Criminology*, vol. 11, no. 2, pp. 1–3.

Smith, J. (2003) *Seeds of Deception: Exposing Industry and Government Lies and the Safety of Genetically Modified Foods You're Eating*, Fairfield, IA, Yes Books.

South, N. (2007) 'The corporate colonisation of nature; bio-prospecting, bio-piracy and the development of green criminology' in Beirne, P. and South, N. (eds) (2007).

Thornton, J. and Beckwith, S. (2004) *Environmental Law* (2nd edn), London, Sweet and Maxwell.

United Nations Environment Programme (UNEP) (1972) *Declaration of the United Nations Conference on the Human Environment* [online], www.unep.org/documents.multilingual/default.asp?DocumentID=97&ArticleID= 1503&l=en (Accessed 18 March 2009).

United Nations Environment Programme (UNEP) (1991) 'The Transfoundary Movement of Hazardous and Nuclear Wastes in the Wider Caribbean Region – A Call for a Legal Instrument with the Cartagena Convention' in *UNEP Technical Report 7*, New York, UNEP.

United Nations Environment Programme (UNEP) (1992) *Rio Declaration on Environment and Development*, 5–16 June [online] www.unep.org/Documents.Multilingual/Default.asp?DocumentID=78& ArticleID=1163 (Accessed 6 June 2008).

United Nations Environment Programme (UNEP) (2006) *A High-Level Meeting on Compliance with and Enforcement of MEAs* [online], http://new.unep.org/Documents.Multilingual/Default.asp?DocumentID=466& ArticleID=5113&l=en (Accessed 12 June 2008).

Walters, R. (2006) 'Eco-crime' in McLaughlin, E. and Muncie, J. (eds) (2006).

Walters, R. (2007) 'Crime, regulation and radioactive waste' in Beirne, P. and South, N. (eds) (2007).

Walters, R. (2009) *Eco-Crime and Genetically Modified Food*, London, Cavendish-Routledge.

Welfare for Animals Global (2002) *Germany* [online], www.wagny.org/germany (Accessed 13 February 2009).

Westra, L. (2004) *Ecoviolence and the Law: Supranational Normative Foundations of Ecocrime*, Ardsley, NY, Transactional Publishers.

White, R. (2008) *Crimes against Nature: Environmental Criminology and Ecological Justice*, Cullompton, Willan.

Winston, M. (2002) *Travels in the Genetically Modified Zone*, Cambridge, MA, Harvard University Press.

World Commission on Environment and Development (1987) *Our Common Future: Report of the World Commission on Environment and Development* (The Brundtland Report), Oxford, Oxford University Press.

Wortley, R., Mazerolle, L. and Rambouts, S. (eds) (2008) *Environmental Criminology and Crime Analysis*, Cullompton, Willan.

Chapter 7
The state, terrorism and crimes against humanity

Penny Green

Contents

1   Introduction

This chapter focuses on another aspect of 'crimes of the powerful': crimes committed by states – specifically state violence. This topic has long been neglected by or not considered to be the 'proper' remit of criminology. This major gap in the discipline is now slowly being addressed.

The chapter outlines a theoretical and empirical basis for understanding the nature of, and extent to which states engage in, 'crimes' and aims to explore:

- the extent to which nation states are protective or coercive agencies

- how states claim and defend their own sovereignty

- the relationship between states and the individual perpetrators of state violence

- the features of state formations that encourage violent governance

- the role, if any, of globalising forces in the exercise of state violence.

Activity 7.1

What do you think of when you hear the word 'state'? Do you think of democracy, protection, leadership, trust, public services, order, government, peace, stability? Or do other things come to mind, such as violence, lies, scandal, distrust, taxes, bias? What informs your view of the state and is it a reliable source of information?

Comment

Traditionally within criminology, the state is most commonly understood as 'protector' against, rather than perpetrator of, crimes. But states also kill, injure, destroy and plunder with far more serious and widespread consequences than those associated with 'everyday crime'. State crime can take various forms, including corruption and intimidation, violation of health and safety regulations, institutional racism and, of most significance to the discussion in this chapter, torture, terrorism, disappearances, ethnic cleansing and genocide. It might rightly be considered the most serious form of criminality because the monopoly of both violence and legal regulation typically enjoyed by sovereign nation states means that they can inflict violations of human rights with impunity on both foreign nationals and their own citizens.

A key characteristic of all nation states is that they have successfully claimed a monopoly of legitimate use of physical force within their own territory (Weber, 1968; Cover, 1986; Tilly, 1992). They are therefore in a position to perpetrate or instigate the world's most serious violence: the infliction of pain, injury or death in contravention of international or national legal or moral norms (Green and Ward, 2004). It is this illegitimate state violence, or state crime, that is addressed in this chapter. It is also important to recognise that 'State violence needs to be understood both as an expression of state power, and as comprising individual acts of aggression with complex social and psychological relations to other forms of interpersonal violence' (Green and Ward, forthcoming).

Criminal state practice is manifested in a range of guises, of which torture, war crimes and genocide are perhaps the most familiar (at least as they are represented by intermittent media coverage). But state crime as a generic category importantly can also include political corruption, forms of organised crime, state–corporate offending and much of the death and suffering attributed to natural disasters (see Chapters 1, 5 and 6).

This chapter looks specifically at torture and terror as illustrative of crimes against humanity. The concept of 'crimes against humanity' was introduced into international law through the International Military Tribunal at Nuremberg following the Second World War. It refers to a wide range of 'inhumane acts' committed against any civilian population. It is broader than 'war crime' in that it also applies in times of peace, and it differs from 'genocide' because it is not restricted to those specific state practices aimed at eradicating a national, ethnic or religious group through mass murder. Since Nuremberg, the concept of crimes against humanity has been given further legal status through the establishment, in the early twenty-first century, of international criminal tribunals for crimes committed in Rwanda and the former Yugoslavia during the 1990s. But it can also be utilised to bring attention to far wider geopolitical processes that implicate superpowers (i.e. the USA, China and the former USSR), as well as European states, in the transmission and perpetration of, and training for, crimes against humanity in states other than their own. The global reach of state crime, for example, has been secured by practices of imperial domination and colonialism and, more recently, through the dissemination of torture technologies and training. Much of the most excessive state violence requires, in addition, 'the stripping of human dignity' (Glover, 1999, p. 337) from victim groups and their subsequent exclusion from what Helen Fein (1990, 2000) has termed the moral 'universe of obligation' that citizens normally afford each other. This is a process of 'dehumanisation', which historically has tended to be a local process preceding genocide and other forms of massacre (e.g. the dehumanisation of Jews, Gypsies and other groups by the Nazis,

Figure 7.1
Iraqi Kurds fleeing the brutal repression of Saddam's Ba'athist regime (Turkey, 1991)

of Kurds by Iraq's Ba'athist regime, of Cambodia's 'New People' by the Khmer Rouge and of the ruling Tutsis by Rwanda's Hutu peoples). However, with the rise in Islamophobia, which followed the attacks on the US World Trade Center and Pentagon in 2001, the world has arguably witnessed a more global pattern of dehumanisation driven by the international 'war on terror'. The image shown in Figure 7.1 is representative of processes of dehumanisation instigated by states against those deemed to be threatening to state power.

Section 2 defines state crime and the concepts that might be embodied in that definition. Sections 3 and 4 then explore in some detail two major forms of state violence – torture and terror. The chapter concludes with a discussion of how state violence is justified and legitimated, and examines debates about whether state crime should be viewed as 'crime' or whether damaging and violent actions of the state are best understood through discourses of 'social harm'.

2   Defining state crime

Activity 7.2

Read through the reports of 'atrocities' and 'perpetrators' given in the three extracts reproduced below.

What do they have in common? Would you consider these events and behaviours to be indicative of 'crimes' committed by nation states? Are they representative of 'state crime'?

Extract 7.1

Radovan Karadzic delays plea to war crimes charges in The Hague

Peter Walker, Mark Tran and agencies

Radovan Karadzic today asked for more time to enter a plea as he made his first appearance before a war crimes tribunal in The Hague.

... the former Bosnian Serb leader – charged with 11 counts of genocide, war crimes and crimes against humanity – complained he had been 'kidnapped' to appear before the court.

He also attempted, before being stopped by the judge, to outline a complex plot under which he claimed Richard Holbrooke, the senior US diplomat who brokered the 1995 Dayton peace deal in Bosnia, wanted him murdered.

... the Dutch judge, Alphons Orie, read out the long list of allegations.

They include charges connected to the Srebrenica massacre and the long siege of Sarajevo. ...

Once the charges had been outlined Karadzic attempted to complain at length about 'numerous irregularities' in the way he was arrested, the manner of his appearance before the court and the alleged plot involving Holbrooke.

He said Holbrooke had the 'intention to liquidate me' before being told by the judge that this was not the moment for such claims.

He protested, calling it a 'matter of life and death' and warning that Holbrooke's arm 'is long enough to reach me here'. He also talked about an alleged deal reached with Holbrooke under which he would retire from public life in return for immunity.

The combative, occasionally tetchy performance – broadcast live on four of Serbia's five national TV networks – echoed at times that of Slobodan Milosevic when he was tried in the same courtroom.

As with Milosevic, Karadzic's case could drag on for years. Milosevic also presented his own defence and the hearing was regularly delayed, both by the former Serb president's ill health and his delaying tactics. He died in 2006 before a verdict was reached.

Karadzic faces charges of genocide, crimes against humanity and war crimes for allegedly masterminding atrocities throughout Bosnia's 1992–1995 war.

Source: *The Guardian*, 31 July 2008

Extract 7.2

Zimbabwe: UN high commissioner calls for halt to political violence

Mark Tran, Allegra Stratton and agencies

Political violence has corrupted Zimbabwe's presidential election, creating a 'perversion of democracy', the UN's leading human rights official said today.

On the eve of a presidential run-off in which Robert Mugabe is the only person standing, Louise Arbour, the UN high commissioner for human rights, reinforced international criticism of the Zimbabwean government by calling for an immediate halt to human rights abuses by the ruling Zanu-PF party and by the opposition Movement for Democratic Change in some cases.

'Victims and their relatives deserve justice. Those who perpetrate crimes must be held to account,' the former UN war crimes prosecutor said in a statement released in Geneva.

'Serious violations of human rights and the associated impunity attributed mainly to groups linked to the ruling Zanu-PF and, in some cases, to the MDC party, are unacceptable and need to stop immediately. Victims and their relatives deserve justice. Those who perpetrate crimes must be held to account.'

Nearly 40 UN human rights investigators in Geneva called on the 84-year-old Mugabe to heed calls to postpone tomorrow's vote, following attacks that have left over 80 of his political opponents dead and caused Morgan Tsvangirai, the MDC leader, to withdraw.

'We are of the view that no election should take place in the absence of conditions that would guarantee the free, full and equal participation of all citizens in the electoral process,' the independent UN experts said in a joint statement released in Geneva during their annual week-long meeting.

Mugabe, who is set to extend his 28-year rule as he is running unopposed, has dismissed such calls and said there could be no interference in his country, even from the African Union.

Separately, the International Federation for Human Rights urged the UN Human Rights Council to hold a special session on 'gross and systematic human rights violations' in Zimbabwe, including killings, torture, arbitrary arrests and intimidation.

Source: *The Guardian*, 26 June 2008

Extract 7.3

Goldsmith calls for inquiry into Iraq torture

Clare Dyer

The outgoing attorney general, Lord Goldsmith, called yesterday for an investigation into how illegal torture techniques came to be used by British soldiers in Iraq. He said it was a matter of grave concern that techniques such as sleep deprivation, hooding and stress positions were deployed against suspects held by UK forces.

He told MPs and peers in a hearing of the joint committee on human rights: 'These techniques were outlawed on a cross-party basis in 1972. We have to seek why anyone thought these were permissible techniques. I think there needs to be an inquiry.

'I certainly agree that there is a matter of grave concern as to how these techniques came to be used, who authorised them and on what basis.'

Lord Goldsmith told the parliamentary committee that he was only aware such interrogation techniques were being used after Baha Musa, an Iraqi hotel receptionist, died in British custody.

Mr Musa, 26, had been detained under suspicion of being an insurgent. He died in Basra in September 2003. Seven members of the Queen's Lancashire Regiment, which is now the Duke of Lancaster's Regiment, faced the most expensive court martial in British history, but all were eventually acquitted.

One soldier, Corporal Donald Payne, 35, became the first British serviceman to admit a war crime, that of treating Iraqi prisoners inhumanely, and was jailed for a year.

Source: *The Guardian*, 27 June 2007

Comment

These three cases involving Bosnia, Zimbabwe and Iraq are typical of how atrocities and corruption practised in the name of the state are reported in the national media. They refer to war crime, crimes against humanity, human rights violations and genocide but rarely, if ever, to 'state crime'. In this way, these behaviours and events are individualised as symptomatic of 'deranged leaders', 'corrupt politicians' and 'bad apples', rather than being reflective of widespread and systematic state practices.

In contrast, this chapter adopts a definition of state crime as 'violations of human rights perpetrated by agents of the state in the deviant pursuit of organisational goals' (Green and Ward, 2004, pp. 2–6). The primary value of this definition is that it addresses the problem that states as legislators are unlikely, other than in exceptional circumstances, to criminalise their own activities or their own agents. As Marshall B. Clinard and Richard Quinney noted, 'those who legitimate and enforce the law – and determine what is to be regarded as legitimate – are in the position of violating the laws themselves without being criminally defined' (1973, p. 158).

Rather than relying on a legal standard of what is 'criminal', the definition given above is instead embedded in a normative human-rights framework (following Schwendinger and Schwendinger, 1975) combined with criminological conceptions of deviance (see Chapter 1). Deviance here is more complex and more encompassing than illegality. It defines behaviour according to the perceptions of significant social audiences who identify and accept that a rule, which is widely understood as a standard of behaviour, has been breached. Such social audiences might include non-governmental organisations (NGOs), other states, significant sections of the population, victim groups and transnational civil society; and the rule that has been breached might refer to domestic law, international law or social morality as determined by civil society and the state. The deviance of state crime must be in pursuit of organisational goals and driven by organisational demands, and not simply be the actions of state agents operating for personal gain.

Before exploring the nature and extent of state crime, we also need to adopt a coherent and intellectually recognised working definition of the state. Friedrich Engels (1968 [1884]) offers a definition that is both succinct and conceptually valuable. He refers to a 'public power' with a right and need to levy taxes, which controls territory and is made up of personnel organised and equipped for the use of force: this public power consisting 'not merely of armed men but also of material adjuncts, prisons, and institutions of coercion of all kinds' (Engels, 1968 [1884], p. 577). This definition also accommodates those 'proto states' which, while excluded from the international community, include all political entities that deploy organised force, control substantial territories and levy formal or informal taxes (such as the FARC – the Revolutionary Armed Forces of Colombia).

According to C. Wright-Mills, certain dominant institutions in society, such as the military, government and corporations, constitute a 'power elite'. Often the worlds of these three economically, politically and socially powerful groups are interrelated – as relationships between the three are harnessed through commercial arrangements and personnel. When power and wealth become the reserve of specific elites, 'these institutions greatly influence the so-called lesser institutions (i.e. family, education)' (Wright-Mills, quoted in Simon and Eitzen, 1990, p. 10).

A helpful paradigm in explaining elite or organisational deviance has been offered by David Kauzlarich and Ronald C. Kramer (1998). They argue for an approach that integrates structural, organisational and social psychological factors. They propose that 'Criminal behaviour at the organisational level results from a coincidence of pressure for goal attainment, availability and perceived attractiveness of illegitimate means, and an absence or weakness of social control mechanisms' (Kauzlarich and Kramer, 1998, p. 148). The sanctions that follow the identification of state organisational or elite deviance may include legal punishment; censure; rebellion; diplomatic, political or economic sanctions; and efforts to damage a state's reputation.

The state's monopoly over the legitimate use of force is crucial to understanding its illegitimate or criminal use of violence, and presents the student of state crime with a fundamental paradox. The German sociologist Norbert Elias (2000 [1939]) argued that, as the state assumes a monopoly of violence (through processes that involve the centralisation of coercion in armies, police forces, prisons, and so on), a related but counter-development takes place at the level of the individual. Individuals surrender interpersonal violence to the state (Elias, 2000 [1939]; Ward and Young, 2007). Society becomes more 'civilised'. It is the assumption of violence by specialised state agencies that creates the conditions for a reduction of interpersonal violence in civil society.

Activity 7.3

Consider the following questions in light of the quotation from Elias given below:

■ How have nation states assumed a 'monopoly of violence'?

■ What implications does this have for both the protection and the coercion of their citizens?

> When a monopoly of force is formed, pacified social spaces are created which are normally free from acts of violence. The pressures acting on individual people within them are of a different kind than previously ... as monopoly organizations of physical force develop and the individual is held no longer in the sway of constant feuds and wars but rather in the more permanent compulsions of peaceful functions ...
>
> (Elias, 2000 [1939], pp. 369, 372)

Comment

Elias's argument can be summarised in the following way: the development of the state monopoly of violence is inextricably linked with the development of humane sensibilities that are increasingly repulsed by cruelty and interpersonal violence. At the very core of the civilising process, however, we also witness a fundamental paradox. While the state continues to monopolise the exercise of violence and promotes and protects civilised modes of interpersonal behaviour and expression in society, at the same time it perpetrates widespread and highly organised acts of extreme violence towards certain categories of its citizens. The paradox, as Penny Green and Tony Ward put it, is: 'If states depend on a monopoly of organized violence ... but cultivate an abhorrence of violence, why does this not lead to abhorrence, or at least a deep unease, at the state's own practices?' (2009a, p. 236). Understanding state crime relies on an understanding of state structures and the role of violence in both the development and maintenance of modern states. The state's monopoly of the legitimate use of force is crucial to explaining the extremes of state violence with which this chapter is most concerned.

3   Torture

Torture is a crime that is corrosive of the body politic – it debilitates not only the victims who suffer it, but also the perpetrators and states that carry it out. In this section we explore current debates surrounding modern torture, drawing on a wide range of political, social and psychological scholarship.

Activity 7.4

Before reading this section, consider your immediate reactions to the following critical questions:

■   What is torture?

■   Against whom do you think it is practised?

■   Is torture a widespread or an isolated phenomenon?

■   Can torture ever be justified?

Comment

The United Nations Convention against Torture and Other Cruel, Inhuman or Degrading Treatment or Punishment defines torture as follows:

> ... any act by which severe pain or suffering, whether physical or mental, is intentionally inflicted on a person for such purposes as obtaining from him or a third person information or a confession, punishing him for an act he or a third person has committed or is suspected of having committed, or intimidating or coercing

him or a third person, or for any reason based on discrimination of any kind, when such pain or suffering is inflicted by or at the instigation of or with the consent or acquiescence of a public official or other person acting in an official capacity. It does not include pain or suffering arising only from, inherent in or incidental to lawful sanctions.

(Office of the High Commissioner for Human Rights, 1984)

This definition was adopted by the United Nations General Assembly in 1984. However, despite almost universal condemnation and an international prohibition from which no derogation is entertained, torture is practised widely in the twenty-first century. By 2006, 144 states had ratified the Convention against Torture and Other Cruel, Inhuman or Degrading Treatment or Punishment, yet cases of torture and ill-treatment by security forces, police and other state authorities had been documented in at least 102 countries (Amnesty International, 2008). While this is an apparent improvement on the years between 1997 and 2000, during which time torture had been documented in over three-quarters of the world (i.e. 150 countries) (Amnesty International, 2001a), the issue remains. For example, images of American soldiers torturing Iraqi prisoners in Abu Ghraib prison, revelations about the use of extraordinary rendition to transfer prisoners to torturing regimes for the purpose of interrogation, and the testimony of those released from the US prison camp at Guantánamo Bay all revealed to a global public the widespread practice of torture.

Figure 7.2
Accounts of the torture, sodomy and abuse of Iraqi prisoners in Abu Ghraib prison first came to light in 2004

In the wake of the al-Qaeda attacks on New York and the Pentagon in September 2001, the Republican Administration of George Bush, capitalising on the climate of fear and chaos, introduced a raft of repressive new security measures that undermined civil liberties in a way unprecedented in recent US history. The PATRIOT Act 2001 enabled the US Government to arrest and detain people in conditions of secrecy for indefinite periods if there are 'reasonable grounds' that may constitute a threat to national security. Those captured in the 'war on terror' have been labelled 'enemy non-combatants' and held in Guantánamo Bay in 'degrading conditions of duress' without charge or access to legal representation. Rather, their cases were to be heard before military tribunals in contravention of guarantees to a fair trial.

Within this climate of fear and repression a new and heretofore unheard of willingness on the part of politicians, academics and journalists to engage in a debate over the legitimacy of torture has emerged. In this debate, proponents of 'preventive interrogational torture' (especially US law professors Alan Dershowitz and John Yoo) have sought to challenge the universal prohibition against torture (see Greenberg, 2006). These advocates of partially legitimised torture have argued that because of a perceived 'new and extraordinary' threat that Western democracies now face from international terrorism, new and extraordinary measures are required to protect national security. Employing the hypothetical 'ticking bomb scenario' – which posits that the only way to locate a deadly bomb that is primed to go off within twenty-four hours is to torture the terrorist who 'knows' where it is – they have argued vociferously for the legitimisation of 'torture lite' as a means to counter terrorism (Dershowitz, 2004; Luban, 2006).

Elaine Scarry (2004), Henry Shue (2004), David Luban (2006) and others have argued, however, that it is a delusion to imagine that the 'cruelty and tyranny' embodied in torture could be confined to and contained in an inherently flawed hypothetical example. The delusion is magnified by the context of an escalating war on terror, which involves the rapid introduction of emergency powers and a raft of repressive anti-terrorist legislation. This was exemplified in George Bush's 8 March 2008 veto of legislation that would have banned the CIA (the US Central Intelligence Agency) from using forms of torture such as waterboarding (a method of torture that induces the experience of suffocation and drowning in the victim) in the interrogation of suspected terrorists, in which he declared in justification: 'This is no time for Congress to abandon practices that have a proven track record of keeping America safe' (Associated Press, 2008).

3.1 The nature of torture

Edward Peters (1996) provides a harrowing historical record of torture practices. These include: beatings such as jumping on the victim's stomach; *falacca* or *falanga*, which involves beating the soles of the feet with rods; *telephono*, where the torturer claps flattened palms over the victim's ears rupturing the tympanic membrane in the process; the use of electricity, including tying victims to a metal bed before applying a current and the use of pointed electrodes placed on the victim's genitalia; burning ('including roasting on a red hot grill'); *submarino*, the submersion of the victim's head in dirty water until the point of suffocation is almost reached; rape and forced sexual assault; suspension in mid-air with knees bent over a rod and tied tightly to wrists; deprivation of water; fake executions; the forced witnessing of the torture of the victim's family or children; being held incommunicado; sensory deprivation; the forced injection of psychotropic drugs or 'faecal matter' (Peters, 1996, pp. 169–71).

Historically, torture has been a tool of repressive governance – not, as popular fictional and mass media portrayals suggest, an instrument of criminal investigation or intelligence gathering. In its political sense, Ariel Dorfman captures the essence of torture when he defines states of terror as the 'aftermath of torture':

> We live in times where it is no longer abhorrent to express the need to apply electricity to the genitals of a prisoner or tear out his fingernails or keep him for days on end in a cage and blindfolded, if that will save our skin, protect our children, foster our security. The times, the country we live in, allow torture to be applied, as it always has been, in our name by allies and so-called friends and partners.
>
> (Dorfman, 2004, p. 5)

Torture, from this reading, is the method by which terror is instilled in a subject population; a strategy of silencing oppositional and dissenting voices and, through this process, silencing the whole community. Torture is a means of terrorising a community. At the level of the personal, Scarry articulates the impact of torture on the individual as 'world destroying' (1985, p. 29). By this she means that the infliction of intense pain by state agents (perpetrators) against prisoners (internal enemies) destroys the possibility of agency for the prisoner, it takes away the possibility of voice. As Green and Ward note, 'If the state perpetrates or tacitly condones the terror there can be no escape, no other world' (2004, p. 127).

Following an extensive survey of the literature on torture, Green and Ward (2004) isolated a number of structural variables that tend to be present in torturing regimes and which might be understood as important explanatory preconditions of torture. These variables include:

- a historical devaluation of a section of the population

- a strong respect for authority

- a monolithic culture that enjoys a high degree of popular identification (i.e. Staub's 'cultural self-concept' [1989, p. 54] evidenced most strongly in countries such as Nazi Germany, modern Turkey, and Cambodia and Argentina in the 1970s)

- the clear designation of an enemy within the dominant ideology (e.g. Jews in Nazi Germany, 'subversives' in Argentina, Kurdish militants in Turkey – see Staub, 1989, p .62).

When these structural preconditions exist, it is easier for individuals to dispense with socialised inhibitions against the infliction of cruelty. This is exemplified in the discussion on victims and perpetrators below.

3.2 Victims

Victims of torture tend to be of two kinds: either they represent or are perceived to represent some form of political, social or cultural opposition to the ruling regime, or they tend to come from the marginalised, criminalised and impoverished sections of society (Amnesty International, 2000). In the years following the 9/11 attacks, the victims of US-sanctioned torture have included those, such as British-born Muslim Moazzam Begg, whose stories exemplify the global interstices through which targeted repression is carried out in the twenty-first century. Over 800 prisoners have passed through Guantánamo Bay, Baghram Airbase and the other secret detention and torture centres around the world.

In 2001, Begg travelled to Afghanistan with his wife and three young children to work as an aid worker in education and water projects. Following 9/11 and the subsequent US bombing of Afghanistan, he relocated to Pakistan. It was here that he was abducted by the CIA in front of his wife and children before being forcibly transported to illegal imprisonment in Afghanistan's Baghram Airbase, labelled an 'enemy combatant' and tortured before being rendered to Guantánamo Bay. He was released in January 2005 after almost three years of confinement without being charged.

Activity 7.5

Read the two extracts below. The first is a testimony from Begg. The second is a newspaper report that identifies how governments sometimes seek to silence or suppress the testimonies of tortured victims. When you have read the extracts, consider the following question: what are the broader personal, political and social implications of torture?

Extract 7.4

While I was held in Baghram, it was probably one of the hardest periods of the whole of the incarceration. One particular month in May, I was subjected to some extremely harsh interrogation techniques, which included being – or having my hands tied behind my back to my legs like an animal, as they call in America 'hogtied,' with a hood placed over my head so I was in a suffocating position, kicked and beaten and sworn at and spat at, left to rot in this position for hours and hours on end and taken again into interrogation, and this lasted over a period of over a month.

That wasn't the worst of it, of course. The worst of it, for me, was the psychological part, because all of this time I had no communication with my family at all. I didn't know what happened to my wife or my children. For all I knew, they could have done terrible things to them. And that was the biggest fear.

(Moazzam Begg, quoted in Democracy Now!, *2006)*

Extract 7.5

Miliband fails in court bid to keep 'torture proof' secret

Robert Verkaik

The Foreign Secretary, David Miliband, has failed to persuade the High Court that evidence which could help prove the innocence of a British resident held in Guantánamo Bay must remain secret.

Lord Justice Thomas and Mr Justice Lloyd Jones ruled yesterday that Mr Miliband had not properly considered allegations of 'medieval' torture made by Binyam Mohamed against his captors.

Mr Mohamed, 30, an Egyptian national who came to Britain in 1994 seeking asylum, says MI6 intelligence supports his case that confessions he made were extracted under torture.

The court, which has already ruled that the Government possesses potentially vital evidence relating to Mr Mohamed's defence against terrorism allegations, gave the Foreign Office a further week to reconsider its application for an order banning disclosure of the information.

The court found that Mr Miliband's evaluation 'failed to address, in light of the allegations made by [Binyam Mohamed], the abhorrence and condemnation accorded to torture, cruel, inhuman or degrading treatment.'

At the same time the Government was accused of misleading MPs who last year investigated claims that Britain was indirectly involved in the kidnap and torture of terror suspects.

Andrew Tyrie MP, chair of the all-party parliamentary group on rendition, said the judges' ruling 'confirmed the concern I have had for several years: that the UK is complicit in extraordinary rendition.'

Mr Mohamed faces a possible US death penalty over claims that he was an al-Qa'ida member.

Source: *The Independent*, 30 August 2008

Comment

Torture inflicts profound damage, not only on victims and their communities, but also on the individuals and regimes that deploy it, as Marguerite Feitlowitz captures so eloquently:

> Torture is a crime that never ends: It is written on the body, inscribed in the mind and seared into the soul. Neither individuals nor regimes nor societies survive unscathed. The secrets and shame, lies, guilt and corruption last for generations – censoring rational thought, inhibiting democratic impulses, hobbling democratic institutions.
>
> (Feitlowitz, 2005)

Torture has a profound impact on the victim, on the victim's family and on the community from which the victim comes. Medical Foundations for Victims of Torture around the world report the intergenerational damage inflicted on children and grandchildren of torture survivors (Bamber, 1995; Marton, 1995). Survivors report a panoply of medical, psychological, social, economic and political traumas that follow from torture. The traumatic consequences of torture are compounded by what Elizabeth Stanley describes as their 'silenc[ing] in the wake of their violation' (2008, p. 57). The impact is also one of political subjugation: 'In this sense torture can be understood as an act of cultural transformation moulding and shaping societies within its framework of, often arbitrary, cruelty – creating in its wake dislocated, apathetic and fearful populations who withdraw from public life' (Green and Ward, 2004, p. 139). Moreover, the newspaper article in Extract 7.5 reports how personal accounts of torture are sometimes prevented from coming to public view. In this case, a senior government minister has actively attempted to silence the views of a tortured detainee, even when such evidence could prevent the detainee from facing a death penalty. This further identifies the pervasive nature of torture to include government and legal institutions that rule to either release or suppress victim testimonies.

3.3 Perpetrators

Perpetrators of torture must be understood in their broadest incarnation in order to fully grasp the global networks that define and sustain this crime against humanity. This section examines, in turn, those torturers who physically carry out acts of torture and those torturers who trade and train in torture technologies.

Torturers

Torturers (those who physically and psychologically inflict torture) are, in almost every documented case, drawn from the ranks of serving police officers and military personnel (Feitlowitz, 1998; Huggins et al., 2002). Being comfortable with strict hierarchical working arrangements and acquiescence to unquestioning obedience to authority appear to be essential preconditions for becoming a torturer. Given these preconditions, a broad range of research supports Janice Gibson's findings that 'individual personality and background information about individuals, by themselves, cannot distinguish individuals who will commit torture or other cruel acts from those who will not' (Gibson, 1990, p. 79). Studies into the Nazi doctors who participated in torture (Lifton, 1986), into the Einsatzgruppen Nazi paramilitary death squads (Staub, 1989) and into torturers under the military regime of the Greek Colonels (1967–74) (Haritos-Fatouros, 1988) equally suggest that torturers are, in many senses of the word, 'normal'. Attempting to explain how normal people can engage in acts of appalling cruelty brings us back to one of criminology's primary questions – what is it that causes individuals to deviate from legal and moral norms? There are, it seems, four potentially crucial factors in the making of a torturer: membership of elite hierarchical coercive state agencies; the existence of institutional enclaves of barbarism; ideological predispositions; and training.

The famous Stanford prison experiment, in which volunteers were given the roles of prisoners and guards in a simulated prison (Haney et al., 1973), demonstrated the relative ease by which non-sadistic individuals could disengage from humane sensibilities and behave in a cruel and sadistic manner in given institutional settings. Similarly, Stanley Milgram, following his disturbing studies into obedience and authority in which subjects were instructed by a scientist to inflict pain on other subjects, wrote: 'This is perhaps the most fundamental lesson of our study: ordinary people simply doing their jobs, without any particular hostility on their part, can become agents in a terrible destructive process' (Milgram, 1974, p. 6). What this and other research (e.g. Lifton, 1986) suggests is that certain institutional settings have the capacity to produce great cruelty. They are, as Robert Lifton describes, 'atrocity-producing' (1986, p. 425).

Abram de Swaan has argued that, in order to create the conditions under which systematic torture can be perpetrated, it is necessary for states to create discrete, compartmentalised enclaves of barbarism in which civilised norms do not apply. In these terrifying spaces de Swaan argues that 'wildness and brutality are let loose, or maybe even instilled, and at the same time instrumentalized, for specific purposes, within demarcated spaces at an appointed time: an archipelago of enclaves where cruelty reigns while being reined in all the time' (de Swaan, 2001, p. 269). But beyond the impact of the 'atrocity-producing' institution there appear to be certain ideological features that offer an important explanatory component in the making of a torturer. Vehement anti-communism, attraction to fascist ideology and high levels of respect, deference and obedience to authority, it has been argued, all appear to predispose a person to the role of torturer (Lifton, 1986; Haritos-Fatouros, 1988; Staub, 1989; Gibson, 1990). As such, 'perpetrators both select themselves for their role and are selected by those in authority' (Staub, 1989, p. 56).

Torture trainers and traders

Engagement in torture normally also requires training and there are well-documented accounts that demonstrate the impact of humiliating and brutalising methods on trainees. Evidence from Greece, Brazil and Argentina suggests that training forms an important initiation rite, 'providing prospective torturers with social modelling and systematic desensitisation to acts of violence' (Gibson, 1990, p. 85), as well as schooling them in techniques that employ scientific knowledge about bodily and psychological capacities. Training implies structural resources. It requires a network of state officials (facilitators and perpetrators) who may include military personnel, police officers, prison officers, medical professionals, judges, magistrates and psychologists (Chomsky and Herman, 1979; Rejali, 1994; Cohen, 2001).

In 2004, the systematic and institutionally sanctioned torture of Iraqi prisoners by US soldiers in Iraq's Abu Ghraib prison came to world attention. Images of grinning American soldiers standing over shackled, naked and hooded Iraqi men in demeaning, sexually humiliating and contorted positions shocked the liberal conscience of the Western world. Rather than the aberrant behaviour of an isolated few, it became clear that the nine soldiers who were court-martialled for the crimes were in fact responding to orders issued from the highest levels of military and government command (Hersh, 2004). Following the leaking of the report, Major General Taguba was summoned to meet with Secretary of Defense, Donald Rumsfeld, in his Pentagon office:

> In the meeting, the officials professed ignorance about Abu Ghraib. 'Could you tell us what happened?' Wolfowitz asked. Someone else asked, 'Is it abuse or torture?' At that point, Taguba recalled, 'I described a naked detainee lying on the wet floor, handcuffed, with an interrogator shoving things up his rectum, and said, "That's not abuse. That's torture." There was quiet.'
>
> (Hersh, 2007)

For his efforts to expose and denounce torture within the US military, General Taguba was forced to resign (Hersh, 2007).

Alfred McCoy, in his analysis of CIA interrogation between the Cold War and the war on terror, argues that Abu Ghraib was simply a culmination of 'CIA torture methods that have metastasized like an undetected cancer inside the U.S. intelligence community over the past half century' (McCoy, 2006, p. 5). Other liberal democracies, particularly France and the UK, have also played a crucial role in the global spread of state terror. Western involvement in torture training and the trade in torture has a long and unedifying history. Despite claims of human rights considerations and 'ethical' foreign policies, a range of liberal democracies offer authoritarian regimes both training in counter-insurgency methods and trade in the instruments of torture. Between 1998 and 2000, Amnesty International identified the USA as the country with the greatest number of manufacturers, distributors, suppliers or brokers of leg irons, shackles, gang chains or thumb cuffs. While Amnesty International identified twenty-two such companies operating in the USA, other countries, specifically Germany, the UK, South Africa, Taiwan, France, Spain and China, are also home to companies manufacturing and dealing in torture technologies (Amnesty International, 2001c).

Begg, whose story was discussed in Section 3.2, reported:

> When I was in Guantánamo Bay, one of the things I pointed out to my lawyer was how it was ironic that these shackles were made in England, just like me and him. It was very bizarre. Those shackles would often cut into my arms and legs and make me bleed. It was those very same shackles I saw being used by American soldiers in Baghram airbase to hang a prisoner from the ceiling. It said 'Made in England' on there too. If these cuffs are used to shackle people up to the tops of ceilings or cages and then [those people are] beaten, it calls into question what those shackles are actually being used for.
>
> (Amnesty International, 2007, p. 17)

McCoy has argued that much of the abuse generated by the terror regimes of Latin America and Asia in the 1970s and 1980s had its origins in the USA: 'While dictatorships in those regions would no doubt have tortured on their own, U.S. training programmes provided sophisticated techniques, up-to-date equipment, and moral legitimacy for the practice, producing a clear correspondence between U.S. Cold War policy and the extreme state violence of the authoritarian age' (McCoy, 2006, p. 11).

The Western Hemisphere Institute for Security Cooperation (WHINSEC), better known in its former incarnation as the School of the Americas (SOA), is a US Department of Defense Spanish language-training establishment with a long history of training the military and police leaders of brutal regimes. Located in Fort Benning, Georgia, the facility has played a crucial role in training torturers, particularly those from Latin American dictatorships. Senior members of the Argentine and Chilean Juntas, military officers from Panama and the officer corps of Guatemala's brutal counter-insurgency military were all trained in the American art of counter-insurgency at the SOA. The SOA's training manuals (1982–1991), which came to light in 1996, advocated torture, beatings, blackmail and executions as central to counter-insurgency and were distributed for training purposes in Colombia, Ecuador, El Salvador, Guatemala and Peru (Kepner, 2001).

The French colonial experience in Indochina and, particularly, Algeria during the 1950s and early 1960s was exported and recrafted in Latin America during the 1970s. Rita Maran records the French military's triumphal advice, 'Torture is the particular bane of the terrorist ... reports of results are magnificent' (Maran, 1989, p. 49). Such acts of state terror have been depicted in internationally acclaimed films; for example, Gillo Pontecorvo's 1965 cinematic masterpiece, *The Battle of Algiers*, provides a compelling account of French terror in the Algerian struggle for independence.

Elsewhere in Latin America the Guatemalan Historical Clarification Commission (set up to investigate human rights violations during the country's long (1960–96) period of civil conflict) charged the USA with a willingness:

> ... to provide support for strong military regimes in its strategic backyard. In the case of Guatemala, military assistance was directed towards reinforcing the national intelligence apparatus and for training the officer corps in counterinsurgency techniques, key factors which had significant bearing on human rights violations during the armed confrontation.
>
> (Cited in Amnesty International, 2001c, p. 44)

What this discussion of both the international trade and training in torture technologies illustrates is that torture itself, while often understood as a local phenomenon restricted to particularly repressive regimes, is essentially a powerful component of global structures of dominance. WHINSEC's training manuals and equivalent training manuals and programmes propagated by the West also have the effect of tying weaker developing states into violent forms of governance.

3.4 Extraordinary rendition

In this section we examine the phenomenon by which ostensibly non-torturing states outsource their torture requirements to torturing states. This practice, known as 'extraordinary rendition', is the final (but perhaps not exhaustively so) means by which the global reach of torture should be understood. In March 2005, *The New York Times* exposed the Bush Government for 'putting prisoners in the hands of outlaw regimes for the specific purpose of having someone else torture them' (*New York Times*, 2005). Following the events of 9/11, President Bush had given broad authority to the CIA to export or 'render' terrorist suspects to torturing regimes for interrogation purposes. These regimes included Syria, Egypt, Jordan, Uzbekistan and the special CIA torture prisons established in Poland and Romania. The US administration has, however, required the cooperation of other European states in the rendition process. Reprieve (a human rights NGO building legal support for prisoners and Guantánamo Bay detainees) documented the role of Scotland in assisting the CIA's torture transfers to some of the world's most cruel regimes. Glasgow Prestwick Airport was identified as a 'crucial "staging point" in the renditions' circuits', specifically as a refuelling port for CIA rendition jets carrying kidnapped prisoners to Poland, Romania, Jordan, Egypt and Uzbekistan: the latter being notorious for torture practices that involved boiling parts of the body, ripping out fingernails and toenails, asphyxiation with a gas mask, and administering electric shocks to genitalia (Reprieve, 2007, p. 1).

According to Reprieve, these CIA missions would have been impossible without the support offered by cooperative states. In early 2008, despite previous denials from Prime Minister Tony Blair, it was also revealed that US aircraft used British facilities on the British Indian Ocean territory of Diego Garcia in 2002 to transport rendered terrorist suspects (Elliot and Gibb, 2008). These revelations were not initiated by the government but rather by the research and persistence of NGOs like Reprieve and of campaigning journalists.

4   State terror and terrorism

Although the United Nations has struggled for decades with, and has yet to agree, a definition of terrorism, in its most commonly accepted formulation 'terrorism' is understood as the clandestine use of violence against civilian targets for purposes of intimidation, or to create a climate of fear, in pursuit of political goals.

This dominant definition is typically ideologically associated with non-state actors; however, it can also be applied to state actors. Two other forms of terror deployed by states fall outside this definition: the violent intimidation of civilian targets by uniformed state agents, which lacks the clandestine character usually associated with the 'terrorist' label; and assassinations and extra-judicial executions where these are used to eliminate specific targets rather than primarily to intimidate others. The latter are frequently carried out by covert death squads with close ties to the state. Terrorism is 'lodged in the space where contests over conceptions of legitimacy and violence overlap' (Ward and Young, 2007, p. 236).

Activity 7.6

Why do you think terrorism is most commonly associated only with non-state actors?

Make a few notes before you read on.

Comment

The understanding of terrorism as solely an anti-state activity holds powerful sway in influential intellectual circles. For example, the 'definitive' global database on terrorist incidents – produced jointly by the Rand Corporation and St Andrews University in Scotland – excludes incidents of state terror and includes incidents involving Western state armies of occupation only when they are victims and not when they are perpetrators of violence (Poole, 2006). It is easy to see how a limited definition of terrorism is perpetuated when commentators rely on databases such as this. It is, however, difficult to find support for this limitation in either empirical, theoretical or historical terms, as explored below.

4.1 Analysing terror

Terrorism first emerged as a modern political idea during the French Revolution: 'It was a violence visited by the state on its enemies, not a strike against sovereignty by its faceless foes' (Eagleton, 2005, p. 1). To accept a definition of terrorism as confined to sub- or non-state actors is to accept the ideologically distorted use of the term by those who employ terror as a means of governance and as a strategy for national security. The appropriation of the term 'terrorism' to apply solely to acts of political violence against state targets therefore requires critical analysis.

Although non-state actors are most commonly associated with terrorism (in terms of mass media and government representations of public enemies), many have argued that the most powerful, brutal and extensive purveyors of terror are governments and their proxies (Gareau, 2004; Green and Ward, 2004; Franks, 2006; Chomsky, 2007). States around the globe, in varying degrees, have engaged in systematic, clandestine, illegal and violent activities in order to induce fear in the population to advance political goals. They have done so overtly, covertly and ambiguously. It may seem contradictory to speak of states overtly engaging in clandestine activity, but this paradox is inherent in the nature of some forms of state terror. Even when acts of terror, such as the Indonesian massacres in East Timor (discussed further in Section 4.2) and the destruction of Kurdish homes and communities in the 1990s in south-eastern Turkey, are performed by uniformed agents of the state, attempts at concealment (at least of the state's role) are usually made: 'Modern state terror is a form of deviant behaviour, which breaks widely accepted norms (usually including the state's own laws) and which must therefore be concealed or denied' (Green and Ward, 2004, p. 107). However, combined with the concealment and denial of torture and murder, modern states must make these acts known, particularly within the targeted communities, in order for them to be effective as terror (Graziano, 1992; Campbell, 2000). One of the most powerful ways in which this is achieved is through the use of 'death squads' and 'disappearances'. For example, as Frederick Gareau has graphically documented:

> The Pinochet military regime [in Chile between 1973 and 1990] deployed a range of unimaginably cruel methods of terror. Opposition prisoners would be heavily sedated and flown in helicopters over the Pacific Ocean. Whilst in the aircraft their stomachs would be sliced open so that when they were thrown into the water far below they would sink without trace.
>
> (Gareau, 2004, p. 82)

Activity 7.7

Make notes on the following questions:

■ Why, if states already exercise a monopoly of violence, do they need to turn to the tactics of terror?

■ Is terror a rational action on their part?

Comment

A useful means of analysing state terror has been through the lens of 'instrumental rationality'. States (and particularly their coercive agencies) tend to be goal-directed organisations characterised by operationally efficient methodologies designed to maximise goal achievement. Drawing on the work of Kauzlarich and Kramer (1998) and Ted Gurr (1986), Green and Ward (2004) explored the rationality of state terror using three concepts: motivation, opportunity structure and social control. In motivational terms they found that states are more likely to employ terror against domestic enemies when:

■ the threat posed by oppositional forces is deemed significant

- the oppositional forces are grounded in strong community support

- the opposition themselves employ political violence

- the opposition has no links to the ruling elite (i.e. is socially marginal)

- there is a strong commitment to ideological goals (e.g. anti-communism).

As with other areas of criminological study, opportunity structures relate to means (legitimate or illegitimate) available for goal attainment. States are motivated to resort to terror and repression for a variety of reasons, not least by the availability, or not, of other means of conflict resolution. If those alternative means are absent and the resources available for repression are present, then states, given the conditions outlined in relation to opportunity structures, are likely to engage in state terror. Charles Brockett (1991) offers the comparative examples of Honduras, Guatemala and El Salvador in the 1980s to illustrate this point: Honduras faced a rebel threat of comparable severity to that of its neighbours, but although it employed a CIA-trained death squad to 'disappear' and torture suspected guerrillas, it never engaged in the extreme and wide-scale murder and destruction that characterised state repression in El Salvador and Guatemala (McClintock, 1985; Schirmer, 1998). Brockett (1991) argues that because Honduras had a weak army, less coercive and exploitative rural class relations than Guatemala or El Salvador, and sufficient land available to concede some of the peasant movement's demands, it did not perceive the guerrilla threat as demanding such an extreme response.

Terror, however, also appears to be underpinned by high degrees of irrationality. Terror regimes are usually energised by ideologies that distort the reality of their political experience. They are also driven by dangerously unrealistic aspirations in relation to social and economic control. In this sense, state terrorists may be seen to act rationally on the basis of irrational 'maps' of social reality. In their irrational ideological worlds all forms of political opposition and social dissent may come to be seen as 'violent subversion' and the murder and torture of those so defined becomes justified as a rational response to great threat (cf. Pion-Berlin, 1989; Graziano, 1992).

The Argentinian officers of the 'Dirty War' (1976–83) – a period of repression and terror, in which an estimated 25,000 or 30,000 people were 'disappeared', tortured and in most cases killed – were convinced of the legitimacy of their war against the evil of international communism (Osiel, 1997). The 'paranoid script' from which they operated served to silence dissent (Suárez-Orozco, 1992, p. 234). Equally, the 'irrational' goals of Pol Pot's genocidal Khmer Rouge regime, particularly that of returning Cambodia to 'year zero' (a radical form of agrarian communism where the whole population had to work in collective farms or forced labour projects), drove policies of execution, starvation, torture, forced labour and disappearances. In pursuit of this ambition, the Khmer Rouge murdered between 850,000 and 2 million people (Chandler, 1999).

4.2 Governance through political violence

Terror, as Noam Chomsky and Ed Herman (1979) argue, is a form of governance that is less a strategy of punishment and more a form of brutal political control. Governance through terror requires extensive physical and technical resources and the monopoly over the systematic performance of violence that only states are capable of acquiring. Only states and powerful proto states, such as the Colombian FARC, have the physical resources and the monopoly of violence required for systematic terror of this kind. As Herman writes, torture as one of the operating tools of terror is thus characterised by 'standard operating procedures in multiple detention centres, applicable to hundreds of detainees and used with the approval and intent of the highest authorities' (Herman, 1982, pp. 113–14).

Two examples, from Cambodia and Argentina, will suffice:

> In Cambodia's Tuol Sleng, the terror complex created by the Khmer Rouge, human rights researchers found torture manuals, torturers' biographies, thorough prison records, detailed accounts of interrogations, confessions and medical examinations and elaborate diagnostic flow charts apparently detailing the interrelationship of enemy networks derived from forced confessions.
>
> (Hawk, 1986, p. 25)

In Argentina at the height of the 'Dirty War', there existed 'a huge torture complex which has at its disposal the most modern and sophisticated equipment, and which requires an increasing number of staff – jailers, drivers, executioners, typists, public relations officers, doctors and others ... a network of some 340 secret torture centres and concentration camps' (Feitlowitz, 1998, p. 8). For the regime, the network was required to destroy the 'hidden enemy', to rid the world of subversive forces (i.e. intellectuals, writers, trade unionists, psychologists, journalists) and to impose a world of Catholic military order.

As Chomsky (2007) reports, states have also increasingly outsourced the exercise of terror for 'public relations' reasons. By privatising the delivery of terror, states themselves can both condemn the brutal excesses of paramilitaries and offer 'plausible denials' in relation to their own role in

Figure 7.3
The Museum of
Genocidal Crimes in
Cambodia was formerly
used by the Khmer
Rouge as a detention
and torture centre in
the late 1970s

the conduct of violence against oppositional and marginal groups. In Colombia, paramilitaries tasked with carrying out the most horrendous atrocities have been widely described as the 'sixth division' of the Colombian armed forces. According to Human Rights Watch:

> ... the relationships described ... involve active coordination during military operations between government and paramilitary units; communication via radios, cellular telephones, and beepers; the sharing of intelligence, including the names of suspected guerrilla collaborators; the sharing of fighters, including active-duty soldiers serving in paramilitary units and paramilitary commanders lodging on

Figure 7.4
About 30,000 people were 'disappeared' in Argentina during the 'Dirty War': a seven-year campaign by the Argentine government against suspected dissidents between 1976 and 1983

military bases; the sharing of vehicles, including army trucks used to transport paramilitary fighters; coordination of army roadblocks, which routinely let heavily-armed paramilitary fighters pass; and payments made from paramilitaries to military officers for their support.

(Human Rights Watch, 2001, p. 1)

The 1975 invasion of East Timor by Indonesia resulted in the murder of 200,000 Timorese people (i.e. one-third of the total population) and thousands more were subjected to atrocities committed by the Indonesian military and its pro-Indonesian paramilitary proxies. Throughout the period of occupation (1975–99) they conducted a campaign of terror against the East Timorese people, including: indiscriminate shooting of unarmed groups of civilians; the ordering of victims to dig their own graves before execution; execution of unarmed individuals at close range; secret burials without any attempt to identify victims; public beheadings; cannibalism and amputation of body parts; public display of decapitated heads, ears and genitalia; immolation; crucifixion; ordering of victims to line up in formation before line-by-line execution; parading of corpses; abductions and disappearances; rape; torture; and the execution of detainees in detention centres (CAVR, 2005).

Terror as a form of coercive governance requires resources commonly available only to states, yet because of issues relating to recognisable deviance and political legitimacy it is also accompanied by systematic patterns of denial. The outsourcing by states of the exercise of terror is part of this process of concealment and denial.

5   Globalisation and state violence

As this chapter has argued, the study of state crime demands an internationalist perspective. While the most brutal forms of state violence and terror might indeed be conducted by authoritarian states (normally in the so-called developing world), Western democratic states, as we have seen, have played a crucial role in the globalisation and legitimation of that violence. According to Michael McClintock, for example, the US military doctrine of counter-insurgency has legitimated state terror globally as a means of confronting dissent and subversion. He identified specific organisational forms that characterise terror states – paramilitary irregulars, elite special forces and powerful centralised military intelligence forces – and located them firmly in the legacy of counter-insurgency doctrine (McClintock, 1992). One of Argentina's most brutal state terrorists, General Ramon Camps, who controlled the Buenos Aires province police force, reported that:

> In Argentina we were influenced first by the French and then by the United States. We used their methods separately at first and then together, until the United States' ideas finally predominated. France and the United States were our main sources of counterinsurgency training. They organized centres for teaching counterinsurgency techniques (especially in the US) and sent out instructors, observers, and an enormous amount of literature.
>
> (Quoted in Gareau, 2004, p. 103)

The report of the Chilean National Commission on Truth and Reconciliation made explicit the 'dyscivilizing' impact of the US doctrine of counter-insurgency. Instruction and training of the Pinochet regime (1973–90), by Western agents, in anti-guerrilla warfare, the laying of ambushes, survival techniques and 'special' methods of killing, 'All of this' the report stated, 'gradually accustomed the student to the fact that ethical limits were receding and diminishing, sometimes to vanishing point' (quoted in Gareau, 2004, p. 80).

But there is another arena in which globalisation impacts on state violence, and that relates to resistance. Within the limitations frequently enforced through political censorship (e.g. media portrayal of the first Gulf War), modern communications have increasingly made possible the physical portrayal of state violence:

> One link between terror and globalisation is that what happens in these enclaves and unpacified spaces affects not only adjacent, pacified spaces, but individuals at a great distance. American and British families are bereaved in Iraq; Muslims and Jews on other continents can identify with the sufferings of their co-religionists in the Middle East. Of course, this is not a new phenomenon.

The novelty of globalisation is often exaggerated. But global media (including the internet) significantly amplify the impact of acts of violence by and against states, and the scope for developing global networks united by solidarity with their victims or perpetrators.

(Ward and Young, 2007, p. 244)

And while transnational civil society, through global networks, may contribute a sense of solidarity and practical support to domestic struggles against torture and terror, it would be wrong to assume that 'globalisation' is an inherently liberating tool. Film footage of the massacre at Santa Cruz cemetery in East Timor on 12 November 1991 provoked international condemnation of Indonesia when it was shown around the world, and certainly placed Indonesia under unprecedented scrutiny in relation to its human rights abuses in the region. But as the Commission for Reception, Truth and Reconciliation in East Timor reported: 'even in the face of strong international demands to bring those who had killed unarmed demonstrators to account, the institutional practices of ABRI/TNI [the armed forces of Indonesia] provided the majority of perpetrators who were most responsible with effective impunity' (CAVR, 2005, p. 205).

Equally, the widely publicised genocide perpetrated against the population of Darfur elicited only a limited response from the international community, while China has explicitly supported the Sudanese Government as it has pursued its economic interests in the region (purchasing two-thirds of Sudan's oil production and supplying arms to Khartoum). The power of China's veto on the UN Security Council has been to block Western moves to impose sanctions on Sudan (Human Rights Watch, 2003).

5.1 States of denial?

Virtually all states that govern through terror and torture adopt strategies of what Graham Sykes and David Matza (1957) described as 'techniques of neutralization'. These are devices which reveal that the offending state is aware that it is infringing a rule, which at some level it recognises as legitimate but in practice disdains. Stan Cohen (2001) elucidates these stages as a 'complex discourse of denial' and justification in which torture and human rights violations are first denied outright, or the victim is denied (as with the Argentinian *desaparecidos* – the 'disappeared' – who were, according to leading member of the Junta, General Viola, 'absent forever'); and then reclassified as self-defence or 'moderate physical pressure', rather than torture. Finally, justificatory admissions are given; for example, as acting 'in the national interest'. Other stages in the process include: the condemnation by the offending state of those who have condemned them implying hypocrisy on the part of the condemners; and appeals to a higher moral authority (religious authority; 'civilisation'), more potent in the eyes of the offending state than the law or social morality.

Activity 7.8

How do you think nation states can justify or neutralise their own violations of human rights?

Select an example of state crime and explore the ways in which the following five techniques of neutralisation (Sykes and Matza, 1957; Cohen, 2001) might be employed by a state or state agency to neutralise their crime:

- denial of injury
- denial of victim
- denial of responsibility
- condemnation of the condemners
- appeal to higher loyalty.

Comment

State terror as a technique of coercive governance is almost always coupled with denial. In this sense states are at least conscious of deviating from rules to which they ostensibly subscribe, and act in a range of ways to conceal their crimes in order to sustain at least some degree of political legitimacy. Both authoritarian and democratic states have adopted terrorist techniques as an instrumentally rational response to political threats, especially but not exclusively to the threat of anti-state terrorism or armed revolt. In authoritarian regimes, state violence typically tends to be targeted against local populations, whereas that perpetrated by Western democratic powers has also extended beyond the local in facilitating global repression.

6   Conclusion

This chapter ends by raising questions that address one of the core concerns of this book: that is, whether social problems, hazards and atrocities (such as terror and torture) would be better considered within a social harm discourse (cf. Hillyard et al., 2004) rather than through the paradigm of 'crime'. For example, is torture more usefully conceptualised as a harm? And what is the political, intellectual or social value in labelling torture and state terror as crime? While some writers (Kauzlarich et al., 2001) equate all human rights violations with state crime, others have argued that this position severs the conceptual link between crime and deviance. Tony Ward has argued that 'deviant behaviour is what criminology is about' (2004, p. 85) and while many state practices can be considered as inflicting social harm of one kind or another on the many (through social and economic stratification and related inequalities of class, poverty, racism, sexism, and so on), to describe entire economic systems as criminal is to abandon the analytical power of the criminological classification. If we do so, we are left with a framework of social harm that is so broad that it includes accepted and legitimate social and economic policy (which, while producing politically unfair outcomes, is nonetheless widely accepted as legitimate) alongside the widely condemned Israeli invasion of Gaza (2008–09) and the kind of terror inflicted by Saddam Hussain and the Latin American generals. Rather, this chapter has argued that we should, as Ward suggests, confine our analysis of crimes committed by states to those acts 'which embody the matrix of actors, rules, audiences and sanctions', that is, to those 'acts committed by state agents in pursuance of state goals which violate human rights and which are perceived by significant social audiences as deviant (violating legal or moral rules), and to which social audiences are disposed to apply sanctions' (Ward, 2004, p. 86).

As Chomsky has said, 'Inquiry very definitely does reveal that state terror and other forms of threat and use of force have brought vast suffering and destruction ... it is shocking to observe such discoveries are ignored in the intellectual culture' (Chomsky, 2007, p. 101). This quotation from Chomsky is a reminder that the issues raised in this

Figure 7.5
Campaigning against state-sponsored torture

chapter have remained largely outside not only of criminological but also of dominant political discourse. There appears to be a general reluctance to acknowledge the depth of destruction, despair and injury that nation states can and do inflict not only on their own populations, but on those of other nation states. Considering the contribution of state agencies to the world's homicide rates, the scale of their economic crimes and the torture and terror they exert through domestic and international modes of governance, the space devoted to state crime in the criminological literature in particular seems negligible. Falling outside the traditional individualised and localised paradigms of criminology, scholars have long regarded state crime as a subject beyond the remit of the discipline. This chapter has been designed to illustrate the poverty of that position.

References

Amnesty International (2000) *Torture – A Modern Day Plague*, London, Amnesty International.

Amnesty International (2001a) *Annual Report*, London, Amnesty International.

Amnesty International (2001b) *Colombia: Stop the Massacres, Stop the Aid!*, London, Amnesty International.

Amnesty International (2001c) *Stopping the Torture Trade*, London, Amnesty International.

Amnesty International (2007) *European Union: Stopping the Trade in Tools of Torture* [online], www.amnesty.org/en/library/info/POL34/001/2007/en (Accessed 15 February 2008).

Amnesty International (2008) *Amnesty International Report* [online], http://thereport.amnesty.org/ (Accessed 29 December 2008).

Associated Press (2008) *Bush Vetoes Bill Banning Waterboarding* [online], www.msnbc.msn.com/id/23526436/ (Accessed 8 October 2008).

Bamber, H. (1995) 'The Medical Foundation and its commitment to human rights and rehabilitation' in Gordon, N. and Marton, R. (eds) *Torture: Human Rights, Medical Ethics and the Case of Israel*, London, Zed Books/Association of Israeli-Palestinian Physicians for Human Rights.

Brockett, C.D. (1991) 'Sources of state terrorism in rural Central America' in Bushnell, P.T., Shlapentokh, V., Vanderpool, C.K., and Sundram, J. (eds) *State Organized Terror: The Case of Violent Internal Repression*, Boulder, CO, Westview.

Campbell, B.B. (2000) 'Death squads: definition, problems and historical concept' in Campbell, B. and Brenner, A.D. (eds) *Death Squads in Global Perspective*, London, Palgrave Macmillan.

Chandler, D.P. (1999) *Brother Number One: A Political Biography of Pol Pot*, Boulder, CO, Westview.

Chomsky, N. (2007) *Failed States: The Abuse of Power and the Assault on Democracy*, London, Penguin.

Chomsky, N. and Herman, E.S. (1979) *The Political Economy of Human Rights*, Nottingham, Spokesman Books for the Bertrand Russell Peace Foundation.

Clinard, M.B. and Quinney, R. (1973) *Criminal Behaviour Systems*, New York, Holt, Rinehart and Winston.

Cohen, S. (2001) *States of Denial: Knowing about Atrocities and Suffering*, Cambridge, Polity.

Commission for Reception, Truth and Reconciliation in East Timor (CAVR) (2005) *Chega! Final Report of the Commission for Reception, Truth and Reconciliation in East Timor* [online], www.etan.org/etanpdf/2006/CAVR/07.2_Unlawful_Killings_and_Enforced_ Disappearances.pdf (Accessed 16 June 2008).

Cover, R. (1986) 'Violence and the word', *Yale Law Journal*, no. 95, p. 1601.

de Swaan, A. (2001) 'Dyscivilization, mass extermination and the state', *Theory, Culture and Society*, vol. 18, nos 2–3, pp. 265–76.

Democracy Now! (2006) 'U.S. exclusive: Moazzam Begg describes abuse at Baghram and Guantanamo and witnessing the killing of two fellow detainees', *Democracy Now!*, 14 March [online], www.democracynow.org/2006/3/14/u_s_exclusive_moazzam_begg_describes (Accessed 16 September 2008).

Dershowitz, A. (2004) 'Tortured reasoning' in Levinson, S. (ed.) (2004).

Dorfman, A. (2004) 'The tyranny of terror: is torture inevitable in our century and beyond?' in Levinson, S. (ed.) (2004).

Eagleton, T. (2005) *Holy Terror*, Oxford, Oxford University Press.

Elias, N. (2000 [1939]) *The Civilizing Process* (revised edn) (trans. E. Jephcott), Oxford, Blackwell.

Elliot, F. and Gibb, F. (2008) 'US aircraft did use British base to transport terrorist suspects', *The Times*, 22 February, p. 4.

Engels, F. (1968 [1884]) 'Origins of the family, private property and the state' in Marx, K. and Engels, F. (eds) *Selected Works*, London, Lawrence & Wishart.

Fein, H. (1990) 'Genocide: a sociological perspective', *Current Sociology*, vol. 38, pp. 1–111.

Fein, H. (2000) 'Testing theories brutally' in Smith, R. (ed.) *Genocide: Essays Toward Understanding, Early Warning, and Prevention*, Williamsburg, VA, Association of Genocide Scholars.

Feitlowitz, M. (1998) *A Lexicon of Terror: Argentina and the Legacies of Terror*, Oxford, Oxford University Press.

Feitlowitz, M. (2005) *The Torturer General* [online], www.pen.org/viewmedia.php/prmMID/77/prmID/918 (Accessed 16 September 2008).

Franks, J. (2006) *Rethinking the Roots of Terrorism*, New York, Palgrave Macmillan.

Gareau, F. (2004) *State Terrorism and the United States: From Counterinsurgency to the War on Terrorism*, Atlanta, GA, Clarity Press/London, Zed Books.

Gibson, J.T. (1990) 'Factors contributing to the creation of a torturer' in Suedfeld, P. (ed.) *Psychology and Torture*, New York, Hemisphere.

Glover, J. (1999) *A Moral History of the Twentieth Century*, Oxford, Oxford University Press.

Graziano, F. (1992) *Divine Violence: Spectacle, Psychosexuality and Radical Christianity in the Argentine 'Dirty War'*, Boulder, CO, Westview.

Green, P. and Ward, T. (2004) *State Crime: Governments, Violence and Corruption*, London, Pluto Press.

Green, P. and Ward, T. (2009a) 'Torture and the paradox of state violence' in Clucas, B., Johnstone, G. and Ward, T. (eds) *Torture: Moral Absolutes and Ambiguities*, Baden-Baden, Nomos.

Green, P. and Ward, T. (forthcoming) 'Violence and the state' in Sim, J., Tombs, S. and Whyte, D. (eds) *State, Power, Crime: Readings in Critical Criminology*, London, Sage.

Greenberg, K. (ed.) (2006) *The Torture Debate in America*, Cambridge, Cambridge University Press.

Gurr, T.R. (1986) 'The political origins of state violence and terror: a theoretical analysis' in Stohl, M. and Lopez, G.A. (eds) *Government Violence and Repression: An Agenda for Research*, Westport, CT, Greenwood.

Haney, C., Banks, C. and Zimbardo, P. (1973) 'Interpersonal dynamics in a simulated prison', *International Journal of Criminology and Penology*, vol. 1, pp. 69–97.

Haritos-Fatouros, M. (1988) 'The official torturer: a learning model for obedience to an authority of violence', *Torture* (Torture Rehabilitation Centre, Denmark), vol. 26, no. 1, pp. 69–97.

Hawk, D. (1986) 'Tuol Sleng Extermination Centre (Cambodia)', *Index on Censorship*, vol. 15, no. 1, pp. 25–31.

Herman, E.S. (1982) *The Real Terror Network: Terrorism in Fact and Propaganda*, Boston, MA, South End Press.

Hersh, S.M. (2004) 'Torture at Abu Ghraib: American soldiers brutalized Iraqis: how far up does the responsibility go?', *The New Yorker*, 10 May.

Hersh, S.M. (2007) 'The general's report: how Antonio Taguba, who investigated the Abu Ghraib scandal, became one of its casualties', *The New Yorker*, 25 June [online], www.newyorker.com/reporting/2007/06/25/070625fa_fact_hersh (Accessed 14 July 2007).

Hillyard, P., Pantazis, C., Tombs, S. and Gordon, D. (eds) (2004) *Beyond Criminology: Taking Harm Seriously*, London, Pluto Press.

Huggins, M.K., Haritos-Fatouros, M. and Zimbardo, P.G. (2002) *Violence Workers: Police Torturers and Murderers Reconstruct Brazilian Atrocities*, Berkeley, CA, University of California Press.

Human Rights Watch (2001) *The 'Sixth Division': Military–Paramilitary Ties and U.S. Policy in Colombia* [online], www.hrw.org/reports/2001/colombia/6theng.pdf (Accessed 15 February 2008).

Human Rights Watch (2003) *Sudan, Oil and Human Rights*, 24 November [online], www.hrw.org/en/reports/2003/11/24/sudan-oil-and-human-rights (Accessed 22 January 2008).

Kauzlarich, D. and Kramer, R.C. (1998) *Crimes of the American Nuclear State: At Home and Abroad*, Boston, MA, Northeastern University Press.

Kauzlarich, D., Matthews, R.A. and Miller, W.J. (2001) 'Toward a victimology of state crime', *Critical Criminology*, vol. 10, no. 3, pp. 173–94.

Kepner, T. (2001) 'Torture 101: the case against the United States for atrocities committed by School of the Americas alumni', *Dickinson International Law Journal*, vol. 19, part 3, pp. 475–530.

Lifton, R.J. (1986) *The Nazi Doctors: Medical Killing and the Psychology of Genocide*, London, Macmillan.

Luban, D. (2006) 'Liberalism, torture and the ticking bomb' in Greenberg, K. (ed.) (2006).

Maran, R. (1989) *Torture: The Role of Ideology in the French-Algerian War*, New York, Praeger.

Marton, R. (1995) 'Introduction' in Gordon, N. and Marton, R. (eds) *Torture: Human Rights, Medical Ethics and the Case of Israel*, London, Zed Books/ Association of Israeli-Palestinian Physicians for Human Rights.

McClintock, M. (1985) *The American Connection, Vol. II: State Terror and Popular Resistance in Guatemala*, London, Zed Books.

McClintock, M. (1992) *Instruments of Statecraft: U.S. Guerrilla Warfare, Counterinsurgency, and Counter-terrorism, 1940–1990*, New York, Pantheon.

McCoy, A. (2006) *A Question of Torture: CIA Interrogation, from the Cold War to the War on Terror*, New York, Metropolitan.

Milgram, S. (1974) *Obedience to Authority*, New York, Harper & Row.

New York Times (2005) Editorial, 'Torture by proxy', 8 March [online], www.nytimes.com/2005/03/08/opinion/08tue1.html (Accessed 19 November 2008).

Osiel, M. (1997) *Mass Atrocity, Collective Memory and the Law*, New Brunswick, NJ, Transaction.

Peters, E. (1996) *Torture* (expanded edn), Philadelphia, PA, University of Pennsylvania Press.

Pion-Berlin, D. (1989) *The Ideology of State Terror Economic Doctrine and Political Repression in Argentina and Peru*, London, Rienner.

Poole, S. (2006) 'Terror' in Poole, S. *Unspeak*, London, Little, Brown.

Rejali, D. (1994) *Torture and Modernity*, Boulder, CO, Westview.

Reprieve (2007) *Scottish Involvement in Extraordinary Rendition*, 3 October [online], www.libertysecurity.org/article1643.html (Accessed 10 February 2009).

Scarry, E. (1985) *The Body in Pain: The Making and Unmaking of the World*, Oxford, Oxford University Press.

Scarry, E. (2004) 'Five errors in the reasoning of Alan Dershowitz' in Levinson, S. (ed.) (2004).

Schirmer, J. (1998) *The Guatemalan Military Project*, Philadelphia, PA, University of Pennsylvania Press.

Schwendinger, H. and Schwendinger, J. (1975) 'Defenders of order or guardians of human rights?' in Taylor, I., Walton, P. and Young, J. (eds) *Critical Criminology*, London, Routledge & Kegan Paul.

Shue, H. (2004) 'Torture' in Levinson, S. (ed.) (2004).

Simon, D.R. and Eitzen, D.S. (1990) *Elite Deviance*, Boston, MA, Allyn and Bacon.

Stanley, E. (2006) 'Towards a criminology for human rights' in Barton, A., Corteen, K., Scott, D. and Whyte, D. (eds) *The Criminological Imagination: Readings in Critical Criminologies*, Cullompton, Willan.

Stanley, E. (2008) 'The political economy of transitional justice in Timor-Leste', in McEvoy, K. and McGregor, L. (eds) *Transitional Justice from Below: Grassroots Activism and the Struggle for Change*, Oxford, Hart Publishing.

Staub, E. (1989) *The Roots of Evil: The Origins of Genocide and other Group Violence*, Cambridge, Cambridge University Press.

Suárez-Orozco, M. (1992) 'A grammar of terror: psychocultural responses to state terrorism in dirty-war and post dirty-war Argentina' in Nordstrom, C. and Martin, J. (eds) *The Paths to Domination, Resistance and Terror*, Berkeley, CA, University of California Press.

Sykes, G. and Matza, D. (1957) 'Techniques of neutralization: a theory of delinquency', *American Sociological Review*, no. 22, pp. 664–70.

The Battle of Algiers, film, directed by Gillo Pontecorvo, 1965.

Tilly, C. (1992) *Coercion, Capital and European States A.D. 990–1990*, Oxford, Blackwell.

Ward, T. (2004) 'State harms' in Hillyard, P. et al. (eds) (2004).

Ward, T. and Young, P. (2007) 'Elias, organised violence and terrorism' in Mullard, M. and Cole, B. (eds) *Globalisation, Citizenship and the War on Terror*, Cheltenham, Edward Elgar.

Weber, M. (1968) *Economy and Society*, vol. 3, New York, Bedminster Press.

Acknowledgments

Grateful acknowledgement is made to the following sources:

Cover

Copyright © UpperCut Images;

Chapter 1

Figures

Figure 1.2: Copyright © Matt Cardy/Getty Images; Figure 1.3 top: Copyright © Greenpeace/Christan Aslund; Figure 1.3 bottom: Copyright © Louisiana Department of Environmental Quality; Figure 1.4: Copyright © Gethin Chamberlain/Guardian News & Media Ltd, 2008; Figure 1.5: Copyright © Mostafizur Rahman/AP/PA Photos.

Chapter 2

Text

Extract 2.1: Barnett, L. (2006) 'We are not pigeons', *Borehamwood & Elstree Times*, 9 March 2006. opyright © Newsquest; Extract 2.5: Ridgeway, W G (2005) 'Dubai, Dubai - the scandal and the vice', Social Affairs Unit www. soacialafairsunit.org.uk Copyright © William G Ridgeway.

Figures

Figure 2.1: Copyright © Rockstar Games; Figure 2.3: Davis, M. (1998) Ecology of Fear: Los Angeles and the Imagination of Disaster, Picador, an Imprint of Macmillan; Figure 2.5: Copyright © Matt Cardy/Getty Images; Figure 2.6: Copyright © APF/Getty Images; Figure 2.7: Copyright © Eraldo Peres/AP/PA Photos; Figure 2.8: Copyright © Karim Sahib/Getty Images.

Chapter 3

Text

Extract 3.1: Warren, P. (2007) 'Hunt for Russia's web criminals', *The Guardian*, 15 November 2007. Copyright © Guardian News & Media Ltd 2007; Extract 3.2: Johnson, B. (2007) 'Police arrest teenager over virtual theft', *The Guardian*, 15 November 2007. Copyright © Guardian News & Media Ltd, 2007; Extract 3.3: Kleeman, J. (2007) 'Get a (new) life', *Marie Claire*, September 2007. Copyright © Jenny Kleeman.

Figures

Figure 3.1: Copyright © eXtremeCast Games; Figure 3.2: Courtesy of Peter Twining www.schome.ac.uk/wiki/the_schome_park_bliki; Figure 3.3: Copyright © DREAMWORKS/Ronald Grant Archive; Figure 3.5: Copyright © Rockstar Games.

Chapter 4

Text

Extracts 4.2 and 4.5: Lewis, P. (2006) 'Nightmare world of suburban sex slaves', *The Guardian*, 8 May 2006. Copyright © Guardian News & Media Ltd 2006; Extract 4.4: UNICEF (2003) Trafficking in Human Beings, Especially Women and Children, in Africa, UNICEF. Copyright © UNICEF Innocenti Research Centre.

Figures

Figure 4.1: Copyright © Tim Ockenden/PA Archive/PA Photos; Figure 4.3: Copyright © Karen Kasmauski/Corbis; Figure 4.4: Bettmann/Corbis; Figure 4.5: Copyright © John Phillips/Photofusion; Figure 4.6: Copyright © Bob Watkins/Photofusion.

Chapter 5

Figures

Figure 5.1 top: Copyright © A2292 Gero Breloer/DPA/PA Photos; Figure 5.1 bottom: Copyright © Eugene Hoshiko/AP/PA Photos; Figure 5.2 top: Copyright © Eberhard Streichan/zefa/Corbis; Figure 5.2 bottom: Copyright © Richard Chung/Reuters/Corbis; Figure 5.3: Copyright © Jai Redman; Figure 5.4: Copyright © Andrew Holbroke/ Corbis; Figure 5.5: Copyright © AFP/Getty Images.

Chapter 6

Text

Extract 6.1: Macallister, T. (2007) 'Greenpeace calls BP's oil sands plan an environmental crime', *The Guardian*, 7 December 2007. Copyright © Guardian News & Media Ltd 2007; Extract 6.3: Godoy, J. (2008) ' Biodiversity: Indigenous peoples fight theft', Inter Press Service News Agency, 24 May 2008.

Figures

Figure 6.1a: Copyright © Design Pics Inc/Rex Features; Figure 6.1b: Copyright © Frans Lanting/Corbis; Figure 6.1c: Copyright © Lin Alder/Still Pictures; Figure 6.1d: Copyright © Michael Nichols/National Geographic Magazine; Figure 6.1e: Copyright © Gari Wyn Williams/Alamy; Figure 6.1f: Copyright © KG-Photography/zefa/Corbis; Figure 6.1g: Copyright © Greenpeace.

Chapter 7

Text

Extract 7.1: Walker, P. and Tran. M. (2008) 'Radovan Karadzic delays plea to war crimes charges in The Hague', *The Guardian*, 31 July 2008. Copyright © Guardian News & Media Ltd 2008; Extract 7.2: Tran, M. and Stratton, A. (2008) 'Zimbabwe: UN high commissioner calls for halt to political violence', *The Guardian*, 26 June 2008. Copyright © Guardian News & Media Ltd 2008; Extract 7.3: Dyer, C. (2007) 'Goldsmith calls for inquiry into Iraq torture', *The Guardian*, 27 June 2007. Copyright © Guardian News & Media Ltd 2007; Extract 7.5: Verkaik, R. (2008) 'Miliband fails in court bid to keep 'torture proof' secret', *The Independent*, 30 August 2008. Copyright © The Independent.

Figures

Figure 7.1: Copyright © Patrick Robert/Sygma/Corbis; Figure 7.2: Copyright © AP/PA Photos; Figure 7.3: Copyright © Chris Rainier/Corbis; Figure 7.4: Copyright © Carlos Carrion/Sygma/Corbis; Figure 7.5: Copyright © 2005 TopFoto/Imageworks;

Every effort has been made to contact copyright holders. If any have been inadvertently overlooked the publishers will be pleased to make the necessary arrangements at the first opportunity.

Index